MEXICAN WOMEN IN THE UNITED STATES

MEXICAN WOMEN IN THE UNITED STATES

struggles past and present

Edited by
Magdalena Mora
and
Adelaida R. Del Castillo

Occasional Paper No. 2
Chicano Studies Research Center Publications
University of California   •   Los Angeles

Commemorating International Women's Day
March 8, 1980

International Standard Book Number: 0-89551-022-7
Library of Congress Catalog Card Number: 80-10682

Second Printing 1982

Managing Editor: Rosa M. Martinez
Associate Editor: Adelaida R. Del Castillo

CONTENTS

PART FIVE—PROFILES

APPENDIX

INTRODUCTION

SEX, NATIONALITY, AND CLASS: LA OBRERA MEXICANA

Adelaida R. Del Castillo
Magdalena Mora

Until recently, the Mexican woman as an historical entity in her own right has received meager, if not inconsequential, treatment. As yet, no existing work fully encompasses the multiplicity of her contributions to Mexican and United States history—her struggles on behalf of her sex, class, and nationality. Moreover, such a work must acknowledge the historical presence, interaction, and collaboration between Mexican communities on both sides of the border. Currently, enthusiastic interest, seminal research, and analysis of the role and activism of Mexican women is emerging.

The primary objective of this Chicano Studies Research Center Occasional Paper is the documentation and appraisal of Mexican women's participation in the struggle against national oppression, class exploitation, and sexism. The essays present the complexity and depth of her participation and attest to her leadership, courage, tenacity, and creativity.

INTEGRATION AND DEVELOPMENT

Popular notions of Mexican women as passive and apathetic overlook the historical militancy of women laborers and political activists.

The activism of Mexican women in student and community organizations in the last decade further belies these notions. Yet, clear political analyses of the role of these women in the political process and inner workings of progressive organizations are few. Hopefully, the experience of women activists in the Chicano Movement, the growth and decline of the white radical women's movement, and political programs aimed at the full integration and development of women as activists and equal members of society, will contribute to a richer understanding of the oppression of Mexican women and its solution.

The first three articles in part one of *Mexican Women in the United States: Struggles Past and Present,* by Del Castillo, Hernandez, and Vásquez refer to the Chicana, and the character of her role as activist and woman in the Chicano Movement. The paradox of her oppression, even within a liberation movement, are discussed. Del Castillo provides a general evaluation of women's participation within the structure of Southern California's Chicano student and community organizations, from the late 1960s to the mid 1970s. Hernandez distinguishes the nature of Chicano student activity and Chicana activism in San Diego via the political orientation and problems encountered by two women leaders at San Diego State College (now San Diego State University). Vásquez, once a leader in Southern California's Chicano student movement, recounts lessons learned through class struggle

Adelaida R. del Castillo is a graduate student in the Anthropology Department at the University of California, Los Angeles. Magdalena Mora is a graduate student in the History Department at the University of California, Los Angeles.

and its effect toward greater equality between the sexes where there once existed a double standard of work and social behavior.

Understandably, the question of female liberation and its implications for Mexican women becomes crucial. But Mexican women are inevitably forced to analyze liberation within the context of national oppression and class conflict. For her, liberation is primarily a political question integrally linked to the liberation of her people and class. Important, too, is the consideration of national and international women's movements and the valuable contributions they have made toward their liberation.

The last three essays in part one address the political integration and development of women by focussing on the issue of female liberation. Dunbar Ortiz discusses the influence of the Civil Rights Movement on ethnic and white radical movements and the character it lent to the nascent radical women's movement. Dixon follows with an analysis of that movement and what happens when radical struggles fall short of working-class unity and focus. Her accounts of sexism and betrayal by male leadership dispel romantic formulas of working-class unity without the equal participation and development of women. Finally, Larguia and Dumoulin present a critical analysis of women's role as consumer, and distinguish between her role as biological reproducer and reproducer of labor power within the family. Moreover, they stipulate conditions for her liberation and equal status as a member of society.

STERILIZATION

National oppression of Mexican people in the United States has most blatantly manifested itself in attacks against the undocumented worker, the exploitation of his labor, and the forced sterilization of Spanish speaking women.

Sterilization in this country has tripled since 1970 according to the May 1976 issue of *Signos Vitales.* Sterilization of poor and non-white populations is disproportionately high. In 1971 Princeton University reported that 33 percent of all women sterilized under federally funded planned parenthood family programs were black. In 1973, one hundred Indian women were sterilized in Claremont, Oklahoma. By 1974, the annual rate of sterilizations performed in this country was estimated at over half a million cases. According to the Ralph Nader Health

Research Group Study report of October 1973, many of the women were not aware of the dangerous and irreversible aspects of the operation. Moreover, they content that poor and non-white women are most often approached to consider sterilization while under the duress of childbirth. During this same period, 1971 to 1974, twenty-four Mexican women were sterilized in Los Angeles without having given informed consent. On May 31, 1978, ten of these women filed a civil action suit against the medical institution in which the sterilizations were performed; on June 30, Senior U.S. District Judge Jesse W. Curtis ruled in favor of the institution attributing the various sterilization incidents to a lack of communication, "misunderstandings," he explained, "are bound to occur."

Part two addresses sterilization abuse and begins with Del Castillo's overview of the predominatly punitive rationale underlying the advocacy of sterilization in this country. Velez-I offers a theoretical exposition of socio-cultural variables involved in oppression and, thus, established the context for his analysis of the involuntary sterilization of the ten Mexican women. He concludes that sterilizations result in the total disruption of the victim's social and psychological well-being.

LABOR ACTIVITY

Easily exploited and often unaware of their rights as workers, Mexican women have become the "ideal" labor force. In the April 1979 issue of the *AFL-CIO American Federationist,* Alfredo C. Montoya, director of the Labor Council for Latin American Advancement, informs there was a "33 percent increase in the number of Hispanic women in the workforce—more than double the 15 percent increase among all U.S. women" for the period 1973–77. Blue-collar employment of Hispanic women currently totals 28.9 percent, twice that of the total blue-collar female workforce. Most of these women work as operatives in the manufacturing sector, a category classified as having the lowest rate of future growth most probably due to mechanization.

Current earnings and the unemployment rate for Hispanics further portend a grim economic future. The unemployment rate for Hispanics in the final quarter of 1978, according to Montoya, was 8.1 percent compared to 5.5 percent for the total workforce. Annually, the Hispanic male workers earns $4,000 less than the national median of $14,850. The Hispanic woman earns over $1,000 less than the annual $8,566 for all U.S. women.

Part three opens with an analysis of the apparel and electronics industries by the *NACLA Report on the Americas* and Bernstein et al, respectively. These two articles are important to a basic understanding of why and how these industries seek ever cheaper production costs through the exploitation of workers. Regionally, the drive for greater profits has taken these industries from the highly unionized areas of the northeastern United States to the relatively unorganized workforce of the West Coast. Ultimately, companies ignore national boundaries and exploit Asian and Latin American workers by paying them wages a fraction of those paid American workers.

Schlein's examination of Los Angeles' garment industry focuses on the exploitation of workers, the majority of which are Spanish speaking women. Labor code violations, dispersion of production processes, and runaway shops enhance their exploitability and frustrate efforts to organize them. Even so, lessons learned and progress made through unionization efforts must be acknowledged.

Schlein believes one reason for the garment industry's deplorable working conditions is the lack of unionization which she attributes to the presence of Latin Americans. In contrast, Phil Russo, director of the International Ladies Garment Workers Union (ILGWU) organizing drive in Los Angeles, was quoted in the July 1978 issue of the *Guardian,* the Socialist weekly newspaper, as saying: "The conventional wisdom in the labor movement was that so-called 'illegal aliens' were unorganizable. But we're proving that that's wrong. We're having phenomenal success here." Years before Russo made this observation, however, Mexican community groups were working with and organizing undocumented workers. Hispanics, notes Montoya, are generally more apt to be union members than the rest of the workforce. Presently, 26 percent are members of unions, slightly above the rate for all U.S. workers.

Mexican workers, in particular, have fought hard for better working conditions and unionization. The national bilingual newspaper *Sin Fronteras* reported that on May 31, 1975 a strike by citizen and undocumented Mexican workers at Toltec Foods of Richmond, California ended in victory for workers. Some 150 members of

the AFL-CIO Bartenders and Culinary Workers, Local No. 595 were able to shut down the company plant and set up a twenty-four-hour picket line for three weeks despite the lack of cooperation from their own union officials and intimidation from the local police and Immigration and Naturalization Service (INS). Equally significant, on May and September of 1976 in Los Angeles, California, and San Antonio, Texas, respectively, *Sin Fronteras* reported citizen and undocumented workers raided at work by the INS refused to show identification documents. Collusion between management and the INS has been evident. INS raids on undocumented workers continually occur at places where organizing drives are taking place and often on pay day.

Exposure of employers schemes to facilitate the exploitation of Mexican workers provides several observations. Employers have sought to cheat workers and create hostilities between Mexicans by paying the Spanish speaking less than those who speak English. Those fast at doing piece work are accused of cheating by employers who either refuse to pay them for work done or lower wages for all piece work. Others purposely miscount bundles of piece work then force workers to do extra work without pay. Once strike activities or unionization drives are initiated employers have tried to curtail them by threatening employees with lay-offs, deportation, or scab replacement. Where a union already exists, management has been known to decertify it.

A case in point occurred at California Originals in Torrance, California. When Local No. 376 of the International Brotherhood of Pottery and Allied Workers went on strike on October 9, 1975 management immediately made use of Vietnamese strike breakers and decertified the union by coercing scab workers to vote for decertification. Furthermore, strikers were weakened when their union withheld economic support. That same year, Local No. 18 of the International Union of Dolls, Toys, Plastic Novelties and Derived Products of the AFL-CIO in Chicago was decertified when workers were deceived into signing blank sheets of paper later used by management in a decertification petition.

At least 50 percent of the participants in these and similar labor struggles are Mexican women. Working conditions for these women, including members of unions, are quite often below the working standards of organized labor. Many work for a maximum wage which is below the minimum wage scale, have no seniority rights, and work under dangerous and unsanitary conditions. Consequently, women who are single heads of household receive annual incomes severely below the poverty level. Yet, the courage and tenacity with which women have fought for better wages and working conditions is exemplary. For these very reasons "Women at Farah: An Unfinished Story" and "The Election Day Immigration Raid at Lilli Diamond Originals" are important contributions to U.S. labor history. They document the hardships and political developments encountered by women as family members, wage earners, and union organizers. The subsequent acceleration toward their awareness of working-class needs becomes evident.

PAST STRUGGLES

Part four opens with Hart's "Working-Class Women in Nineteenth Century Mexico." In it he discusses the nature of incipient labor activities in nineteenth century Mexico, Socialist influences, and the participation of working-class women in them. The industrialization of Mexico during the latter half of that century resulted in an influx of rural workers to urban areas, many of these were women employed in the manufacture of textiles. Although women were not allowed formal participation in leadership, they were among the first to join labor movements. It was not until close to the end of the century on March 5, 1876 that women were allowed to participate as delegates to the first Congreso General Obrero de la República. Three years later, Carmen Huerta was elected president of the Congreso.

Working-class movements in Mexico significantly influenced labor activities in the southwestern United States via the leadership and cooperation of political activists across the border, again women were important participants. By the turn of the century, revolutionary agitators were more strongly and clearly defending the importance of women in liberation movements. In particular, Ricardo Flores Mágon through his essay "A La Mujer" makes a graphically progressive statement on the situation of working-class women and their responsibility to revolution as members of an oppressed class.

Sara Estela Ramirez, a journalist and literary figure, is part of a core group of women leaders within the Partido Liberal Mexicano. The group is responsible for assuming public roles which

persecuted leaders of the party could not undertake. The importance of Zamora's work reveals her political significance and her literary importance as woman and activist.

Finally, part four ends with Monroy's essay on the ILGWU's organizing drives among Mexican garment workers from 1933 to 1939. He notes a regional shift from the east to the west coast by capable Jewish union organizers and a hierarchy of union leadership with Mexicans at the bottom.

PROFILES

The collection of essays in part five focus on the lives and times of individual Mexican women. Their hardships and struggle for social injustice, against poverty and exploitation have fostered a fighting spirit and helped many to see the importance of class solidarity. Personal experiences such as these are an integral part of our history and demonstrates the desire and capacity of Mexican women to struggle for social and economic rights. They attest to the level of working-class and national consciousness among broad sectors of Mexican people residing in the United States at various points in our history.

CONCLUSION

Overall, the class, national, and sexual oppression of the Mexican woman has without a doubt limited her full participation in society and the advancement of Mexican people as a whole. At this place in time, emerging political statements on and about her should contribute to a better understanding of this triple oppression. Together these selections represent important aspects of the Woman Question as it concerns Mexicans today.

ACKNOWLEDGEMENTS

We are greatly indebted to the authors and previous publishers of material presented here. Through their cooperation this book was made possible. We are equally grateful to Juan Gómez-Quiñones, Carlos Vásquez, and Carlos Velez-I for supportive criticism and direction. To Rosa M. Martinez, whose careful editing of the manuscript contributed invaluably to its presentation, our sincere appreciation.

PART ONE

INTEGRATION AND DEVELOPMENT

MEXICAN WOMEN IN ORGANIZATION

Adelaida R. Del Castillo

INTRODUCTION

Having based much of the following on personal observations, I should mention some pivotal points involving my exposure to Chicano Movement activities in southern California. My introduction to the Chicano Movement took place in late 1967 during a two week stay with the Teatro Campesino in Del Rey when I was seventeen. My student activities as a "Chicana" began soon after, in 1968, during my last year of high school. In 1969 I became an UMAS-MEChA member at the University of California, Los Angeles and served as co-chairperson on one of the chapter's communications committees.[1] In 1971, I left school and worked with a group of Chicana feminists who published a journal entitled *Encuentro Femenil* in 1973 and 1974. For myself, as for many others, experiences such as these initiated valuable insight into racism and sexism in this country and contributed effective political direction to the growing activism of the Chicano Movement.

It appeared, however, that a resurgent nationalism of the Chicano Movement drove many to confuse stereotypic traditional male/female concepts for actual viable roles. Paradoxically,

while Mexican students fought for the democratic rights of Mexican people in general, the manner in which they implemented much of their political and organizational activities particularly limited the democratic participation of women.

The question of women's equality in the struggle for class liberation and a national self-determination has posed and exposed contradictions in nascent political movements—the Chicano Movement was no exception.

In 1975 I began work with a community organization concerned with the defense and mobilization of Mexican people via a working class perspective. Consequently, Marxist-Leninist defense of the liberation of women as indispensible to the liberation of the oppressed provided greater clarity concerning the role and significance of women in struggle. Democracy, writes Lenin, is measured not only by the status of the working class but by that of women as well. If women are considered inferior or denied privileges enjoyed by men, there can be no democracy. In effect, democracy entails complete equality for women and "freedom from the guardianship and oppression of men."[2]

It became clear to me, nonetheless, that the problem of integrating women quantitatively and qualitatively into organizational and political work would not resolve itself without a concrete political and organizational program on women.

I would like to thank Magdalena Mora and Juan Gómez-Quiñones for their criticisms and discussion during the preparation of this paper. © 1980 by Adelaida R. Del Castillo

THE STUDENT EXPERIENCE

The 1968 student walkouts in the Los Angeles area exposed the quality of education in barrio schools as being among the poorest in the nation, resulting in some of the highest high school dropout rates anywhere. Here, the majority of Mexican girls who dropped out of school did so because of pregnancy or marriage. Those who remained most often were not considered college material by school counselors who steered them into homemaking or business courses. At most, some acquired secretarial skills.

The development of special admissions programs eventually made it possible for Mexicans to enter college who, for academic or financial reasons, would not have been able to do so. For many, especially women, attending college was their first experience out of the home environment, and suddenly, their first confrontation with predominantly non-Mexican surroundings. As a consequence, feelings of alienation in the school housing dorms and inadequacy in the classrooms was not uncommon.

Student organizational involvement became important because it provided women with a sense of identity, common goals, and an ethnic and class peer group with which to relate socially and politically. It substituted for what was lacking in the rest of the college community.

Organizational needs welcomed women's willingness to participate by utilizing their secretarial and homemaking skills. Women took minutes of meetings, typed, answered phones, and cooked. They would set up and tend booths at fundraisers and dances, and stayed behind to clean up. Such responsibilities came within the traditional sphere of women's work, and women were expected to perform accordingly.

Work of this nature often substituted for political sophistication and camouflaged political timidity on the part of many women who were not well acquainted with movement issues, who lacked confidence as independent thinkers, or who found it difficult to articulate ideas. Consequently, women were viewed as innately marginal to intellectual and political processes. Dependence on male direction and leadership reinforced this assumption as did actual movement leadership, which was male in the majority, and undeniably gifted and dynamic.[3]

FEMALE LEADERSHIP

Leadership role models being unmistakenly male, both within the general Chicano Movement and the student sector of that movement, presented problems for women who actually filled these roles. Generally, women students were expected by their male peers to involve themselves actively but in subordination.

Some women assumed positions of organizational leadership when male leadership failed to assert itself. This did not mean, however, that men were willing to accept women as leaders. Some men considered this a direct affront to their masculinity. At times, women who were sensitive to the propriety of traditional male/female roles conceded visible leadership roles to men.

A case in point involved a university where the formation and development of UMAS was largely attributable to female leadership. When the organization sponsored a conference featuring as guest speaker Rodolfo "Corky" Gonzalez, of Denver's Crusade for Justice, opinions concerning female leaders surfaced. It was considered improper and embarrassing for a national leader to come on campus and see that the organization's leadership was female. Consequently, the organization decided that only males would be the visible representatives for the occasion. The female chairperson willingly conceded. Still, at another state college, the election of its first female UMAS chairperson caused the derision of that organization's male membership by males in other campus UMAS groups.

To insure concerted action, some women in leadership sought to deal with the alienation and lack of cooperation of male members by relying on male friends to act as liaisons. These liaisons were especially important in recruitment and could be utilized, it was rationalized, until the men came to accept the legitimacy of a female chairperson. Also, women made sure they had the support of compañeros when addressing black student leadership which resented negotiating with women.

These women were often the force behind the initial formation of a campus organization by communicating and encouraging other students to meet regularly. They sought and maintained communications with other campuses and community groups. They organized and attended conferences and caucuses through which they developed their political awareness and ability. They wrote student proposals and confronted the school administration and other campus groups for the implementation of programs.

Often, assuming leadership also meant the risk of having one's personal integrity and emotional stability threatened. The revengeful and denigrative campaigns against women by men were the most effective and successful. Commonly, women in leadership were labeled unfeminine or deviant. At times, women were accused of being sexually perverse or promiscuous, and men were deliberately used to betray them. When a woman leader had a compañero, he was frequently taunted or chided by the other men for failure to keep her under his control.

The influence men had on each other and on other women in their peer group facilitated the alienation of female friendship. Eventually, the political, social, and mental stress resulting from these campaigns forced resignations if not total abandonment of student activity on the part of victims. The groups of men who consequently took over often allowed the atrophy of the organization through lack of leadership, commitment, and consistency of work.

When women did not immediately assume leadership, organizational work experience and political development allowed them the opportunity to work their way up. Often this development could be hastened through the guidance and support of male leadership who recognized their potential. These women were relatively few. Women in general became part of networks of loyalty to particular males in leadership who were themselves referred to, in the idiom of students, as "heavies."

A "heavy" was a leader and a capable strategist, although not necessarily an elected organizational leader or officeholder. They were student leaders in their own right. Inversely, officeholders were not necessarily considered heavies. Consequently, women who were elected officers, such as secretaries or treasurers, remained outside the strategic meetings of these individuals. These meetings took place outside the formal structure of the organization, and membership was generally not aware of them. The meetings normally preceded organizational meetings, and resulted in decisions some of which the organization would formally adopt.

Women in this group were able to exercise leadership without having to risk attacks from the male rank and file. On the contrary, respect and admiration were given to them for talented and exemplary work. Their main problem was that other women envied them, and were reluctant to recognize their leadership, which they sought to undermine through petty gossip.

HINDRANCES

Chicano student organizations of the late sixties and early seventies had to concern themselves with the immediate development, implementation, and maintenance of target programs. Their major contribution was the creation and establishment of educational recruitment programs. But the implementation and maintenance of many of these programs forced organizations to assume a principally bureaucratic character at the expense of other organizational and political responsibilities. The political and leadership development of membership was one such responsibility.

Leadership abilities were generally seen as inherent. Student organizations were not structured or geared to develop the leadership potential of its general memebership and, in this sense, denied them democratic participation when they failed to mature in the decision making process. Often, women who were present in organizational processes were nevertheless vocally absent and were allowed to continue in that manner without a question as to the status of their development.

Sexist attitudes played a major role in bypassing the organizational and political development of women. It was generally assumed that women were central only within a personal sphere of human interaction as wives, mothers, and lovers. Comparisons were frequently made between vocal black and white women and nonvocal Mexican women. These comparisons ignored the Mexicanas' history of political activism.

Often, students indulged in the very stereotypes they sought to overturn. Few were aware of the daily struggle of Mexican women at low-paying and demeaning jobs, or the collaboration of women on welfare, fighting state and national bureaucracies. Many of these women were single parents; many could not afford the luxury of being full-time mothers. Given the general economic status of Mexican people, it was willful to assume that Mexican women could remain isolated at home, since most had need to support their families.

Men found it difficult to relate to women other than as sexual conquests. It was not beyond some men to request sexual cooperation as proof of commitment to the struggle, by gratifying the men who fought it. This caused confusion for women new to the struggle, inexperienced, yet willing to do what they could to associate, contribute, and identify with it. It was not unusual for a female, in the same class with her boyfriend, to take notes while he listened, type his term papers before typing her own, and tolerate his psychological and/or physical abuse as well as put up with his infidelity.

The immediacy of completing practical organizational work also precluded involvement in political work. At one state college, a group of young women who sought to learn more about movement issues were riduculed by some of the men. These women eventually began meeting with other women who were willing to discuss political issues with them during the lunch hour. Soon the men criticized them for neglecting their responsibilities; office phones were not being answered and typists were not available when needed. Consequently, the women stopped meeting.

ORGANIZATIONAL STRUCTURE

Student organizations lent themselves to a division of labor which dichotomized between obscure female and visible male activity. This is not to say that women performed minimal or insignificant work. On the contrary, student women, in performing much of the organization's basic tasks, were crucial to the operation of the organization. In contrast, men generally took ultimate responsibility for the leadership of the organization. Their work was identified with strategy and coordination while women were clearly involved with implementation. Reasons for this dichotomy had much to do with exposure to experiences of leadership and political activities, educational preparation, and traditional expectations.

Women participated and were the auddience to meetings, conferences, marches, rallies, and pickets. Quantity characterized the presence of attendance and played a crucial role in the implementation of student strategies. Participation in this area was easily accessible to most students and required minimal political awareness or organizational commitment.

Implementation of work required more political commitment and consistency than being well-versed in political issues. Work entailed meeting frequently and secretarial responsibilities, writing, public relations, fundraising, leafleting, and cooking.

In comparison, the organizational activities of "heavies" were characterized by their almost exclusively male presence, their selectivity, and their responsibility for the ultimate direction of the student organization. Successful organization depended on the capacities of leadership to correctly perceive political events in the campus and community, plan effective strategy and programs, and recruit, maintain, and develop the support of students and community. In the early years, student leaders on several campuses were exemplary in their sacrifice and commitment to the struggle which often disrupted personal commitments and academic goals, as it did for most students who gave the struggle priority.

Within student organizational structure, the difference between quantitative and qualitative participation was basically distinct as work categories; one more or less dominating the other. In considering the role of women it cannot be denied that they participated in meaningful work. All work is meaningful given a constructive goal. As stated earlier, women were generally confined to work which was more quantitative than qualitative and limited to traditional female roles in both the activist and personal sphere of interaction. The full potential of women as persons and activists was thereby confined and stifled.

FEMINISTS

The underestimation of the intellectual and political capacities of the Mexican woman produced some very extreme results. Unfortunately, the least desirable was among the most common. Varying degrees of an inferiority complex led many women to depend on others for direction, credibility, and identity, both personally and politically. Many of these women eventually withdrew from school.

Other women concentrated much of their

efforts in the personal exploration of male/female relationships at which they were believed to be at their best. Some women vicariously sought meaning and strength through their affairs with different men, preferring those in leadership. But the momentary nature and often exploitive character of these relationships led to disillusionment and frustration. It was not unusual for these women to become the object of ridicule and gossip, further isolating them from their peer group and eventually forcing their withdrawal from organizational activity.

Whether women voiced it or not, they were well acquainted with varying degrees of sexism. Feminist consciousness jelled primarily through subjective encounters with it and through deficiencies in organizational function and structure which denied them equal participation. Sex served as a major criterion for the distribution of labor.

At first, it was difficult for women to articulate these observations without a conceptual point of reference with which to explain sexism. Voicing them could result in social, organizational, or political isolation. Eventually, however, the popularity of the Anglo feminist movement served as an important impetus in the articulation of sexism in the Chicano Movement. Within the context of Chicano struggle for liberation, women saw a major contradiction in the subordination of the Chicana woman. Organizational reaction to these criticisms were, nevertheless, severe.

Women were accused of diverting organizational attention from issues of priority. Their criticisms and feminist arguments were thought to be relevant only to Anglo women and divisionary to the movement. Social and organizational ostracism was effectively used in the isolation of these women. Antisexist criticism was interpreted as hatred of men and women were warned, "El problema es el gavacho no el macho!"

The movement could not understand or sympathize with female liberation which the media presented as the whims of bra-burning, man-hating, Anglo middle-class women. Misconceptions of what liberation meant for Mexican women drove activists in the movement to conclude in Denver's 1969 National Chicano Youth Conference that Chicanas did not want to be "liberated."

Chicanas themselves could not readily accept Anglo concepts of feminism, most of which were ethnocentric and which failed to acknowledge Mexican women as members of a different class and cultural group. It was politically incorrect for Mexican women to blame Mexican men for their oppression when both were oppressed by socioeconomic conditions—high unemployment rates, poor housing, lack of medical care, and inferior education. True that the sexist behavior of men contributed to the oppression of women, but this could not fully explain the oppression of Mexican women.

Popular women's issues publicized by Anglo feminist currents were generally identified with one's right to personal freedoms and the revolution of male/female relationships. Too often, male privileges served as the yardstick by which to measure liberation for women. The impression was given that middle-class women's concerns were the concerns of all other women regardless of race, culture, or economic differences.

Although Chicanas acknowledged the legitimacy of issues popularized by the general feminist movement, they knew that their liberation would have to go beyond the issue of mere equality with men because Mexican males were no better off, politically or economically. But Chicanas who failed to perceive their liberation in class terms failed to correctly identify the source of their oppression. This made them susceptible to bourgeois feminist positions that embraced capitalism as ideal and espoused professionalism as remedial to social problems.

In contrast, Chicanas in San Diego, for example, advocated class struggle as the solution to women's oppression. However, these positions were largely influenced by forces deriving from outside the movement and were hardly popular within it.

Chicana feminism itself was delineated not so much through cohesive political statements as through the focus of issues and activities. Chicanas took the offensive on the woman question by concretely addressing issues which were of major importance to Mexican women. Realizing that any work focusing on Mexican women would have to be implemented outside orthodox student organizations, they regrouped into exclusively female discussion workgroups and/or worked with community-based women's service organizations.

They explored areas of concern in student

and community newspapers, newsletters, documents, and journals which they themselves organized and published. Although Chicana issues were similar to other women's issues, they were also undeniably distinct.

When Chicanas addressed issues of health and medical care, language, poverty, and racism were important variables. Mexican women and their families were often denied services because they could not speak English or afford the services. The racist sterilization of Mexican women and their use as guinea pigs in birth control experiments made easy victims of poor women who also had problems understanding English. Equally unjust were the high disproportionate numbers of Chicanas who were unemployed or on welfare. If Anglo women were asking for better, more rewarding jobs, Chicanas were asking for the right to work. Employment for many of these women was not a choice but a necessity which, in turn, reflected their immediate need for adequate childcare. In addition, the educational level of Mexican women was lower than that of black or white women. Her chances of filling positions made available by affirmative action programs were again disproportionately lower because she lacked the skills and the experience.

Although the movement had no formal position on the status of Mexican women, feminist activity filled this void by providing observations and interpretations on her predicament. Chicana feminists were recognized as spokespersons for Chicano women in general and frequently spoke on campuses, radio, and television talk shows, and testified before government commissions on the status of minority women.

Communication with other feminists in northern California and throughout the Southwest was established through travel and conferences, culminating in the First National Chicana Conference in 1971. The conference was held in Houston, Texas, and involved the participation of more than six hundred Mexican women from the Southwest and Midwest. Events at the conference vividly characterized the polarization existing between feminists and nonfeminists.

Nonfeminists expressed the popular sentiments of the movement by reiterating that men were not the problem and that it was the responsibility of women to be supportive of them and of the movement in general. They walked out and held their own conference in a nearby park.

The remaining women resolved to send tele-grams to the American Medical Association condemning the use of Mexican women as involuntary participants in birth control and other drug related experiments. They called for free, legal abortions, birth control, and twenty-four hour childcare centers controlled by the community. The Catholic Church was condemned as being instrumental in the oppression of Mexican women and Chicano awareness and self-determination was advocated.

Feminist contributions to the movement in general were significant. Chicanas introduced and qualified a list of issues relevant to Mexican women. These included welfare rights, employment, childcare, birth control, involuntary sterilization, health and medical care, affirmative action, and the family. Community service programs initiated by women specifically addressed the need for skill development and employment. In addition, feminist activities allowed young women exposure to political experience, encouraging initiative and leadership qualities normally denied them in male-dominated organizations. Furthermore, they questioned whether middle-class feminism was representative of women's concerns in general. Pressure from feminists and the overall attention given women's issues eventually made it necessary for movement groups to acknowledge and address the issue of women. Finally, the labor and activities of women in this period of movement history complied consistently with a history of female activism in the Mexican struggle for self-determination.

But the liberation of Mexican women could not survive merely on issues which failed to place it within a general sociopolitical perspective able to identify the roots of women's oppression. The liberation of women had to be linked with the liberation of a people and a class in as much as they were an integral part of these.

IDEOLOGICAL DEVELOPMENT AND CONCURRENT ORGANIZATIONAL STRUCTURE

As the student movement grew less and less effective as a leadership force in the movement, community activity, particularly in Los Angeles, provided an encouraging contrast. The political line and presence of some of these organizations served to recruit community members, workers, and students. By the mid-1970s these groups were the most visible in their defense of the class interests and democratic rights of Mexican people. Through democratic centralism, collective work, discussion, and criticism, membership was obliged to comply with organizational and political responsibilities.

EXPLOITATION OF WOMEN

The relationship between the working class and the capitalist is undeniably antagonistic. The capitalist must continually strive to make profits if he is to remain in power and the worker must continually fight for decent wages if he is to remain alive. Their interests conflict, and one group succeeds only at the expense of the other.

Much of the oppression resulting from the exploitation of one class by another manifests itself in the oppression of women. The personal, sociopolitical, and economic oppression of women contributes directly and indirectly to the power of capitalist oppression. If women as laborers are oppressed and exploited in their status as a reserve army and cheap source of labor, then their exploitation has direct consequences for all workers when female labor is used to hold down wages, prevent unionization, maintain insufferable working conditions, or replace the labor of strikers. Their social inequality serves to justify their economic and human exploitation through their devaluation as persons entitled to democratic rights. The human devaluation of Mexican women has led to their systematic sterilization by government supported agencies. Interpersonal oppression of women, whether intentional or not, in effect, only reinforces this devaluation. The political mobilization of women, then, is crucial to any struggle of class liberation.

THE ORGANIZATION

The status of women in organization is reflected in their organizational and political roles which in turn reflects democratic participation. The organizational structure encountered in one particular national organization based in Los Angeles comparatively contributed to the democratic participation of both men and women. This Marxist-Leninist group adhered to democratic centralism and the practice of criticism and self-criticism, and when these were applied with honesty and consistency, they contributed significantly to the development of political, organizational, and leadership capacities. The number of women in the organization approximately comprised half of the membership with some nuclei being composed entirely of women. This specific characteristic did not differ greatly from student organizations where the number of women was equally as high and where it was not unusual for some committees to be entirely female.

Democratic centralism requires participation at all levels of the units which make up the organization and, although national leadership is centralized, it is theoretically obliged to consider the direct input of its rank and file units essential to effective collective work.

Collective work and study were political responsibilities within the organization, and the nucleus strove for organizational, political, and theoretical development by involving the participation and discussion of its individual members in all areas of work, whether it concerned planning, evaluation, criticism, or discussion of study. Anticollective behavior such as lack of participation, intimidation, individualism, and arrogance were targeted for rectification through criticism and self-criticism.

Consequently, the leadership development of the general membership was comparatively greater and superior to that under student organizational structure.

Collective work discouraged division of labor based on sex, creating similar work tasks for both men and women. Selection of leadership depended on theoretical and political competence, consistency of work, and was largely chosen by one's immediate peer group. Both men and women were equally responsible for completing assigned areas of work whether these involved writing documents, leading study groups, selling newspapers, leafleting, manning booths, childcare, providing night security, office work, or cleaning.

The consistency and dedication with which many women met their responsibilities clearly showed their ability as a force in collective leadership.

OBSTACLES

Male/female interaction, nevertheless, continued to reflect several tendencies reminiscent of past organizational relationships. The most obvious was the exclusively male leadership at the national level. This situation changed in 1977 when the rank and file elected women to fill two of the seven top national positions.

The lack of national female leadership revealed the general situation of women in the organization and their unequal political development. This was undoubtedly due to limitations arising from objective conditions such as lack of organizational and political exposure, as well as subjective prejudices largely attributable to sexism.

If women were expected to participate equally in democratic centralism as well as contribute to the liberation of their people, then their organizational and political development was imperative. Although women continued to have difficulties with matters concerning self-confidence, assertiveness, articulation, and political awareness, it was normally assumed that these problems would more or less resolve themselves through general work activities without a program of action to address them directly.

Sexist behavior and attitudes on the part of some men, however, showed no signs of rectification. On the contrary, some found it expedient to ideologically and physically intimidate women who failed or refused to comply with their political or personal position. Once again, women served as links of communication in internal political networks of loyalty to male figures who, in turn, provided them with political direction and protection. Sex and family connections were sometimes used to recruit women and maintain them in these relationships. Slander and attacks on personal integrity were used to discredit women and remove them from leadership when necessary.

Organizational attention was given these and other problems once women in the organization initiated concern through informal and formal discussion. Consequently, the integration of women and the development of women's issues were formally adopted by the organization as legitimate political goals at its national meeting in 1977. Sexist behavior and attitudes were equally discouraged.

Although the need for the liberation of women was acknowledged in theory, the organization tended to place the relevance of this matter in an either/or context which resulted in the issue being avoided altogether or isolated from all other organizational priorities. The nature of women's issues was analyzed in a manner which

was interpreted as directly challenging the priority of working-class issues. Failure to recognize the crucial role of women as an integral part of the working class left the impression that one could only be developed at the sacrifice of the other and, in effect, allowed liberal attitudes towards sexism and the unequal status of women in the organization. Consequently, the organization dragged its feet in the implementation of a concrete program for women.

PRAGMATIC CONSIDERATIONS

Childcare

The presence of women in organization eventually results in the presence of children in work areas, meetings, and social functions.

Lack of a childcare program made it difficult for married and single mothers to involve themselves fully and competently in organizational work, eventually forcing parents to choose between giving priority to their political activities or their children.

On the one hand, work suffered when women were late, unable to complete work assignments, or attend meetings because of their children. On the other hand, when the women had no other recourse but to bring their children to work, the children noisily played in an area already too small to work in. When the children wanted to eat, sleep, or go home, it was not always possible since work took priority. Mothers either brought them lunch or fed them at the nearest hamburger stand, and the children slept in the office while their parents worked until the late night or early morning hours.

It was difficult for parents to reconcile organizational activities with the circumstances under which they placed their children. Children were not receiving needed attention in matters dealing with, for example, homework, punctuality at school, and recreation with peers. This situation forced some women to lessen their activities to a minimum or withdraw totally. Consequently, the work of the organization suffered when it lost the talents some of these persons brought with them.

The organization eventually initiated childcare on Saturdays. When it took place consistently, the children looked forward to it and enjoyed the activities in which they participated. Children were also organized into children's brigades and marched with the organization in mass demonstrations carrying the red flags of their group and chanting for the liberation of their people and class; they were truly impressive. Activities such as these compensated for many things.

Any organization which recruits the involvement and commitment of women must commit itself to the development and maintenance of effective programs of childcare and education so important to a class struggle. Children too must learn to work collectively and aspire toward socialist ideals. Work itself and the involvement of women cannot continue to suffer because adequate childcare programs are lacking.

Recruitment

Presently, the number of Mexican working women exceeds 40 percent and is continually rising. Many of these women are unorganized and exploited in some of the lowest-paying and least desirable jobs in this country's economy.

Yet, the organization failed to seriously consider placing the recruitment and organization of working-class women on the list of its priorities. The quantity of working-class women in any progressive organization must increase as must the quality of their political development made possible through the implementation of systematic programs.

Arguments by some state that qualitative change in the status of women must first be preceded by quantitative change in the organization's number of female decision makers; but this may not always be feasible. Consider, for example, who first decides to allow female leadership in a male dominated organization. Also, some women are unaware of the need to promote other women to leadership. Most importantly, if quantitative change in the number of female cadre is conditional to their qualitative transformation, their lack of development is mechanically and superficially attributed to numbers.

A Women's Commission

The formation of a women's commission within the organization could have been vital to the development of programs and work with women in general. It could have assisted in the identification of target areas for work, conducted investigative work or necessary studies, and developed and implemented programs. It might have more effectively coordinated and overseen the consistency of all work in this area.

Protection of Women

Traditionally, destructive behavior towards women has been hidden behind the facade of privacy, asserting that a man has a right to beat his wife, his lover, or women in general. The women felt that if we could not condone the abuse of one class by another, clearly we could not condone the abuse of one sex by another. Any organization which adheres to class liberation will make every effort to rectify tendencies and practices which result in brutality to women. Privacy does not exist where the human rights of half the population are concerned.

Oppression of women is convenient only to the oppressor, and in some ways many of us contribute to this oppression; but the struggle for the liberation of women must be removed from the individual realm and made a collective responsibility. Ultimately, the clarity or ambivalence with which an organization chooses to deal with these responsibilities reflects its overall commitment to class liberation. If women have endured some of the greatest injustices throughout history, then their status may serve as a criterion by which to judge the progress of a people's liberation.

CONCLUSIONS

Chicano movement organizations in the late sixties and early seventies brought about an uneven, yet definite process of exposing women to organizational and political activism. Recruitment into the local and national struggles of the movement for many women occurred while they were students in high schools, colleges, and universities. There they were exposed to campus and community politics.

The increase in the number of women in political activities did not, however, change the general nature of their organizational roles. Women continued in traditional maintenance roles through their work and homemaking activities as office workers, secretaries, cooks and cleanup crew. Male/female relationships were often qualified by the movement's romantic conception of a woman's place in the revolution. Consequently, avenues for her full development as a political activist remained limited.

The impetus and motivation toward a fuller more significant integration and development of women was provided later by two distinct social influences emerging within the broader context of Mexican activism. For one, Chicana feminism was an immediate response to the sexism of the movement. It sought solutions outside of movement traditional structures. When it spoke of liberation, it spoke of the liberation of women in general. When it spoke of the liberation of Mexican women, it addressed particular issues which, in actuality, applied to an entire class and ethnic group; but class contradictions among women were interpreted as racial. When feminism failed to make the connection between the liberation of a class, an oppressed nationality, and women, it failed as a social and political force, and it failed to rectify the inequality of Mexican women in organization.

In contrast, a Marxist-Leninist perspective placed the liberation of women within the context of class struggle and the liberation of a people. The petty-bourgeois feminist assumption that the interests of one class of women were representative of all women was misleading and denied that class interests determine political interests.

By the mid seventies several sectors within the movement of Mexican activists in southern California had developed ideologically and assumed organizational structures strongly conducive to the development of class consciousness among Mexican women. Specifically, class consciousness helped to democra-

tize the structure and function of the organization by requiring both labor and leadership from male and female members alike. The gradual acceptance of Marxist concepts by Chicanos gave a wider social perspective to the aims, issues, and political activities of the movement. Women could no longer remain isolated political entities, nor could Chicanos continue to delineate a political arena for themselves at the exlcusion of any Mexican.

Clearly, the liberation of Mexican women cannot begin only after the working class has been liberated. It must be a concurrent struggle, for women are part of that oppressed class, and, in addition, part of an oppressed sex. Women themselves must assume responsibility for changing both the objective conditions and the subjective influences resulting from sexism. It is no longer enough to explain why the oppression of women exists within the movement, we must now ask why it persists.

NOTES

1. United Mexican American Students (UMAS), which later changed its name to Movimiento Estudiantil Chicano de Aztlán (MEChA) were the more active Chicano student campus organizations in the late sixties and early seventies.
2. *The Woman Question: Selections from the Writings of Karl Marx, Frederick Engels, V.I. Lenin and Joseph Stalin.* (New York: International Publishers, 1973).
3. For an overview and critical analysis of Southern California's Mexican student movement see Juan Gómez-Quiñones, *Mexican Students Por La Raza: The Chicano Student Movement In Southern California 1967–1977* (Santa Barbara: Editorial La Causa, 1978).

LIVES OF CHICANA ACTIVISTS:
The Chicano Student Movement (A Case Study)

Patrícia Hernandez

INTRODUCTION

The Chicana activist is an intriguing subject for study. She is different from the usual portrayal of the Chicana-Mexicana in the mass media. She is well-educated, often university taught, in addition to being self-taught. She has denounced many traditional roles, choosing to spend her time leafleting, organizing, and studying. She is immersed in la política.

The Chicana activist is not just a "women's libber." She charges United States society with racism as well as sexism. She constitutes an integral part of her people's struggle against discrimination, low-paying jobs, and inadequate housing and education.

The Chicana activist is found among those who have accepted a class struggle analysis of this society, and who have, therefore, joined the larger political struggle against the capitalist system. This type of Chicana has embraced a Marxist-Leninist political line, and thus has dealt with being on the outside of system politics. She is not in the mainstream of women's politics; she is not accepted by many elements of the Chicano movement. Her involvement

requires discipline, commitment, caution, and discretion. It requires her undivided attention.

This essay concerns itself with the personal lives of two Chicana activists who began their political careers with the Chicano Student Movement in the late 1960s. Today, over ten years later, they remain strong political activists. This essay attempts to show the personal effects of politics on their lives during the years of 1968 to 1976. The interviews were taped as the women were questioned concerning family reactions, relationships with friends, time spent in political activity, marriage roles, and motherhood. Aliases have been used to preserve their privacy and freedom. One woman is married and has a daughter, the other woman remains single.

In order to get the full impact of the experiences of these women, their activities are shown within the political context of the Chicano Student Movement at San Diego State College (now San Diego State University). Both women were students there during the formative years of the student movement. They both held leadership positions in the MEChA (Movimiento Estudiantil Chicano de Aztlán) student organization. What happened at San Diego State is in itself a unique chapter in the history of the Chicano Student Movement. Strong student control of MEChA and of the Chicano Studies Center

Patricia Hernandez attended the University of California, Los Angeles and was active in the student movement.

was held by Marxist proponents until a severe political split took place which resulted in the loss of student dominance. Both women were intensely involved in this ideological dispute. The information presented in this study comes from primary documents of the time; position papers from the students and the community, letters of resignation, and taped interviews with students and faculty were also used.

This essay is useful for a number of reasons. First, it allows us a rare view into the personal lives of Chicana activists, revealing the extent of their political commitment. Moreover, the Chicano family is brought into focus as it attempts to deal with the influence of politics, on itself and on the lives of its children. In addition, this paper could add a new perspective from which to view the Chicano Student Movement. The movement left indelible marks on its participants, particularly on the women.

To the Chicano Student Movement came many young women who were away from home for the first time, and who were still imbued with the traditions of the familia. For most of them, this was their first experience with rallies, protests, and organizational conflicts. For some, it would be the beginning of a politically active life which would continue long after their school days. During these first years, young Chicana women made important decisions about the conflicts between traditional cultural roles and new revolutionary roles. Predictably, the changing role of the Chicana is also dealt with in this paper.

This essay adds to the history of the Chicano Student Movement in general, and to the account of San Diego State University in particular. But, more importantly, it contributes to the history of the Chicana-Mexicana activist. Chicana activism is not a phenomenon without precedent. It has been manifested by the heroines of the War for Independence, the French Intervention, and the Social Revolution of 1910 in Mexico. Historically, Mexicana women have also been active in movements for women's suffrage and civil rights. History finds them involved in politics, forming ligas of their own. In 1911 the Liga Femenil Mexicanista was formed under the auspices of the first Congreso Mexicanista in Laredo, Texas. The Chicana-Mexicana has also been an integral part of the labor struggles of agricultural, cannery, and industrial workers. Her efforts, therefore, in the more recent Chi-

cano Movement should not be viewed with surprise.

The first part of this essay briefly summarizes the Chicano Student Movement at San Diego State; it focuses primarily on political developments. The second part will concentrate on the lives of Carmen and Gloria. This inquiry seeks to particularize the young Chicana activist of today. Unlike most past investigations, here we will concentrate on their personal lives.

SAN DIEGO STATE COLLEGE

Chicano students at San Diego State began to organize themselves as early as 1967. The Mexican American Youth Association (MAYA), was the first organizational name which was also used nationwide. In 1968 or 1969, the name was changed to Movimiento Estudiantil Chicano de Aztlán (MEChA). The Chicano Student Movement on campuses was part of the larger Chicano Movement of the 60s. The farmworker's struggle to unionize campesinos; Rodolfo "Corky" Gonzales' Crusade for Justice in Denver, Colorado; and the Land Grant Movement in New Mexico led by Reis López Tijerina, all represented part of the Chicano Movement. Chicanos were clearly responding to their social and economic conditions of inadequate housing and education, low-paying jobs, high unemployment, drug abuse in the barrios, and lack of political power.

Nationally, Chicano students began to marshall their forces, choosing, at times, confrontation tactics to gain their objectives. Students at San Diego State, as well as on other campuses, raised basically the same issues as those raised by the community. However, they also focused on educational issues concerning institutions of higher learning. They pushed for the establishment of Chicano studies, student supportive services, and for increased Chicano enrollment.

By spring 1969, six classes were offered in Chicano studies at San Diego State. By 1970, federal funds had been obtained through Model Cities Program for developing an escuelita in the barrio. Chicano enrollment was augmented due to the gains made by students in demanding more viable minority programs.

These accomplishments, however, did not distinguish San Diego State from any other campus. Most Chicano students throughout the state fought for and gained similar concessions. What was different about this campus were the conditions under which MEChA and the Chicano Studies Center operated. Basically, two factors were at play which eventually collided, exposing the severe political contradiction which existed among Chicanos on that campus. The first factor was that the development of the Chicano Center coincided with the administrative push for university status at San Diego. The second factor was the policy of student control of MEChA and of the Chicano Center.

As a state college, the campus was arranged in divisions rather than in schools or colleges. The transitional period from a college to a university allowed for a certain amount of flexibility in new and developing programs. From 1969 to 1970, the Chicano Studies Center was not easily accommodated in the existing structure; therefore, it was allowed to exist outside traditional structures. Moreover, it had a separate source of funding. In 1971, MEChA members met with the deans of the College of Professional Studies and the College of Arts and Letters. They discussed the feasibility of the Chicano Center becoming part of one of the two colleges. MEChA students chose to remain outside the university structure. In 1973 the university no longer asked for compliance; the administration merely stated that the Center would be included in a school or college by fall 1974; MEChA objected.

MEChA's opposition to entering a college was based upon a number of rationales among which student control was central. Almost from its inception, MEChA was in a process of creating a strong body of students who would control and direct Chicano studies and Chicano programs on campus. If the Center were placed within a college or school, student control would be lost, since university rules and regulations would not sanction it.

By 1973 Chicano students, through MEChA, instituted the following measures to insure student control. Their implementation was facilitated by the fact that the Center was operating outside of university traditional structures.

1. The hiring and firing of all faculty, administrators, and staff would be controlled by students.

2. Students would be involved in all faculty affairs. Voting rights were recognized for

students at faculty meetings. This would insure that all faculty matters, such as curriculum development, faculty committees, grading policies, etc. had student input.

3. Self-grading was encouraged in all Chicano studies classes. It was felt that Chicanos could understand and decide what was best for them.

4. Full-time faculty positions were split among students and faculty so that students could team-teach. This was felt to be one step in eliminating the traditional student teacher role which, they felt, kept students dependent on their teachers for direction.

5. Students sought to implement salary sharing.

6. Students desired access to all files at the Chicano Studies Center.

7. There was to be a student co-chairperson of the Center.

8. There was to be student control of the political direction of the Center.

MEChA members, during this time, also discussed the question of political theory and the need for a viable political philosophy. After many day-long meetings, MEChA adopted a "class struggle" analysis, then they formed a number of Marxist-Leninist study groups. This, however, did not occur without dissension. The Chicano Movement had begun as a struggle against discrimination and exploitation of Chicanos. It emphasized building Chicano pride and culture. Now many activists were realizing the limitations of such an analysis. They advocated a class interpretation which would unite the working-class people against the system that exploited their labor. In essence, these two positions reflected the nature of the political dispute which erupted as the university moved to absorb the Chicano Center and eliminate student control.

When the school administration announced the incorporation of the Chicano Center, MEChA proposed a motion calling for the resignations of all Chicano faculty, staff, and administrators. Although the motion was eventually recalled, it was successful in exposing the idiological struggle within. Some of the students and faculty did not agree with the political direction which had been taken. Some faculty members resented and refused to cooperate with the policies of team-teaching or salary sharing. Many Chicanos wanted to retain a nationalistically oriented, independent movement. These people, along with members of the community, charged the Marxists with elitism, undemocratic, and "un-Chicano" practices.

The Chicano community of San Diego intervened in the political struggle at the university. However, to this day, the question of who constituted the "community" is still argued. Marxist students say the community group did not represent the workers; nor was it representative of the community in general. In any event, the community was negative to the class struggle advocates. They felt that the Chicano Center was being used to brainwash people in a philosophy that did not meet the needs of Chicanos on campus or in the community. It is interesting to note that the response from some community based people changed over time. In the beginning, the community had been very supportive of the student organization and of the students in general.

In fall 1974, the Chicano Studies Center was incorporated and became part of the School of Arts and Letters. The action was probably facilitated by the internal ideological split. At one point some faculty members informed the administration of the activities and of the structure of the department. Once this was done, the university stepped in immediately and demanded that the department comply with all university rules and regulations such as hiring and firing, student participation, and class content.

It is difficult in such a brief summary to give a precise account of the Chicano Student Movement at San Diego State University. What I tried to present was the essence of the political development. Moreover, and perhaps most important for this essay, the question of student control surfaced as central to the MEChA organization of San Diego State. To that extent, the organization differed from other MEChAs in the state. The ideological split was not in itself an unparalleled phenomenon. In fact, it occurred within many student organizations. It is reflective of the political shifts that were taking place within the Chicano Student Movement at that time. MEChA at San Diego State was dissimilar to the extent that the political dispute meant the loss of student control with regard to the

Chicano Center. Here, the proponents of Marxism were attempting to run the Center on the principles of a collective. They had actually instituted the measures listed earlier. Thus, the ideological struggle not only meant the loss of MEChA but also the loss of the Center.

The personal effects on those involved in such an intense struggle would, no doubt, be difficult to measure. The two women interviewed, in the following pages, were involved first as students, and second as full-time faculty members of the Chicano Studies Center from 1971 to 1974. Following the political dispute, their contracts were not renewed. The university stepped in and enforced the M.A. requirement which neither of these women could meet. Moreover, one of the women was married to a Chicano administrator there. If she were rehired, it might appear that her husband had exercised influence.

In retrospect, the women still view the occurrence as painful. They have memories of alienated friendships, hurt feelings, and broken relationships. They remember the experience as exhaustive. The gains made, especially in the beginning years, are now seen as reformist. The Chicano Student Movement has been assessed by them as having been contradictory in regard to the Chicana. Although exposing a philosophy of liberation, the movement continued to oppress women. The Chicana's political development went through stages at San Diego State. These two women were actively involved in organizing and educating Chicanas, both in the community and on campus. In the following pages we look into the lives of Carmen and Gloria as they interacted with their friends and family during their student movement days.

PERSONAL LIVES: BACKGROUND

Gloria and Carmen both came from "traditional" Chicano families. When Carmen told her father she was going to college, he asked her, "Why? After all, you're just going to get married anyway." Gloria's family was also strongly influenced by their cultural-religious background. Simply stated, la mujer was expected to get married, have kids, and stay home. That's how it had always been.

The social and economic condition of both families corresponds with the usual pattern found in Chicano circles. Both fathers were self-taught mechanics at one time or another. They both changed jobs often. Carmen's father was also a seasonal farmworker. They lived in the Imperial Valley in the city of Calexico where the majority of the people are Mexican-Chicano laborers. Both mothers augmented the family income by being housekeepers, taking in ironing, or babysitting. In recent years, Gloria's mother had been working in a small department store. After five years of employment, she was promoted to sales clerk. In Calexico, as in any barrio, this was considered a good job.

Although Gloria and Carmen grew up in similar economic conditions, their development took different forms. While Carmen, between the ages of five to fifteen, got piano lessons from her aunt, Gloria led gangs of pachucas in barrio gang wars. Once in high school, Carmen joined the school band, where she played the clarinet and flute as well as the piano. She also ventured into student govenment, where only a few Chicanos were ever seen. She learned to swim and later became a lifeguard at the local neighborhood swimming pool. This was not the usual route for Chicanas, in fact, Carmen's experiences were quite out of the ordinary. Gloria, on the other hand, continued her gang activity until her high school junior year. However, at about sixteen, she began making an effort to do well in school. She decided that she did not want to spend her life working hard like her parents had done; she wanted a decent job. As a result, she joined Future Teachers to learn about that profession.

It is most revealing that two women with substantially different experiences became political dissidents. One woman can be described as having achieved a certain amount of assimilation, and experiencing a reasonable amount of success in a number of areas. The other one, scarred by street fights, and finding herself heading towards the same economic situation as her parents, struggled hard to change her course. Both women now discuss their past experiences and disagree as to whether it made them susceptible to political involvement.

INITIAL INVOLVEMENT: 1968-1969

Like most Chicanas in college, these young women were admitted under the Educational Opportunity Program for minorities (EOP). Increased Chicano enrollment in those years was the direct result of Chicano student demands the previous years. EOP provided some financial support, however, it was not sufficient and students were forced to work. Both Carmen and Gloria worked in the Chicano barrio as translators or counselors with younger Chicanos. Carmen remembers when she tried to hold down three jobs, carry a full load of classes, and remain politically active in MEChA. Gloria's mother would cross the border many times into Mexicali in order to buy groceries for her. Both of them agreed that those were hard days.

Carmen was only eighteen when she started at San Diego State where she said she met with racism and sexism. She got involved in MEChA because she was frustrated and needed to talk things out. After a few months, Carmen took a leadership position which required her to develop speaking abilities and leadership qualities. In 1969 she became chairperson for the Chicano Council for Higher Education (CCHE). She travelled around the state, coordinating meetings, activities, and conferences for the nineteen state colleges. Carmen also taught a class on the Chicana in 1969, before she became a faculty member of the Chicano Studies Center.

Gloria went to San Diego State in 1969. She became politically active after her second semester. Feeling that something was lacking in the classes, she began attending different political meetings on campus, including black students' meetings. Once in MEChA, however, she took on a number of leadership positions. In the beginning she was, at one point, elected secretary of MEChA, but declined the position, at which point she spoke on how women were looked upon as those who would type, file, cook, and do the work behind the scenes. After this talk she was elected treasurer.

During this time, the women's issue was beginning to surface among Chicanas. Both Gloria and Carmen later became catalysts in organizing Chicanas on the campus. MEChA, at San Diego State, became one of the earliest and strongest Chicana organizations on a college campus; between 50 to 150 Chicanas were usually present at any given meeting.

THE FAMILY CONTEXT

Carmen stated that her parents did not react strongly to her involvement. "They had always been anti-Anglo, so they didn't really react.

They accepted and respected what I was doing, especially because of our support of the farm-workers' issue." Carmen took her parents to MEChA meetings when they came to visit her. Unlike many other parents, they had no problem accepting the term "Chicano;" only her sister opposed the use of the word and her involvement.

Today, Carmen says her parents do not really know "who she is." She senses that they may think she is a socialist because of the literature she sends them. Carmen's mother has read such books as *Origins of the Family, Private Property and the State,* by Engels. Mailing literature to relatives is something Carmen does regularly.

Gloria's story is different. For approximately one year she did not tell her parents about her involvement. When she would see them their main concerns were, "How are you doing in school?" and "Do you have enough to eat?" In her second year, 1970, Gloria finally did tell her parents—their response was mixed, but positive. She said they did not fully understand, and at times, they would be frightened by television or newspaper reports of Chicano events.

Gloria and her parents eventually began to discuss politics which caused her parents to review their life experiences and identify the discrimination and inequalities they suffered. This exposure was the impetus for Gloria's father to demand a raise at his mechanic's job. He was receiving minimum pay for doing highly technical work. Consequently, he quit and was unemployed for six months until he was called back and given a raise.

Because of Gloria's efforts and encouragement, her brothers and sisters began to develop politically. She brought them to San Diego State College where they were introduced to the Chicano Movement. In those days they worked together and had similar politics. Today, that has changed—they disagree with her political direction and they no longer work together. There is still close contact among them, and at family gatherings politics dominate the discussions.

When asked if her family relationships have changed because of her political involvement, Gloria responded, "It's helped my relationships. I have developed politically and understand certain socioeconomic factors that come into play in terms of people working." She talked about her father, for example. She said she could better understand why he drank heavily.

She can see why, after working hard in the hot sun all day, he wanted to come home and drink. Gloria said that the relationship with her father, especially, has improved. Reactions from family and friends, however, were not always positive. Gloria remembers when the pressures of politics got too heavy, she would go home to rest, many times in need of money, food, or emotional support. Her mother would ask, "Gloria, why do you do this to yourself? Why don't you put your personal life first."

Close friends from the community had trouble, too, understanding Gloria's involvement. At a party with the "old crowd" in 1969, Gloria and her movement friends from San Diego State College were faced with a confrontation because of their beliefs. In 1970, at a bautismo, Gloria again found herself torn between movement friends and community friends and relatives. Parents got involved and old family grievances erupted. Gloria got the baby's parents involved in a political discussion, a matter her parents did not like. She said she felt torn apart because these were people who almost raised her, but who did not agree with what she was doing. On the one hand, she wanted to keep her relationships, on the other hand, she was committed to certain principles.

To this point, the effects of political activity has been measured in terms of responses from others. Now we look at the internal effects this activity had on the two women. These effects stem from the amount of time spent in activity, decisions made on the basis of political commitment, and decisions concerning marriage, motherhood, and traditional roles. As mentioned earlier, these women presently see their gains in the Chicano Student Movement as reformist. Nonetheless, the following discussion centered on their dedication and commitment in those early days.

When we discussed the amount of time Gloria and Carmen spent in political activity, Carmen stated that meetings took up a lot of her time. Depending on the issues, some meetings lasted an entire day and some even through the night. As chairperson of CCHE, Carmen was frequently out of town for entire weekends. In addition to the time spent on political activity, Carmen worked either on or off campus in order to support herself. Along with her work, she also attempted to maintain high grades and develop basic writing, reading, and speech skills, which she lacked when she entered college.

During those first years, both women experienced a difficult change in terms of the time spent with their families. At first, they went home at least two or three weekends a month. But, gradually, they found that more and more of their time was spent on other movement activities. It became painful to explain their absences to their families. "It wasn't that we didn't want to be home, it's just that it was necessary to be somewhere else."

The amount of time and effort put into politics naturally affected other areas of their personal lives. Gloria, for example, told about the effect of politics on her health. By 1970, she became physically sick and mentally exhausted. By now, MEChA had gained a Chicano Studies Program, supportive services, and other objectives they had fought for. The situation had deteriorated so much for her, however, that she transferred to Sacramento State College, hoping to regain her strength. However, as a political activist, Gloria could not refrain from involving herself once again in the Chicano struggle. Soon, she was immersed in community activities and meetings. She did, however, concentrate more on school and frequently made the dean's list. Before she left Sacramento, she became ill again due to a combination of political pressures and family problems. About to lose their home, Gloria's parents looked to Gloria to take on the responsibilities of the family. Gloria headed home.

As to their involvement with men, these two women had radically different experiences. Carmen was married at an early age of nineteen. Gloria, at the time this paper was compiled in 1976, was still single. Being twenty-eight and unmarried contradicts traditional Mexican lifestyle. Gloria, although once engaged, broke her engagement approximately one year after she became involved in the Chicano Student Movement. Ironically, while she was developing into a political dissident, her fiancé was fighting a war in Vietnam. When he returned, Gloria tired to get him involved in her political struggle but to no avail; they just could not relate to each other anymore. Gloria says it was difficult to end the relationship because both families had been planning the marriage and furniture and gifts had been bought for them.

Gloria says it is still very difficult for her to deal with traditional roles. She is aware that certain behavior is expected from her. For example, Gloria was instilled with the idea to get married at an early age. Because she has not, she finds she must repeatedly explain why and defend her actions. In any case, were she to marry, she feels it would never result in a traditional male and female relationship. She feels that marriage partners must be supportive of each other. They must reeducate themselves about traditional roles so that they do not oppress each other.

Gloria has discarded many traditional ideas, especially those that are materially based. At times however, she finds herself having to compromise for the sake of her parents. As to her political activity, she tells them only part of what she is doing. "They could not handle it if I told them everything," she says. They still nag her about settling down with a family and a husband.

During her eight years as an activist, Gloria had two lengthy relationships with movement men whom she worked with. She candidly speaks of the difficulty she had when a relationship was not going well. Her political work suffered and she could not be as effective as she wanted to be. At times, when Gloria felt lonely or defeated because of politics or because a relationship was going badly, she received emotional support from other women. The women talked and helped each other by sharing their experiences. Gloria felt that many women activists quit their political work due to pressure from a husband or boyfriend. In some cases, it was a matter of not wanting to sacrifice time and energy.

Carmen, on the other hand, has been relatively content with her marriage to an activist in the Chicano Student Movement. Through the years they have gone through separations and difficult times, but, for the most part, they have remained close. The lack of time together has been, and continues to be, one of the greatest sources of tension between them. When Carmen was chairperson for CCHE, their relationship went through its worst time because she was gone so often. Carmen feels that if her husband had not been involved in the movement, their relationship would not have survived.

Traditional roles have been exchanged in their marriage, many times with great struggle for both of them. Carmen does not cook, her husband does. A three day separation took place over this issue before it was resolved. This marital dispute was closely monitored by Carmen's peers to see if she could put her theory into practice. Many of these women had criticized her for marrying so young.

Carmen agreed with Gloria that marriage should be a supportive partnership. She also stated that political unity was imperative in a marriage between two activists. This unity would allow the freedom necessary to help each other develop politically. However, it has occasionally been absent from Carmen's marriage. Carmen states she is not sure at what point she would choose her political commitment over marriage. "It would depend on the circumstances. For instance, if a strong political party was emerging that needed very committed people . . . I don't know, I'll resolve that if I come to it."

Now, Carmen sees her marriage and political work as having equal importance. Carmen talks about one point in her life when she chose her marriage over politics. The organization she was with required a lot of time and work. She was attending study groups which were held at all hours. One study group was scheduled at midnight, another at 5:00 a.m. At least six hours a day were devoted to study groups. At that time Carmen's marriage was lacking political unity. She and her husband were at different political levels and he wanted her to spend more time at home. The situation came to a head when her daughter became ill. Carmen chose to take care of her instead of going to the study group. She was severely criticized for her decision. At that point, she realized she had to begin to take care of matters at home; they had priority at that point in time.

Carmen maintains some traditional ways. She believes respect for the elderly and for children is very important. Carmen stated that in the future, her daughter's opinion would be well respected. However, she says that because sometimes she is very tired she is impatient with her daughter. But, for the most part, Carmen is satisfied with her role as a mother. She, perhaps does not spend as much time with her child as she would like to, but she believes that, "It's not so much the quantity as the quality of time spent together."

Both Carmen and Gloria agreed that the task of raising children should be a collective effort which aunts and uncles, friends and relatives should share. They feel that children should learn from a number of relationships. She said that political women should share the responsibility of caring for each other's children. Child care should be handled collectively if necessary.

Carmen looks forward to having more children. This will, no doubt, have an influence on her political life, but she thinks motherhood and activism are compatible.

CONCLUSION

By 1976, Carmen or Gloria could still be found at study groups, leafleting, or involved in organizing laborers. Gloria stated that she takes time off from her work only when necessary. She was just beginning to take weekends off. Carmen is still trying to balance her life between marriage, motherhood, and politics. When asked if at any time they felt like quitting, they both answered yes.

Being a political activist means a lot of work without pay. Both women agreed that one must be economically self-sufficient in order to do political work. Gloria is so involved in political work that she works only part-time at a salaried job. Recently, she taught a class at a state college. There is no doubt that her economic condition is affected by her political commitment. She has her M. A. and is qualified for a good job. However, the work of educating women and politicizing people is more valuable to her. She, as well as Carmen, look at the future with hopes of realizing their political goals.

Personal fulfillment to Gloria is being able to give more political direction to people, especially to Chicana women. She relates well to women of all ages. She and Carmen presently have ongoing women's study groups. Carmen looks forward to an involvement in a strong political organization. Also, she plans to become an integral part of the labor force as a welder. She feels this will enable her to put theoretical learning into practice. Her economic status has not suffered by her political commitment. She has been able to work at a job and still continue her political activities.

Today, life for Carmen and Gloria is more intense than it was in the student movement days. Both are cautious about how they do things, and they are more experienced in political work.

Carmen and Gloria are, perhaps, somewhat representative of the young Chicana activists of today. They are serious in their business and involved in a struggle. Hopefully, this paper has shed some light on the extent of their commitment, on the effect of politics on their lives, and on their daily struggles as students, and as Chicana activists.

BIBLIOGRAPHY

Primary Sources

Position Paper by Proponents of Marxism-Leninism (May 1974), San Diego State College.

Analysis of Chicano Studies: Student Control or University Cooperation by Proponents of Marxism-Leninism (September 1974), San Diego State College.

Letter of Resignation to SDSU from a full-time professor of Chicano Studies Center (August 20, 1974).

Paper of Historical Background of Chicano Studies Center by Proponents of Marxism-Leninism, San Diego State College.

Memorandum from Associate Vice-President for Academic Affairs, San Diego State University to Chicano Studies Department (August 6, 1974).

Position Paper by Chicano Community Representatives (April 1974), San Diego State University.

"Community Plan" supporting the original concept of MEChA (May 1974) San Diego State University.

Letter from the Chicano Federation of San Diego County to certain proponents of Marxism-Leninism, San Diego State University.

Taped Interviews

"Lives of Chicana Activists," with Chicana activist, Gloria (alias), 85 minutes, February 22, 1976.

"Lives of Chicana Activists," with Chicana activist, Carmen (alias), 95 minutes, February 22, 1976.

"Chicano Student Movement at San Diego State University," with Chicana activist, Gloria (alias), 70 minutes, September 1, 1975.

"Chicano Student Movement at San Diego State University," with Chicana activist, Carmen (alias) 70 minutes, September 1, 1975.

"Chicano Student Movement at San Diego State University," with professor who resigned, 120 minutes, August 8, 1975.

WOMEN IN THE CHICANO MOVEMENT

Carlos Vásquez

A resolution which emerged from the women's caucus at the 1969 Chicano Youth Conference held in Denver, Colorado read: "We have come to the consensus that we do not want to be liberated." This was indicative, at the time, of two dynamics in the Chicano Movement: (1) a reaction to attempts by Anglo "left" groups particularly the Socialist Worker's party to promote petty bourgeois feminism in the movement; and (2) the lack of ideological clarity and unity among Chicanas on the woman question. This situation was to change dramatically over the next few years.

In the early stages of the Chicano Movement and throughout its later years, sexism was clearly present in many forms and on many occasions. There existed a double standard of work and social life among men and women involved in the same struggle. Women did the petty work, men did the leading. Women's opinions were belittled or ignored and rarely was the woman allowed meaningful positions of leadership. Tokenism was utilized for women who agreed with the positions of the dominating males of the group or organization, while those who differed were ostracized as "Anglo" or "bourgeois" feminists.

Carlos Vásquez teaches Mexican History at California State University, Los Angeles, and is a graduate student in the Department of Latin American History at the University of California, Los Angeles. © 1980 by Carlos Vásquez

To circumvent inevitable changes in the status of women in the movement, attempts were made to romanticize the problem away. Qualities of "Las Adelitas" and the "beautiful Aztec princess" were attributted to the women. This was a way of replacing the religious pedestal on which the Mexican woman had been kept in subservience, with romantic, political, and cultural pedestals used for the same end. By romanticizing the conditions of the woman, she was supposed to remain quiet and obedient.

In another vein, we grabbed onto the concept of the traditional Mexican family and by this means sought to box the woman into a role of mother, housemaid, and little else. This limited her participation in the political struggle and made it virtually impossible for her to participate with the same level of intensity as her compañero.

It was in the midst of this confusion and struggle within the movement that Northamerican "left" groups tried to secure a toehold in the Chicano Movement with their definitions of feminism. These attempts provoked a reaction from the Chicano movement and forced Chicanas to come to grips with the true nature of the struggle in which they were involved. They had to differentiate it from that which promoted a feminism which demanded little more than equal participation in the exploitative and racist activities of white middle-class males. It was necessary to differentiate between those who saw the enemy as men, and those who came to understand that sexism emanates from exploitative class relations and that the resolution can only be found in class struggle.

In the process, many Chicanas were "burned-out." Those identified as bourgeois feminists were ostracized both by the men of the movement and by the women who saw this as just another form of assimilation and not as a true consciousness of struggle among women of an oppressed people. It was easy to see who was fighting for women's rights and who was fighting for the rights of an entire people.

Out of these struggles emerged two kinds of female leaders. There were those who differed little from the most egotistic and opportunistic of the men. These women usually made a name for themselves, but were unable to hold onto positions of respected political leadership. Although women's efforts were occasionally infected with long-winded, self-importance, this is less a tendency among women leaders than is among too many compañeros.

The struggle served to sharpen the contradictions between those who saw the need for change and were willing to work for it, and those who merely tried to cover up basic chauvinist attitudes. The strong, persistent compañeras who were prepared to study and to take struggle between the sexes and within our people to the most personally expensive levels, made the difference among those who came to change their attitudes of reactionary machismo and chauvinism. Their commitment to love and respect women, and still be strong in their commitments to their people, earned them respect among men and women.

As practical workers, women proved to be the more consistent and persevering. Eventually, the antagonisms initially caused women to assert their identity, their dignity, and their contributions to the people's struggles, produced creative dialogue and struggle which forced many males to change and allowed many women to develop. Many men, seeing the energy, the talent, intelligence, and efforts this unleashed, welcomed the women. Others did not and in still more subtle ways continued to perpetrate sexism and chauvinism.

We learned many lessons from the struggles to define the role of women in the movement. Women are central to the construction of a new society and for the preparation of those generations who must fight to win it. We learned that women's participation in the struggle strengthens and, in fact, solidifies the movement. It is not so much a struggle between the sexes as it is a struggle to insure that women play an equal role in a people's struggle for self-determination. We learned that women's oppression is a triple oppression of sex, nationality, and class. We learned that sexism deprives the movement of over half of a people's forces. Today, a revolutionary movement can succeed only when its forces are free from the restraints of sexual chauvinism.

All these lessons were made clear through struggle. But not all men, nor even all women among our people, have internalized or learned them. We have much to do and a long way to go in defining the correct role of women in our struggle for self-determination. But clearly, the Chicano Movement did much to begin the process of insuring that women play their correct role among the political forces which our people create.

TOWARD A DEMOCRATIC WOMEN'S MOVEMENT IN THE UNITED STATES

Roxanne Dunbar Ortiz

The United Nation's Decade for Women (1976–1985) has recently begun, following the 1975 International Women's Year in the United Nations. Nineteen seventy-nine was the Year of the Child in the United Nations, in conjunction with the Decade for Women.

A perspective on the past ten years of the women's movement in the United States is needed. A review would be useful for women who have been involved in the women's movement and for women who are just now becoming involved, but particularly for minority women who are building women's organizations within their liberation movements in the Unites States.

An analysis of the social and economic situation of women in the United States would be a most useful contribution. However, this brief analysis does not have that broad focus. Rather, it is intended to present a perspective on the "Women's Liberation Movement" and to provide some indications of the future direction of the struggle of women in the United States. Though this paper is particularly directed toward minority women in the United States, it should prove useful for all women interested in or involved in the women's movement in this country.

Roxanne Dunbar Ortiz is a Professor of Native American Studies at California State University, Hayward. © 1980 by Roxanne Dunbar Ortiz

ORIGINS

Though many women who have been involved in the "Women's Liberation Movement" were not activists in the Civil Rights Movement of the late 50s and early 60s and the Anti-War Movement from 1966 to 1975, the emergence of "women's liberation" in 1968 is inseparable from those broader movements. In fact, it may be said, in part, that women's liberation grew out of those movements as a response of women activists to the male supremacy which existed in those movements. However, it may be more correct to say that the strong leadership of black women in the Civil Rights Movement raised the consciousness of the young white women who were involved in that movement. The ideology of "women's liberation" was based, first, on the ideology of the Civil Rights Movement and the Anti-War Movement, and secondly, on the negation of male domination in those movements, which became, in large part, a rejection of leadership per se. Even though "women's liberation" developed its own internal programs, it emerged from the larger movement and grew from there. Therefore, whatever ideological problems and directions exist in "women's liberation" are problems generally existent in our contemporary movements in the United States, and are products of the cultural and socioeconomic dynamics of this society. These problems appear not only in the three broad mass movements of the past two decades—Civil Rights, Anti-War, Women—but also appear in the national liberation movements of Afro-Americans, Mexicans, Puerto Ricans, Native Americans, and the labor movements as well. Therefore, an analysis of "women's liberation" reveals generalities associated with movements in the United States rather than specific characteristics only of "women's liberation."

The emergence of the Civil Rights Movement in the South in the 1950s marked a whole new era in United States social history. That movement may more appropriately be described as a continuation of the long struggle for black liberation; but, because the movement has been so extremely influential, it is best described here as the Civil Rights Movement. Though black people, and certainly all colonized peoples in the United States, have never stopped struggling for freedom and liberation, the historical time, the emergence of new leadership, the expansion of the mass media and literacy, the urbanization of the majority of Americans, decolonization movements throughout the world, the repressive McCarthy era, and many other social and economic factors brought about the widespread (worldwide) impact of the Civil Rights Movement in the United States. This movement, coupled with the U.S. involvement in Vietnam, brought about a powerful and effective Anti-War Movement which dominated the mid-60s, and brought about unprecedented international consciousness within the United States. Hardly any person in the country remained unaffected by these mass movements.

Masses of people, particularly youth from middle-income families, became activists during the 60s to a greater or lesser degree. Exposure to the liberation movements in the world brought about support not only for the Vietnamese in their resistance to U.S. imperialism, but also for African, Asian, Arab, and American national liberation movements. Support for the Cuban Revolution and visits to Cuba became common among activists, and millions of Americans were thereby exposed to the ideas and practice of socialism. Coming out of a period of extreme repression against those who espoused socialist ideals and a period of "Americanism" which created, at the minimum, confusion and

fear, and at the maximum, virulent anticommunism, antiactivism, racism, and repression, many of America's youth found some of the ideas of socialism compelling. The Communist party, reduced as it had been by the repression of the McCarthy era, did not provide the primary leadership for the mass movements of the late 50s and 60s. Although many activists and organizations proclaimed their identification with socialism, most condemned the Communist party as reactionary, revisionist, reformist, or even dead. Most chose to take sides in the Sino-Soviet dispute, and nearly all identified themselves with the Chinese (Maoism), while at the same time supporting liberation movements which were Soviet-allied, such as Cuba, South Africa, and Vietnam.

"Women's liberation," when it emerged in 1968, was heir to the admixture of left ideologies prevalent in the broader Anti-War Movement. The organization which was the base for a number of key initiators of "women's liberation" was Students for a Democratic Society (SDS), which had itself been an outgrowth of the Civil Rights Movement, in particular the Student Non-Violent Coordinating Committee (SNCC). SNCC had been multinational, though primarily white and black, until it reorganized itself under new militant leadership as a black organization at which time SDS and Southern Student Organizing Committee (SSOC) formed themselves as virtually all white following the direction of the new SNCC leadership which said that white people should organize whites, in order to bring about the liberation of black people. As the United States war in Southeast Asia intensified, SDS became the principle anti-war organization capable of amassing great numbers of students and youth in teach-ins, sit-ins, demonstrations, and protests against the war.

Most women activists in SDS had also been Civil Rights Movement organizers. With the growth of SDS and the Anti-War Movement, thousands of young women and men entered the movement who had not been active in the Civil Rights Movement. Concurrently, the mass movement of farm workers, mainly Mexican people born in the U.S., had vitalized the liberation struggle of Mexican people who had been colonized by the United States when half of Mexico's territory was conquered by the U.S. in

1848. The Chicano Liberation Movement emerged. With the occupation of Alcatraz in 1968, the Native American resistance was reactivated. Similarly, the long struggle for Puerto Rican independence experienced an upsurge in growth and influence. Still, the Civil Rights Movement set the style, not only for the Anti-War Movement but also for these re-emerging liberation movements of oppressed nationalities; and it set the style for the re-emerging "Women's Liberation Movement."

Although the broader mass movement never ceased to pose a united front strategy and ideology, the emergence of new leadership and ideology in SNCC came to dominate organization methods. The ideology of "organize your own people around their oppression" became the rule. The strategy of militancy and confrontation came to dominate the movements around 1968.

Nineteen sixty-eight was the apex of all the autonomous movements. The single thread which provided a basis of unity was opposition to the war in Vietnam, though none of the emerging militant individuals and organizations posed the end of the war as their primary goal. At the same time, the apex of unity in the broad, mass movements also existed. There emerged remarkable alliances which indicated the potential of a united front strategy in the United States. The Poor People's Campaign of 1968, led by Martin Luther King before his death, brought together national minorities and poor whites with a progressive class perspective in its program and method of organizing. The working-class perspective inherent in this campaign and the consciousness of racism was an almost unique phenomenon in the history of social movements in the United States. The Vietnam Veterans Against the War was a multinational, primarily working-class organization which formed in opposition to the Vietnam War. The Chicano Moratorium organized tens of thousands of people in opposition to the war in Vietnam. The National Welfare Rights Organization, mostly poor women from all nationalities, was an effective mass movement striking at the heart of the profitable welfare state.

The need for a united movement was clear in 1968 and leaders groped for the means to create one. Key leaders were assassinated and murdered. It is no accident that the women's movement re-emerged from the contradictions and growth of this mass movement which opposed the United State's socioeconomic system and its imperialist foreign policy. The potential breadth of a mass women's movement was breathtaking to envision. But, like other movements, the women's movement inherited no clear program in 1968. "Women's liberation," the militant wing of the women's movement, immediately formulated its position along the lines of separatism and confrontation (of men), using that tendency of the civil rights movement as an analogy and a theoretical base. Yet, at the same time, the struggle for unity was also a powerful force.

As in the other broad movements, a number of professional people identified themselves with "women's liberation." This element was not right wing and reactionary, generally, but rather reformist and liberal, and though politically naive, on the whole they were progressive. Some of the more conservative women who began to identify themselves with "women's liberation" were not newcomers to the fight for women's rights. In fact, "women's liberation" was the latecomer to the field of women's organizing, nationally and internationally. Women for Peace, Women Strike for Peace, Women's International League for Peace and Freedom, the National Organization for Women, and others were already established mass women's organizations. Internationally, women's organizations within the socialist countries and within liberation movements of the colonized world had existed from the birth of those countries and movements.

Every mass movement exhibits a variety of manifestations from conservative through militant. Often the scale coincides with age and generational differences in the United States. "Women's liberation," the particular phenomenon which emerged in 1968, was analogous to other militant segments of the movements of the late 60s. Militancy itself became fashionable and media-promoted. The Black Panther party, Brown Berets, and the American Indian Movement were characterized as militant by the media, as was "women's liberation." To a great extent, these new formations did represent the anarchist element of the broad based mass movements. Ideas of instant revolution, instant consciousness raising, confrontation, ultra-democracy, collectivism, and autonomy of small groups marked these organizations. However, they also contained within them the goals of unity, struggle, and sincere commitment. They were also open to the infiltration of police provocateurs and authorities seeing the advantage of promoting violent tendencies and imprisoning or killing leaders. Significantly, the leadership within these new formations were also new to the movement, the new blood, restless and angry, who had not gone through long years of organizing, demonstrating, and learning from experience, were tired of waiting. In "women's liberation" development, this lack of experience produced facile analysis: "separatism," "feminism," notions of a "woman's state," and "man-hating" as a political strategy.

Practically analogous patterns developed in the other capitalist countries of Europe as well as in Canada and Australia, signifying the similarity of socioeconomic conditions under capitalism which, in turn, set the tone for social movements in those countries.

The militancy of "women's liberation" is less indicative of real hatred and resentment for men, or of viewing men as the enemy, than it is of an already formulated model of organizing which had developed and which the leaders of "women's liberation" applied to organizing women. Notions of self-fulfillment and personal identity and "having one's own thing" were strong forces in the movements and remain so today. Another strain of anarchist revolutionary fervor also emerged (Weatherman) which denied self and identity, but called for the abolition of the family, sex role playing, etc. Stable and experienced movement leadership tended to shun the militant fringe elements of the movements though attempts were made at education and influence.

THE WOMEN'S MOVEMENT TODAY

Programs hammered out by women during the height of "women's liberation" activism remain today. Although some have proclaimed that the women's movement is dead or controlled by reactionary forces, this is questionable. The International Women's Year Conference in Houston in November, 1977 drew 20,000 women, many of them minority women, far more than any conference during the height of activism. Demands for the right to abortion, equal pay for equal work, job promotion, end of job and edu-

cation discrimination, antirape, protection for battered wives, and child care still predominate in the women's movement. These broad demands cross class and racial lines and touch masses of women. Within the movements and organizations, women have emerged as leaders and spokespersons in ways almost unimaginable a decade ago. In fact, millions of women and men in the United States have been profoundly affected by the women's movement in the past decade. In terms of absolute political and economic gains, there have been few. One thing should be clear by now: The capitalist system cannot afford democracy.

"Militancy" and "man-hating" is outside the mass women's movement today, if it exists in movement form at all. Mysticism and false ideologies get much publicity, but are not specific to the women's movement. The Jesus movement, cultism, communal living, sexual experimentation, matriarchism, are isolated and exist among people who have not received political education. In the past five years, mass movement in the United States has been contained. There have been protests and demonstrations among all groups and growing labor movements, yet these have not reached masses of people, and the mass media has downplayed political movements and promoted mysticism with extreme care. Yet, organizing has gone on. Women, activated by their oppression as women, and particularly women from the working class and minority peoples, take the women question very seriously indeed. The struggle for equal rights for women is a permanent part of our future goals in the United States. The form the organizing will take and the direction of the women's movement will depend both on the larger movement and social conditions including the international situation.

BASIS OF MALE SUPREMACY

Male supremacy, on a personal level, manifests itself in certain behavior patterns expressed by men and women toward women. Male supremacy is a relatively recent historical phenomenon. Vast data and oral history indicate that noncapitalist societies do not practice male supremacy and the suppression of women. On the contrary, women share economic and political power with men. Male supremacy has developed historically with the rise of dominant ruling and ownership classes. Masses of women and men were pauperized and dispossessed of their land and productive base with the rise of feudalistic and capitalistic formations. As labor became the most valued commodity under feudal and capitalist production, women, the reproducers of the labor force, were reduced to only that primary function. The general status of women diminished in all areas of the world where such systems came to dominate, which, with colonialism, was in all areas of the world to a greater or lesser degree.

Male supremacy, like racism, is useful to a profit-making economic system because it also allows for extensive exploitation of cheap and free labor. Since the industrial revolution (development of factory production), women, who make up half the population, have constituted a surplus labor force. Employed or unemployed, women also provide free household and child care. The responsibility for household work and child rearing falls on the individual family, rather than the community, as in noncapitalist societies. Therefore, owners incur no expense in rearing their future laborers. Lacking the former self-sufficient economic and political systems of shared power and responsibility, women, then, are forced into an abnormal dependency upon men for support and upon the political/economic system for jobs and welfare.

WHY POWERLESS MEN EXPRESS MALE SUPREMACY

The advantages of male supremacy for owners and rulers are easily explained—profits and power. However, the advantages accruing to powerless men are more difficult to explain. First, male supremacy becomes an almost automatic behavior pattern for men and women since we are subjected to an educational and social system which promotes male supremacy and the notion of the inferiority of women. Women are oppressed by such attitudes, and powerless men are blown up with an artificial and ridiculous sense of power which pacifies them much as alcohol, drugs, and some religions do. Often, it appears that many poor women and men regard each other as more of a threat than the social system. Of course, it is easier to fight each other than to fight a powerful system. But this must be seen as internalized violence, also perpetuated by the ruling system. Women are

often pacified and repressed by male supremacist behavior. The skills and energy of women are often left untapped in movements, or women contribute only as menial laborers.

Men often justify their male supremacist behavior, and women rationalize their own sometimes subservient behavior, based on "tradition." If, in fact, tradition reflects male supremacy, then that aspect of tradition should be abandoned. To rely upon some supposed tradition of male supremacy perpetuates a self-defeating practice. It is doubtful, in fact, that male supremacy was existent in most noncapitalist societies. Europeans noted women leaders, warriors, extreme mutual respect between men and women, lack of arguing, and stability of relationships in Africa and America. The colonizers saw both men and women in those subjected areas as inferior and inhuman. Colonial officials consistently refused to negotiate with women officials. With the destruction of people's economic bases, women and men lost power, and the male supremacist superstructure was imposed.

Worldwide, there has been a downfall in the status of women, especially in the past 400 years. The economic and political bases of democracy and shared power have been eroded and self-subsistent, noncapitalist relations have been replaced with exploitative and commerical exchange relations. Male supremacy is an outgrowth of capitalist economic relations historically and is necessary for the perpetuation of capitalism.

FUTURE DIRECTION

In terms of women organizing to struggle against male supremacy and for equality, the demands women have been making are absolutely legitimate. In terms of behavior, person to person, men and women have changed considerably. However, the actual economic and political situation of women has not changed, and in some areas, such as the professional world, it has declined. Most movements in this country begin on the assumption that the United States is a democracy (as it claims). Perhaps the political *structure* has democratic potential. There are many types of political structures, but none assure *democracy.* Only ownership of the means of production and distribution assures real political power. A tiny minority owns the land, its produce, and controls the labor and distribution of goods and services in this country. That conclusion is not original by any means. However, the logic that follows is often that "getting a piece of the pie" is the solution. Whether an individual, a commune, Native American reservation, new nation, or whatever, getting a piece of the capitalist pie, even if ethical considerations are set aside, is an unrealistic impracticable and illusionary goal. The possibility for competing economically with the existing multinational corporations which own and control this country in collusion with local, state, and federal elected officials, is non-existent. Therefore, a *political* solution is the only practical strategy for a change in power relations and the establishment of democracy. What that means, necessarily, is the substitution of a socialist political economy for the capitalist political economy. Economic equality and political democracy may only be achieved with fundamental change in the social relations of production, and that can only come about when the *people* control the government, and the government administers production, distribution of goods and social services. The struggle for socialism, then, is fundamental to the establishment of women's equality.

Within this context of a constant struggle for social equality and justice in the United States, other realities are an integral part. Racism in the United States has bred national liberation movements of oppressed minorities and native peoples. Indian nations and communities have the absolute right of self-determination which in some cases may mean political independence from the United States. Similarly, Puerto Ricans assert the right to a separate, independent nation. The two large national minorities, blacks and Chicanos, have the right to self-determination. Therefore, any projected unified women's movement must recognize and *support* the rights of self-determination of exploited minorities and colonized native peoples.

The Women's Movement has great potential in helping to create a unified movement for social change in this country. Any notions of separation of women as a political entity, or the establishment of a matriarchy is absurd. That does not mean women's organizations should not exist. They must. They are terribly important. But so are the goals and programs these organizations project. Within each national liberation movement in this country, strong women's organizations are developing. A broad based women's coalition which crosses national and class lines is essential. Such a movement, to be powerful and effective, must support the rights of self-determination of colonized peoples, struggle for the eradication of racism, oppose U.S. imperialism abroad, call for the end of U.S. warmaking and arms development and oppose exploitative economic relations.

NOTES ON TERMINOLOGY

Language has been a powerful political weapon in formation of male supremacist concepts and ideology. Women have responded with alterations in language in an attempt to educate women and men to transform their male supremacist attitudes. But there are problems with some of the terminology that has developed.

"Sexism" was coined by women militants in 1969 and has become a commonly used word to describe the attitudes of men and women which reflect male supremacy and "male behavior." The term is an analogy to "racism" and tends to cloud the historical and material distinction between male supremacy (a product of feudalism and capitalism) and racism (a product of colonialism and national oppression). The term also implies behavioral and sexual change rather than material change. "Sexism" was found useful to incorporate all forms of *sexual* discrimination, namely homosexuality, again evading the *material* basis of male supremacy —*women* as a cheap, surplus labor force and as unpaid mothers rearing the next generation of workers. Within this fundamental material context, the discrimination against homosexuals is unconnected. Certainly the equal civil rights of homosexuals is a valid cause. It is simply not a part of the economic basis for discrimination against *women*. "Sexism" clouds the roots of the problem. The term "male supremacy" is the more scientific and accurate term.

"Feminism" comes from the nineteenth century women's rights movement, which, significantly, grew out of the mass anti-slavery movement. Whatever "feminism" meant to nineteenth century women activists, it has been a confusing term in the contemporary women's movement. Like "sexism," the term "feminism" emphasizes the psychological behavior patterns that result from male supremacy and exploitative economic relations. "Feminism" goes further though and asserts "feminist" values as ones that should be embraced by men and women. "Humanism" or human rights, human values are the proper terms.

Anthropological stereotypes of American Indian and African socioeconomic systems have produced the vague and unscientific usage of "matriarchy/patriarchy." Male supremacist approaches to democratic, non-capitalist societies identified *shared power* as matriarchal. No such system has ever existed where women dominate and rule, nor will this ever be the case. The historical process went from democracy based on shared economic and political power (though sex-role division of labor occurred) to the development of small ruling classes which dominated, economically and politically, over peasantries and out of that base built a proletariat, composed of women and men. Breaking up democratic, self-subsistant social systems was necessary for the development of capitalism. If "patriarchy" can be used to describe the results, it cannot refer to the dominance of *men* economically. The term patriarch comes from the Roman Code. The Roman government was composed of wealthy patriarchs who legally had the power of life and death over their wives, their children, and their slaves (men and women) as well as the peasantry (men and women) on lands claimed by the patriarchs. This model of the ruling class family with the patriarch as dictator has come down as the idealized social unit under capitalist systems. Such a family structure and ideology of male supremacy has been forced on the dispossessed under capitalism. The extent to which an economically and politically powerless father and husband can exert "patriarchal" control is almost totally limited, and mainly serves to divide the poor and stimulate violent relations within the family. But it is not men per se who hold power. There is a ruling class who are owners of land, resources and labor. Some are women, though the general downfall of the status of women historically has indeed created discriminatory patterns to which even women of the ruling classes have been subjected. But their fight, if they fight for equal ruling class power, is hardly relevant to a mass women's movement. The terms matriarchy and patriarchy should be abandoned. They are not useful contemporary terms.

Women organizing women to participate in the movement for social change and the restructuring of society seems so natural that there would be no question as to the necessity for this to happen. Of course, women must deal with centuries-old prejudices in men and women. The debate which has emerged: "Should there be an 'autonomous' women's movement?" is the wrong question. Women who claim to seek a separate women's culture or nation are not dealing with reality. The media has publicized this fringe fantasy to the point that nearly all men and women view it as a real possibility. Autonomy is a political situation or goal for *communities* and *nations* made up of women, men and children. The term is inapplicable to women's organizations and movements anytime, anywhere. But *women organizing women* to participate in the social movement for change is vital.

Finally, the term "women's liberation" itself; I have enclosed the term in quotes throughout, partly to distinguish the particular development in 1968 and partly to question the use of the term "liberation." The American social system is not noted for its scientific usage of language. Generally, language is used to deceive, distort and develop false ideologies. A scientific usage of liberation has developed worldwide with the decolonization movements in Africa, Asia, the Mideast, and the Americas. These are movements of political and economic self-determination and independence, the formation and building of new nations, liberated, out of the wreckage of colonialism. The usage in reference to women's struggle for political and economic justice, equality, and participation is not analogous and confuses and clouds distinctions. The founders of "women's liberation" sometimes called "female liberation," consciously borrowed the term liberation from those decolonization movements. It is time to drop the term and talk about a *women's movement,* which organizes women to the specific issues of women and to understand economic basis of those ills, in solidarity with liberation movements of all colonized peoples.

THE RISE AND DEMISE OF WOMEN'S LIBERATION: A CLASS ANALYSIS

Marlene Dixon

The history of the rise and demise of women's liberation is a primer for a study of the fatal weaknesses that infected all the New Left struggles of the 1960s. The collapse of women's liberation shortly followed the general collapse of the New Left in the early 1970s. Hindsight makes clear that the fatal flaw of the New Left lays in its inability to recognize the determinative role of class conflict. It was consequently unable to distinguish between class antagonisms within mass movements, a product of the failure to comprehend that revolutionary movements arise and flourish only within revolutionary classes.

Many of the errors of the New Left are perpetuated today, whether it be in the so-called socialist-feminist movement or in the so-called antiimperialist movement. Each such tendency, in its own way, has failed to learn from the recent past. Yet, as women, we must not fall prey to the dictum "history repeats itself," for the massive institutionalized exploitation and oppression of women continues, virtually untouched by all the fulminations of the 1960s, just as American imperialism flourishes with unhampered brutality. Nevertheless, any critique of the New Left must recognize that it

Marlene Dixon is editor of *Synthesis—A Journal of Marxist Debate.* Reprinted with permission from *Synthesis.* © 1977 by *Synthesis.*

was, in itself, a powerfully progressive force in all of its manifestations.

Consequently, we cannot fail to recognize that the women's liberation movement resurrected the "woman question" and rebuilt on a world scale a consciousness of the exploitation and oppression of women. For nearly forty years women had been without a voice to articulate the injustice and brutality of women's place. For nearly forty years women had been without an instrumentality to fight against their exploitation and oppression. From the mid-1960s to the early 1970s, women's liberation became that new instrumentality. From the United States and Canada to Europe, to national liberation struggles in Africa and Asia, to revolutionary China itself, the reverberations of the movement set in motion a new awareness and new movements for the emancipation of women. Whatever the faults and weaknesses of women's liberation in the United States and Canada, it was a historical event of worldwide importance.

Nevertheless, what happened to the women's liberation movement in the early 1970s is precisely what happened to each mass movement of the last decade: internal differentiation along class and political lines. In the case of the women's movement, the remnants of women's liberation have come to be dominated by a middle class leadership, reducing a vigorous and radical social movement to a politically and

inp.

ideologically coopted reformist lobby in the halls of Congress. The problem before us is to understand the course of the class conflict that resulted in the final cooptation and decline of the autonomous women's movement.

CONSCIOUSNESS RAISING: THE BEGINNING

The autonomous women's movement was a necessity of the time, a product of the political realities of the 1960s, a transitional movement which was a direct product of the male supremacist structure of the New Left and the legitimacy it permitted for the expression of male dominance in everyday life. The New Left was an instrument for the suppression, oppression, and exploitation of women. The formation of the autonomous movement was the only reply possible. Women set about organizing women in order to avoid the wrecking tactics of the men and to openly fight against the exploitation and oppression of women. Women would never have been able to do so within the male-dominated New Left. Women clearly recognized that the politics and practice around the woman question on the part of student and other left groupings were deformed by their own practice of male supremacy. Women were forced to conclude, on the basis of experience, that only by building a base among women would it be possible to put a correct priority on the question of the emancipation of women, to confront the entire left and force them to a recognition of the centrality of women's emancipation in all revolutionary struggles.

The origin and importance of the small consciousness-raising group is to be found in the basic organizing tool of the autonomous movement: organize around your own oppression. There were many foundations for such a position. First, the major task faced by early organizers was to get women to admit that they in fact were oppressed. The socialization of women includes a vast superstructure of rationalizations for women's secondary status; the superstucture of belief is reinforced through inducing guilt and fear (of not being a "true" woman, etc.) as a response to rebellion against women's traditional role; consequently, women are raised to be very conservative, to cling to the verities of the hearth, to a limited and unquestioning acceptance of things as they are. However, organizers very quickly learned that under the crust of surface submission there had built up in countless women an enormous frustration, anger, bitterness—what Betty Friedan called "an illness without a name." Women's liberation gave the illness a name, an explanation and a cure. The cure was the small group and the method was what the Chinese Communists call "speaking bitterness." The bitterness, once spoken, was almost overwhelming in its sheer emotional impact.

For many new recruits, consciousness raising was the end-all and be-all of the early movement, a mystical method to self-realization and personal liberation. But for others, especially for left-wing radical women, the original aim of the small group was supposed to have been the path to sisterhood—that unity expressed in empathic identification with the suffering of all women—which would lead from the recognition of one's own oppression to identification with the sisterhood of all women, from sisterhood to radical politics, from radical politics to revolution. Early organizers had correctly understood that women could be organized on a mass scale in terms of their own subjective oppression and by appealing to the common oppression of all women (irrespective of class). Aiming at radicalizing the constituency of women's liberation, early radical organizers talked a great deal about the common source of oppression (hoping to foster the empathic identification that would provide the bridge to cross-class unity). They talked much less about the fact that the common oppression of women *has different results in different social classes*. The result of the class position, or class identification, of almost all recruits to women's liberation was to retranslate "organize around your own oppression" to "organize around your own *interests.*" The step from self-understanding to altruistic identification and cross-class unity never occurred because the real basis for radicalization, common economic exploitation, was absent.

"Organize around your own oppression" was indeed a Pandora's Box of troubles. Middle-class women used this maxim to justify the pursuit of their own class interest: "We are oppressed too." "We must take care of our own problems first." Middle-class women also justified ignoring the mass of working-class women by asserting that "ending our oppression will end theirs," i.e., the fight against discrimination would equalize the status of all women.

The transformation of the small group from its original political consciousness-raising function into a mechanism for social control and group therapy was a result of the predominantly middle class character of women's liberation. The fact that there were so few women in women's liberation who were directly experiencing material deprivation, threats of genocide or enforced pauperizaton—that is, so few who were driven by conditions of objective exploitation and deep social oppression—made it almost inevitable that the search for cultural and life-style changes were substituted for revolutionary politics.

What radicals had not taken into account was the fact that middle-class and wealthy women do not *want* to identify with their class inferiors; do not care, by and large, what happens to women who have problems different from their own; greatly disiike being reminded that they are richer, better educated, healthier and have more life chances than most people.

Therefore, behind the outward unity of the women's liberation movement of the 1960s, centered as it was around a public ideology based upon feminism, sisterhood and the demand for equal rights, there raged an internal fight between the so-called feminists and politicos. This fight was disguised in many ways, most effectively by personalizing it or by casting it as a battle against "male-identified" or "elitist" women, in which the pejorative politico" implied both sins summed up by the phrase "anti-woman." All of these pseudo-psychological arguments were manipulative verbiage which mystified the fact that class politics vs. reform politics, and therefore class conflict for hegemony over the leadership of the movement, were the real stakes of the combat. Certainly, participants at the time often were not consciously aware of the true nature of their struggle, but from the vantage point of hindsight, the true meaning of these struggles is manifestly clear. While in the beginning, roughly from 1967 to 1969, the left was in a relatively powerful position, by 1973 a coalition of the center and right had gained control of the women's movement.

THE RISE OF CLASS CONFLICT

The early and primitive ideology of women's liberation stressed psychological oppression and social and occupational discrimination. The politics of psychological oppression swiftly transmuted into the bourgeois feminist ideology of "men as the enemy," for psychological world-views pit individual against individual and mystify the social basis of exploitation. Nevertheless, the politics of psychological oppression and of invoking the injustice of discrimination were aimed at altering the consciousness of women newly recruited to the movement in order to transform personal discontent into political militancy. Women, being in most cases without a political vocabulary, could most easily respond to the articulation of emotion. (This, of course, explains the impassioned, personal nature of the early polemical literature. It was indeed "speaking bitterness.") Furthermore, women of almost any political persuasion or lack of one can easily accept the straightforward demand for social equality. Explaining the necessity for the abolition of social classes, the complexities of capitalism and its necessary evolution into imperialism, etc., a much more formidable task, often elicited more hostility than sympathy. On the other hand, the stress on discrimination and psychological theorizing aimed directly at the liberal core of North American politics. In turn, sex discrimination affects all women, irrespective of race, language or class (but the fact that it does not affect all women in the same way or to the same degree was often absent from discussion).

The primacy of ideologies of oppression and discrimination (and the absence of class analysis exposing exploitation) and the ethnic of sisterhood, facilitated the recruitment of large numbers of women from certain strata of the middle class, especially students, professionals, upper-middle-class housewives and women from all sections of the academic world.

Given the predominantly apolitical disposition of women in general coupled with their initial fearfulness and lack of political experience, the task of revolutionary political education was an uphill battle from the beginning. The articulation of a class analysis in both Canada and the U.S., too often in a style inherited from the competitive and intellectually arrogant student left, frightened women away or left them totally confused and unable to understand what the fuss was all about. In a purely agitational sense, the feminists' anti-male line had the beauty of simplicity and matched the everyday experience of women; the left-wing radicals had the disadvantage of a complex argument that required hard work and study, an "elitist" sin. However, the anti-male line had its difficulties too, rooted in a fundamental contradiction which faces all women. It was impossible to tell women *not* to resent men, when it was plain in everyday life that the agents of a woman's oppression at home and on the job were men. On the other hand, women were unwilling and unable to actualize anger against sexism into a hatred of men.

Because of this contradiction there existed a predisposition to take a rhetorical anti-male stand (throwing men out of meetings to keep them from being obstructionist, expressing anger and contempt towards men to display defiance and thus give moral support and courage to new women, etc.), overlaying a profound ambiguity regarding what was, or ought to be, the relationship between men and women.

The result was a situation which might be termed dual leadership, made up of the early left activist organizers, the politicos, and the newer level of middle-class women, the feminists, the latter seeking, by virtue of their class position, wealth and education, to bring the goals, ideology and style of the movement into line with their politics and class interests. The ethic of sisterhood publicly smoothed over these two opposing conceptions of the enemy, i.e., who and what is going to be abolished to accomplish the liberation of women. Thus, the public ideology of women's liberation built unity around certain basic feminist tenets acceptable to the mixed class composition of the mass movement: (1) first priority must be placed on the organization and liberation of women (glossing over differing and contradictory positions on the definition and means to attain liberation); (2) action programs ought to put first priority upon woman-centered issues; (3) socialist revolution would not in itself guarantee the liberation of women.

The class conflict seething under the nominal agreement on the basic tenets of feminism was ideologically expressed in two contradictory

lines of analysis corresponding to the dual leadership situation. The feminist line stemmed from the assertion that "men are the principal enemy" and that the primary contradiction is between men and women. The politico line stemmed from the assertion that the male supremacist ruling class is the principal enemy and that the primary contradiction exists between the exploited and exploiting classes, in which women bear the double burden of economic exploitation and social oppression. The leftist line stressed that the object of combat against male-supremacist practices was the unification of the men and women of the exploited classes against a common class enemy in order to transcend the division and conflict sexism created between them. Women's liberation was called upon to combat sexism by combatting the dependency and subjugation of women that created and perpetuated the exploitation and oppression of women. The position on men was explicit: men in the exploited classes, bribed through their privileged position over women, acted so as to divide the class struggle. The source of divisiveness was not men per se but the practice of male supremacy.

One can immediately see that the leftist analysis, pointing to class and property relations as the source of the oppression of women, was much more difficult to propagandize than the feminist anti-male line. In everyday life what all women confront is the bullying exploitation of men. From the job to the bedroom, men are the enemy, but men are not the same *kind* of enemy to all women.

THE MATERIAL BASIS OF BOURGEOIS FEMINISM

For the middle-class woman, particularly if she has a career or is planning to have a career, the primary problem is to get men out of the way (i.e. to free women from male dominance maintained by institutionalized discrimination), in order to enjoy, along with the men, the full privileges of middle class status. The system of sexual inequality and institutionalized discrimination, not class exploitation, is the primary source of middle class female protest. Given this fact, it is men, and not the very organization of the social system itself, who stand in the way. Consequently, it is reform of the existing system which is required, and not the abolition of existing property relations, not proletarian revolution—which would sweep away the privileges of the middle-class woman.

The fact that the fight against discrimination is essentially a liberal reform program was further mystified by the assertion that the equalization of the status of women would bring about a "revolution" because it would alter the structure of the family and transform human relationships (which were held to be perverted through the existence of male authoritarianism). The left line held that equalization of the status of women is not, nor could it be, the cause of the decomposition of the nuclear family. The organization of the family is a result of the existing economic structure; just as the origin of the contemporary nuclear family is to be found in the rise of capitalism, so it is perpetuated in the interests of monopoly capitalism. Furthermore, equalization of the status of women would be no more likely to introduce an era of beautiful human relationships than did the introduction of Christianity bring obedience to the Golden Rule or the Ten Commandments. The claim that status equalization would bring about a "revolution" is of the same order as the claim made by the Suffragists that giving women the vote would usher in an era of world peace. Abolishing discrimination would not lead to a "revolution" in the status of women because it would leave the class structure absolutely untouched. Gloria Steinem might build a corporation, a woman might become a general or a corporation vice-president, but the factory girl would remain the factory girl.

The tactical *and* ideological error of the left in this struggle was to try to win the *entire* mass movement to their position. The failure to recognize class struggles led to the defeat of the leftist position not only because of the predominant middle-class background of the movement, but also because the left had not only to fight the petty bourgeois reformers, but also the anticommunist, cold war ideologies with which almost all North Americans have been so thoroughly infected. Without disciplined organization and a working-class base, a left position will *always* lose in a mass movement, or be reduced to self-defeating opportunism.

SISTERHOOD: ROOT OF BOURGEOIS FEMINISM

The politics of oppression and the politics of discrimination were amalgamated and popularized in the ethic of sisterhood. Sisterhood invoked the common oppression of all women, the common discrimination suffered by all. Sisterhood was the bond, the strength of the women's movement. It was the call to unity and the basis of solidarity against all attacks from the male-dominated left and right, based on the idea that common oppression creates common understanding and common interests upon which all women can unite (transcending class, language and race lines) to bring about a vast movement for social justice—after first abolishing the special privileges enjoyed by all men, naturally.

The ideology of sisterhood came to emphatically *deny* the importance, even the existence, of class conflict in the women's movement. To raise class issues, to suggest the existence of class conflict, to engage in any form of class struggle was defined as divisive of women, as a plot by men to destroy women (after all, were not Marx and Lenin *men*?) as weakening the women's struggle, and the perpetrator was proven beyond the shadow of a doubt, to be a *traitor* to women, male-identified, an agent of the enemy in the sisterhood. Sisterhood was a moral imperative: disagreements were to be minimized, no woman was to be excluded from the movement, all sisters were to love all other sisters, all sisters were to support all other sisters, no sister was to publicly criticize other sisters.

Sisterhood, and the outward unity it provided, also disguised and mystified the internal class contradictions of the women's movement. Specifically, sisterhood temporarily disguised the fact that all women do *not* have the same interests, needs, desires: working-class women and middle-class women, student women and professional women, minority women and white women have more *conflicting* interests than could ever be overcome by their common experience based on sex discrimination. The illusions of sisterhood were possible because women's liberation had become in its ideology and politics predominatly a middle-class movement. The voices of poor and working-class women, of racial and national minority women or even of housewives with children were only infrequently heard. Even when these women were recognized, they were dismissed with a token gesture or an empty promise. When the isolation of the left was complete, almost all internal opposition to bourgeois feminism disappeared.

The collapse of sisterhood was principally a result of the disguised class and political conflict which became acute throughout 1970–71. Under the guise of rejecting "elitism" left-wing women were attacked mercilessly for being "domineering," "oppressive," "elitist," "male-identified," etc. In fact, the early radical leadership was in this way either discredited or driven out of the movement, to be replaced by "non-oppressive," "apolitical," manipulative feminist or "radical feminist" leadership. This was the period of the "trashing." At this time a clearly defined right-wing also emerged, the reactionary "radical feminists" who were, by and large, virulently anti-leftist and anticommunist.

In the end, political debate became almost completely nonexistent in the small group, which was essentially reduced to being a source of social and psychological support. Rivalries, disputes and feuds often grew up between small groups in the same city (each doubtless accusing the other of being "elitist"), frequently having the effect (along with the major programmatic and ideological divisions between feminists and politicos) of making even the minimal workings of a women's center impossible.

REACTIONARY FEMINISM

The bourgeois feminist line, "men are the enemy," branches into two ideologies: liberal feminism and reactionary (or "radical") feminism. The first, liberal feminism, does not openly admit that its ideology is a variant on "men are the enemy" but disguises that assumption behind a liberal facade that men are "misguided" and through education and persuasion (legal if need be) can be brought around to accepting the equalization of the status of women. Since the questions of the origins of injustice and the roots of social power are never very strong in any liberal ideology, there is little besides legislative reforms and education to fall back on.

Reactionary feminism, on the other hand, openly asserted as its fundamental tenet *that*

all men are the enemies of all women and, in its most extreme forms, called for the subjugation of all men to some form of matriarchy (and sometimes for the extermination of all men). It offered a utopia composed of police states and extermination camps, even though reactionary feminists very rarely followed through to the logical outcome of their position.

Reactionary feminism was not an ideology of revolution (the likelihood of victory seeming remote even to its advocates) but an ideology of vengeance. It was also a profound statement of despair that saw the cruelty and ugliness of present relationships between men and women as immutable, inescapable. Reactionary feminism may have been politically confused, and it was certainly politically destructive, but it powerfully expressed the experience and feeling of a whole segment of the female population.

The root of reactionary feminism was in the sexual exploitation of women. Its strength lay in the fact that it did express and appeal to psychological oppression, for this oppression is far worse than the conditions of economic exploitation experienced by petty bourgeois women. In the last analysis reactionary feminism was a product of male supremacy, and its corollary, sexual exploitation. Male supremacy, itself reactionary, breeds reaction.

With the virtual expulsion of the left leadership the "radical feminists" assumed leadership over the portion of the movement not yet co-opted into the reformist wing. The excesses of the right: man-hating, reactionary separatism, lesbian vanguardism, virulent anticommunism, opposition to all peoples' revolutionary struggles (including Vietnam), served to discredit women's liberation and to make public the split in the movement between the reformists and the radical feminists. Of the expulsion of the left, no mention was made, keeping up the masquerade as an "anti-elitist campaign." The triumph of the right resulted in the disintegration of the women's liberation movement. In the shambles to which the movement had reduced itself, left and right opportunists were swift to seize the opportunity to take control. The leftists watched the predictable occur with despair while the reactionary, so-called "radical" feminists, with their shriek of "elitism" still issuing from their mouths, found the movement they had sought to control snatched out of their hands.

THE FAILURE OF PROGRAM

Women's liberation never produced a coherent program. Programmatic development requires theoretical development, and women's liberation was incapable, on the basis of its class contradictions alone, of generating a coherent political analysis. What program and agitation existed clearly reflected the class nature of the movement. The wide variety of national and local single-issue programs undertaken by isolated women's groups reflected the overriding problems of younger, middle-class women: the need for legal abortion (rather than a demand for universal health and nutritional care, including abortion and birth control services, which working-class and poor women desperately need); demands for cooperative, "parent controlled" day-care centers (rather than universal day-care with compensatory educational programs which the majority of working-class parents and children need); the creation of women's centers to provide young women with a "place of their own" in which to socialize, to work for abortion on demand or to secure illegal abortions (rather than creating "organizational" centers capable of organizing with working-class women for struggles on the job or in the community).

The cold truth of the matter is that the women's centers often differed very little from the standby of the suburban housewife—community work, complete with good deeds, exciting activities, lively gossip and truly thrilling exercises in intrigue and character assassination. Within these centers working-class women often wandered about in a state of frustration and confusion. They knew something was very wrong, but they did not know what.

Given the almost exclusive attention to sexual exploitation and the consequent psychological oppression, the focus was not upon male supremacy as part of class exploitation, but upon its result, the practice of male chauvinism; not upon the need for revolutionary social and economic changes, but upon individualized struggles between men and women around the oppressive attitudes and objective sexual and social privileges of men. Furthermore, emphasis upon male chauvinism had the effect of privatizing the contradiction between men and women, transmuting the conflict into problems of personal relationships, rather than politicizing the conflict as part of the overall capitalist system of economic and class exploitation.

The internal failures of the movement may be summed up in a brief series of criticisms. Mass movements contain within them class contradictions; women were far too slow to recognize class struggle for what it was within the movement. Furthermore, lack of a correct theoretical analysis led to the left's inability to generate correct programs to guide internal class struggle. The movement was thus reduced to single-issue mass campaigns which had to coalesce around the lowest common denominator, reform. Leadership thus passed to liberal reformers or left opportunists who opposed straightforward class conflicts or open recognition of the inevitability of such conflict. The movement isolated itself, for these and other reasons, from the concrete struggles of working-class women, in the home and in the factory, who make up the majority of oppressed and exploited women. The final and perhaps the most important lesson to be learned is that a movement without coherent politics, organization and discipline cannot be a fighting organization.

In short, women's liberation, for all its rhetoric and all its pretensions, for all its brave start, has outwardly become what it really was (indeed, what it had to be): an anti-working class, anti-communist, petty bourgeoisie reform movement.

TOWARD A SCIENCE OF WOMEN'S LIBERATION

Isabel Larguía
and
John Dumoulin

"The division of labor ... is based on the natural division of labor in the family and the separation of society into individual families opposed to one another, is given simultaneously ... the unequal distribution ... of labor and its products, hence property ... the first form of which lies in the family, where wife and children are the slaves of the husband. This latent slavery in the family, though still very crude, is the first property, but even at this early stage it corresponds perfectly to the definition of modern economists who call it the power of disposing of the labor power of others."

Karl Marx and Frederick Engels
The German Ideology
(New York, International Publishers, 1947), p. 21.

It is generally believed that women are marginal to the process of production: that their incorporation into the process began with their participation in the commodity economy, in which they were destined to perform an auxiliary role; that their fundamental duties are in the home and in the family where they have a woman's role, unrelated to the economy.

Such ideas, widely held by both people in general and specialists, are based on profound ideological confusion. They denigrate women in various ways. They deny the economic value of the work women have generally performed, and they claim, at the same time, that women are born with physical and spiritual characteristics, the nature of which leads them to carry out a specific type of work. This ideological confusion prevents a complete understanding of the functioning of the economy. What is more important, it conceals one of the oldest and most enduring bases of class society.

Marx and Engels discovered how, in the process of formation of a class society, the family was crystallized into a means of control over the labor power of women, into a means of private accumulation. Their principal investigations responded to the urgent necessity to arm the working class with a scientific knowledge of the basis of their exploitation, thus demystifying bourgeois society and revealing the internal dynamics of the capitalist, commodity economy. They also analyzed the division of labor and the evolution of private property, with its close links with the individual family, revealing

This article was first published in *Casa de las Americas,* Havana, Cuba in March 1971. It was translated from Spanish and published in *NACLA Report on the Americas* (formerly *NACLA's Latin America and Empire Report*), December 1972. The North American Congress on Latin America is an independent nonprofit research organization founded in 1966, focusing on the political economy of the Americas. *NACLA's Report* is published bimonthly from 151 West 19th Street, New York, New York 10011. © 1972 by *NACLA.* Reprinted with permission.

how under capitalism it continues to be "the economic unit of society." They produced valuable studies on the oppression suffered by women, and the ideological superstructure which justified it.

The family, as we know it today, arose with the breakdown of primitive society. It is not by chance that the word "family" referred originally to the right of private property held by the paterfamilias over its members as well as over the material goods that made up his household. The "household" emerged as the first form of private enterprise, as the property of the head of the family, for production, exchange, and competition with other households, and for the accumulation of the surplus product.

The original meaning of the word "economy" is, the art of managing household affairs. The property rights of the head of the family implied inheritance through the paternal line, the total ownership of women, as well as control and expropriation of female labor power.

Such had not always been the case. In primitive society, work and all other social activities were carried out collectively, and both property and kinship relations reinforced these collective bonds. It was only with the emergence of the patriarchal family that social life was divided into two clearly differentiated spheres: the public and the domestic. These two spheres underwent unequal development whereas great historical transformations occurred in the former, the latter, which developed much more slowly, acted as a brake on the former.

With the development of commodity exchange and the division of society into classes, all economic, political, and cultural changes centered around the public sphere, while in the household only the individual family unit, as we know it today, was strengthened. Women were relegated to the domestic sphere by the division of labor between the sexes, at the same time, throughout the ages a very powerful ideology developed which even today determines the image of women and their role in social life.

In order to discover the bases of this ideology and the enormous importance it has had in the development of class society, it is necessary to specify the privatized activities performed by women within the bosom of the family. Thus, the following pattern emerges:

1. strictly biological reproduction;

2. education and care of the children, the sick and the elderly;

3. reproduction of labor power consumed daily.

When these three features are combined, biological reproduction is systematically confused with *the private reproduction of labor power,* not only that which is used up by men and women in the process of social production, but also the early training of the new generation of workers.

Such confusion is the basis for pseudoscientific notions which modern society hails as justification for the division of labor between men and women. The biological factor could not have determined the changes which have occurred in the family since primitive society, inasmuch as it has remained identical throughout the entire existence of the species; nor does it explain the role of women in work and their resulting social position. Furthermore, biological reproduction affects men as much as women, with the exception of the nursing period and, in a few societies, the last months of pregnancy.

Women do not perform domestic tasks because it is "natural" to do so. Ethnological studies of pre-class societies have destroyed the traditional nineteenth century image according to which women have, from the onset of history, spontaneously dedicated themselves to weaving and cooking, while men worked in distant fields, waging epic battles against the indomitable forces of nature.

For example, the Routledges indicated in *With a Prehistoric People* that in the group studied, men were incapable of lifting loads of more than sixty pounds, while women were able to carry a hundred pounds or more. As the authors state, "When a man says, 'This task is too heavy for me, it should be performed by a woman,' he is merely confirming a fact."

In *The History of the USSR* by Briusov and others, we read, "In the neolithic metropoli(ses) of Transbaikal, hunting weapons—bows and arrows—were found in both men's and women's graves, which is characteristic of a matriarchal order."

If we prefer to disregard ethnology and archaeological findings, the daily press offers ample information about the struggle of Vietnamese women. During the Tet offensive, for example, more than two million took up arms.

VISIBLE AND INVISIBLE LABOR

The egalitarian position held by women in primitive society was determined by the value of their productive labor, performed collectively. Beginning with the breakdown of collective structures and their replacement by the patriarchal family, women's labor was progressively individualized and limited to the *making of use-values for direct and private consumption.* Excluded from the world of the surplus product, women became the *invisible* economic base of class society. The labor of men, on the other hand, crystallized, through the different modes of production, into *economically visible* objects, destined to create riches upon entering the exchange process. Under capitalism, through the sale of his labor power, man defines himself essentially as the *producer of commodities,* be it as the owner or operator of the means of production. His social position and his class are determined by his activity and by the position he occupies within the world of production of goods for exchange.

Women, expelled from the economic universe where surplus is produced, nevertheless fulfilled a fundamental economic function. The division of labor assigned to them the task of reproducing the greater part of the labor power which moves the economy, through the transformation of raw materials into use values for direct consumption. They thus provide food, clothing, household maintenance, as well as the education of the children.

Economists today understand that men must produce new material goods in order to reproduce the means of production and subsistence (machines, foodstuffs, clothing, etc.) which are continuously used up. This process of constant replacement of production is known as *reproduction,* and occurs within each business enterprise as well as within society as a whole. But what is not understood is that this simple economic reproduction takes place at two distinct levels which correspond to the abovementioned division of labor. One of these is the most primitive form of enterprise, *the household.* If it is true that male and female workers daily reproduce labor power by means of the creation of goods for exchange, and accordingly

for their indirect consumption, it is also true that housewives *daily reproduce a great part of the labor power of the entire working class.* Only the existence of an age-old alienating ideology of sex prevents a clear perception of the economic importance of this form of direct and private reproduction of labor power.

To put it crudely, if the proletariat could not rely on this type of female labor power to provide it with food, clothing, etc. in a world where collective replacement is not provided for, the hours of surplus labor would be significantly reduced.

In evaluating a country's economy and its possibilities for development, it is not enough to compare the surplus value a worker produces with that part of the worker's labor which pays for his family subsistence. The worker and his family do not subsist merely on what they buy with his wages; the housewife and other household members must also invest many hours in domestic work. In order to gain an understanding of the contribution of housewives, let us assume that they dedicate only one hour a day to the maintenance of each human being living today (an absolutely conservative estimate); we would arrive at a number well over *three billion hours of invisible labor performed.* Under present conditions, the proletariat can produce surplus value in the social economy thanks only to these hours of invisible labor. Therefore we can say that women's labor in the household is converted into surplus value by the wage-labor force.

We must think in terms of the total labor supply, the entire labor force that maintains and develops an economy. We can estimate the relative magnitude of the surplus generated when we compare it with the total work done for the market as well as for direct consumption. This second dimension is not usually taken into account, reflecting the fact that economists limit themselves to the categories of commodity production, i.e., those of capitalism.

Capitalists have no direct relationship to subsistence production, although they exploit it indirectly. The enormous quantity of subsistence labor—especially in the non-industrialized countries—added to the low standard of living, allows capitalists to pay the lowest wages and to extract enormous profits even when productivity is relatively low. The economists' omission reflects the discrimination against women and the confusion between biological reproduction and the private reproduciton of labor power.

The division of labor created skilled male workers, concentrating in their hands the creation of the surplus product. By means of these skills, men were liberated from most of the reproduction of their own labor, permitting them to devote all their energies to social production and public affairs. Thus men's work was crystalized into objects, into economic and socially *visible* commodities. Women's work in the bosom of the family did not directly produce a surplus product nor a visible commodity; women were isolated from the sphere of exchange where all values were connected with the accumulation of capital. Women's work remained hidden behind the facade of the monogamous family, and is *invisible* even today. It seemed to vanish into thin air, because unlike men's work it did not produce *visible* products. Thus, this type of work has not been considered to have value, even though it uses up many hours of arduous effort. *Consequently, those who expended the effort were excluded from the economy, from society and from history.*

The invisible product of the housewife is labor power. It is only under capitalism, with the creation of the working class, that labor power becomes a commodity. Capitalism links women more directly with the monetary economy, because they actually produce for the market— the labor market. But they are not the owners of the labor power which they produce: the power belongs to their husbands and sons, who sell it. Furthermore, the prevailing bourgeois approach does not recognize the nature of this new commodity and claims that the capitalist buys "labor" rather than labor power. In this way the housewives' efforts remain invisible as before. The conceptual confusion between biological reproduction and reproduction of labor power lends physiological overtones to social consciousness; the result is that *domestic work is considered a secondary sexual characteristic rather than an economic category.*

Thus, the housewife does not sell her labor power or its products; rather, her invisible labor power is simply confiscated by means of the marriage contract, obliging her to look after the family, shop, process, and serve, in exchange for her keep and the attainment of a social status determined by that of her husband....

Since her specific labor is invisible, her contribution to the development of productive forces remains hidden. So flexible is the intrafamilial division of labor between the sexes, that the relationship can easily adapt itself to any form of class society, be it feudal, capitalist or otherwise.

Within this domestic context, housewives of the working-class sector ("ladies of leisure" are not included), have the special status of a subclass. Housewives, like slaves, do not participate in the exchange process as producers— either among themselves or with any other class—unless they become part of a collective working unit. They do not form part of the public parade of gentlemen, serfs, slaves, capitalists or other groups. They do not participate in public property relationships through which production surplus is created and expropriated. Their situation (which seems unique, though similar in some respects to patriarchal slavery and in others to subsistence peasantry), is that of contributing to this process as a satellite, through the direct reproduction of the labor power of the rest of the workers.

DIVISION OF LABOR: CONSOLIDATION OF OPPOSING SEX MODELS

"Division of labor and private property are... identical expressions: in the one the same thing is affirmed with reference to activity as is affirmed in the other with reference to the product of activity."

Marx and Engels
The German Ideology, p. 22.

"The ruling ideas are nothing more than the ideal expression of the dominant material relationships...; hence of the relationship which make the one class the ruling one, therefore the ideas of its dominance."

Ibid, p. 39.

Aristotle: "It is a general law that naturally dominant elements and naturally dominated elements exist.... The rule of the free man over the slave is one type of domination; that of man over woman is another...."

Napoleon Bonaparte: "Nature intended women to be our slaves.... They are our property...

they belong to us as a tree that bears fruit belongs to the farmer. . . . Women are nothing but machines to produce children.''

Jean-Jacques Rousseau: ''The entire education of women must be relative to men. To please them, to be useful to them, to make themselves loved and honored by them, to educate them as children, to care for them as adults, to counsel them and console them, and to make life sweet and agreeable to them—such are the duties of women at all times and should characterize them from their earliest childhood.''

P. J. Moebius: ''If women's capabilities were developed to the same extent as man's, their generative organs would suffer and we would have a repulsive and useless hybrid.''

John XXIII: ''God and nature gave women different tasks which perfect and complement the work assigned to men.''

Bourgeois science has produced numerous theories designed to prove the biological inferiority of women. Just as slavery, imperialism and fascism gave rise to innumerable pseudoscientific theories intended to demonstrate the inferiority of oppressed peoples and to justify genocide, an impressive number of theories designed to keep women ''in their place'' have been contrived by psychoanalysts, biologists, doctors, sociologists and anthropologists.

The radically opposing sex models that prevail are the product of the division of labor. Based on obvious biological differences, a vast cultural superstructure has been erected, postulating not only physical types, but also temperaments, character traits, preferences, tastes and talents, which are all assumed to be *biologically inherent* in each sex; they are considered to be secondary sex characteristics—immutable, inevitable and ahistorical.

In a comment on Adam Smith, Karl Marx wrote: ''By nature a philosopher is not in talent and intelligence half so different from a street-porter as a mastiff is from a greyhound; the abyss between them exists because of the division of labor.'' And, ''The difference in natural talents between different individuals is not so much the cause as the effect of the division of labor.''

If for a moment we were able to free ourselves from all the prejudices and the distorted personal experiences which have formed our ideology of sex, we would recognize that the opposing models of today are not due to basic biological differences but to the thousands of years in which the division of labor has prevailed.

Throughout the history of class society, the fundamental task of women has been to stay in the home and maintain the family. In this long process juridical structures and cultural·traits that reinforced the situation were developed and implanted. Morality, legislation, and culture consolidated and buttressed the opposing sex models.

Women were made responsible for the perpetuation of the species; the co-participation of men was not taken into account. Simultaneously, there emerged the belief that women were incapable of performing ''heavy,'' ''dangerous,'' or ''responsible'' tasks.

Whereas in the classical female typology reproductive behavior is determining, in masculine typology, labor for the creation of exchange and for juridical and military defense of the goods produced is the primary factor.

The standards of behavior that crystallized throughout the ages predetermine absolutely the educational formation and social destiny of the new human being, according to sex classification. The education of the girl-child, especially in underdeveloped countries and exploited classes, inhibits her from engaging in rough play and games, to the detriment of her physical and personality development. All interest in mechanics, in work tools, is forbidden to her.

Restricted to the narrow limits of the home, the first and inevitable gift a girl-child receives is the traditional doll, toy pots and pans, chairs, brooms, sewing kits, combs and mirrors; why is she not given a gun or a carpentry set? Along with these early playthings, she receives a long decalogue of ''don'ts,'' which tend to instill in her the fear of exploration of the outside world. She is molded into a decorative, pretty, ''feminine,'' object, and from the beginning the conviction is fostered in her that she was born to please through her sex, rather than expressing herself through work. All her creative forces are channelled into the reproduction of the species and the private reproduction of labor power.

As children, both males and females receive the tools which they will use as adults in the form of toys. Their regular use conditions the users to acceptance, physically and psychologically. Thus, the secret division of labor is assured and the base of class society remains unchanged—thanks to this early recruiting of invisible labor power.

Class culture—poetry, fiction, popular music, the mass media, customs and habits—carries forward the thorough and devastating work begun in childhood. Prisoners of this constraining anthropological pattern, women inevitably see their best creative energies diverted toward a hypertrophied culture of love and reproduction. By the time women reach adulthood, they are, objectively speaking, atrophied beings, who look upon themselves as a human byproduct. The system of values with which they have been provided, and to which they desperately cling in a world hostile to their full development, convinces them that their social advancement can come only from the exercise of their sexual traits. Meekness, passivity, abnegation, and pathological fear of independence are required of the classic woman. Our Western Christian society knows how to strangle with silken cords. It is not necessary to bind the feet of our young women; it is enough to create in them monstrous inhibitions, enough to provoke the death of audacity, energy, and curiosity.

Thus are created the internalized bonds which make women conservative, insecure and afraid to launch an open struggle for their full liberation. Even when rejecting the traditional "feminine mystique" and the burden of class culture, even when joining the revolutionary struggle, they tend to seek the approval of a superior masculine authority. This corpus of "virtue," (with the social pseudonym of "femininity") alienates women from their human condition, and is conducive to private reproduction of labor power.

The expectations that the young man must satisfy are exactly converse. As the future *visible* worker, he must develop his physical strength to the maximum (a development repressed in women), as well as his combative intelligence and courage, characteristics defined by that wornout word, "masculinity." Sad examples of the contrast provoked by the division of labor are the public figures with which capitalism bombards men and women for their respective emulation and identification; the President and Marilyn Monroe.

The existence of a dual morality sanctions oppression of women in everyday relationships. This morality requires of men the demonstration of sexual aggressivity, which in some societies becomes obsessive; and from women, the corresponding masochistic provocation. The ideology born from the male-female polarity finds its familiar expression in false gallantry and wolf-whistles, and inculcates in women the conviction that they are nothing more than objects of masculine possession. The average women does not realize that not only are her "beauty," her "poetic and ideal self," possessed; the ultimate aim is the confiscation of her invisible labor power through the marriage contract.

Romanticism became the most formidable smokescreen behind which exploited slave labor could be concealed. The chubby Cupid which fluttered around our grandmothers was in reality a most effective policeman in the service of private property.

THE INDUSTRIAL REVOLUTION: THE SELECTIVE INCORPORATION OF WOMEN INTO THE WORKING CLASS

With the full development of capitalism, the family unit began to undergo important changes, but the exploitation of women in the home remained unchanged. Only their incorporation into the proletariat began to modify substantially the situation of the mass of women. The formation of the working class created a group of free workers which had virtually no material possessions. Inheritance and paternity, pillars of the family in class society, lost their economic significance for a large part of the population. Small producers however, in developed and underdeveloped countries (where they continued to exist in large numbers), maintained patriarchical relationships.

Industrialization required a rise in the cultural level of the exploited classes. The bourgeoisie favored universal elementary education, which required state participation in the training of new generations of workers, training in which the family shared a role. The prospects for extending education were increased; however, the basic division of labor between the sexes was not modified.

Capitalism introduced some substantial changes in the legal status of married women, granting them, at least in principle, the rights of an individual. Engels writes:

> By changing all things into commodities capitalism dissolved all inherited and traditional relationships, and in place of time-honored custom and historic right, it set up purchase and sale, "free" contract. . . . But a contract requires people who can dispose freely of their persons, actions and possessions, and meet each other on the footing of equal rights. To create these "free" and "equal" people was one of the main tasks of capitalist production. (*Origin of the Family, Private Property and the State,* International Publishers, New York, 1942, p. 70.)

Finally, this principle was extended to the marriage contract:

> . . . the love marriage was proclaimed as a human right, and indeed not only as a *droit de l'homme,* one of the rights of man, but also . . . as *droit de la femme,* one of the rights of woman. (Ibid., p. 72.)

Nevertheless, the exercise of this right—as with all other liberal rights—remained subordinate to the realities of the division of labor.

The Industrial Revolution required the massive incorporation of women into industrial production. A female proletariat was created—a new force in history, which assumed enormous importance in the development of society. Through mass elementary education, the opportunity of invading the outside world was conceded to young women (and young men).

Despite the relative modifications that this change produced in traditional sexual patterns, these modes continue to have a powerful influence on the range of occupations open to women. Even though the struggle of middle-class feminists, who possess the relative security conferred by their social and economic status, enabled them to force some openings in architecture, engineering, etc., women are still not accepted as welders, lathe operators, or masons.

The division of labor between the sexes is merely the faithful reflection of the secret division of labor which frees men for public activi-

ties, while isolating the majority of women within the narrow confines of the private reproduction of labor power. It is not by chance that women have been accepted in the textile and clothing industries, in food processing, and in the services as teachers, nurses, secretaries, elevator and telephone operators and domestic workers. *These activities are merely the projection into the public sphere of the tasks performed by women in the household.* With the exception of wartime, in which necessity forces the incorporation of women into heavy industry, they tend to be systematically excluded from all technologically advanced branches of industry. In certain capitalist countries, the bourgeoisie in power tends to conceal this savage discrimination with a facade of health and safety regulations on the job. Thus, the idea that women can perform only *auxiliary tasks* is fixed in the social consciousness of the proletariat.

The ideal of beauty held by the ruling class—disseminated by the mass media—tends to reinforce in women the fear of healthy development of their physical strength. The division of labor within the proletariat helps to consolidate the old prejudices concerning the sexes in the work area. These prejudices pursue two aims:

1. to justify the payment to women workers of lower wages than men (about 45 percent lower), for the same work and same level of skills.

2. to assign to women "light" production tasks, in order to justify the female workers' obligation to continue reproducing labor power in the home after completing the factory work day.

THE SECOND SHIFT

In *The Origin of the Family, Private Property and the State,* Frederick Engels expressed concern for the future of women, declaring that they would have to choose between being housewives or workers. He could not imagine, and in our judgment he was right, that women could undertake both tasks. But due to just one more irrationality of the capitalist system, women are burdened with both tasks, with the weight of superexploitation which wipes out for them the benefits of the shorter hours won by the working class.

The second shift was not denounced politically until very recently, in spite of the fact that it placed women in the same situation as those (nineteenth century) English workers who worked twelve hours and more a day. Domestic work, invisible and apparently lacking in value, continues to be considered a secondary characteristic, and is given a biological quality; hence, it is considered the most natural thing in the world for women workers to bear the burden of the second shift.

Though women have advanced greatly by participating in *visible* labor, they have done so in exchange for a sacrifice which is conveniently overlooked by the ruling class. They work one shift in a factory, receiving a salary for this work; upon returning to their "home sweet home" a second workshift awaits them, non-salaried, unskilled, stupefying drudgery, which banishes from their minds any illusions of equality with men and of their new much-touted social independence.

From table 1, of the weekly working hours of French women in 1959, we may draw several conclusions:

1. For a mother, the second workshift is as long as her socialized workshift; if she has two children or more, it is longer.

2. Since the second workshift increases with the number of children, working mothers are forced to limit their socialized workshift, a third of which is thus sacrificed. It

would seem that working women are unable to carry a workload of more than eighty-four hours per week (against forty-nine for men); however, the Chase Manhattan Bank estimates that North American working women expend about one hundred hours a week.

3. With respect to the social utilization of labor power, full-time housewives spend far more hours solving problems than paid women workers face.

The childless housewife requires *twice the amount of time* a women worker does to attend to her household. Mothers spend some thirty hours per week more on housework when they have no outside occupation. What causes this? A very marked psychological factor intervenes—the tendency of the housewife to occupy herself obsessively with household duties and to overprotect her children, discharging on them all the energies repressed by the division of labor. This same tendency leads her to give up other activities (cultural, recreational and political). In the words of Betty Friedan, "House-wifery expands until it fills all available time." The working woman has wages at her disposal which permit her to socialize part of the second shift through the utilization of launderies, restaurants, daycare centers and other services.

The conservative political forces of France and other highly industrialized countries, while admitting that women work more than eighty-four hours per week, propose as a solution the reactionary measure of part-time work. Such a solution would *tend to defend the traditional division of labor* and impede the socialization of the second shift and the increase in social wages.

Given that the reproduction of labor power is still considered a secondary sex characteristic rather than a specifically economic function, men consider their participation is degrading. The worker who is a militant activist on the job does not realize that part of the surplus value which the owner appropriates is created by his own wife, with himself as intermediary (in this respect he is fulfilling the role of a foreman).

In the sex typologies of class society, the repressive function belongs to man. How does a woman experience this repression? A woman might well describe her situation as follows,

TABLE 1
Weekly Working Hours for Women

No. of Children	Women Workers			Housewives
	Paid Work	Housework	Total	
0	50	27	77	54
1	45	39	84	71
2	37	47	84	76
3 or more	34	50	84	78

SOURCE: *La femme dans la societe: Son images deres les differents milieux sociaux,* by Chombart, de Lauwe and others, Paris Editions Ouvieres, 1964.

If I protest my situation, the whole of society will put me "in my place," utilizing morality and culture which do not tolerate outbursts of "feminine hysteria." *Machismo* acts as a vigilant policeman, preventing me from losing control and stripping away any process of humanization and awareness on the part of men. The husband who understands his wife, who shares the cleaning, washing and ironing equally, is considered in certain social circles to be physically and mentally dificient. Arrogant, curt, disagreeable, playing the tough guy, threatening—such is the symbol of classic virility. It does not demand ritual sacrifices; worse yet, it is a vampire that sucks from us millions of hours of invisible unskilled, unpaid labor. Implacable border guard of the division of labor, it appears at each step the new woman takes on the road to her liberation. Emulating the *big stick* policy, it was present during the early years of my childhood, to inhibit me and hamper the full development of my physical strength. It appears in all sectors of work activity, to snatch work tools from my hands, to close to me the roads to political leadership, to impede my access to the army, and to all branches of high-level production. When it cannot impose itself by force, the symbol of virility assumes a gentle disguise. Feigning a protective, paternal concern, it claims that good working conditions and the integrity of the family will "protect me." When force is unsuccessful, it retreats (temporarily), adopting an air of wise, self-sufficient irony.

I know it well, I know its ideology and its reason for being. Like the eunuch who keeps the keys of the harem, it is entrenched in the social consciousness, to guarantee a semi-slave labor force for the private reproduction of labor power. It is there to serve the ruling class, to confuse the people, to prevent women from realizing our creative potential, which, if turned to social labor on a mass scale would provoke an immense advance. It is there because if all my sisters understood to what extent they are deformed, to what extent they are exploited, the collapse of the foundations of class society would be hastened.

WOMEN, PRISONER OF CONSUMER SOCIETY

We should not underestimate the enormous ideological and economic importance that sex has today for the survival of class society. The values of liberalism, with its emphasis on individual rights, its total philosophy and culture of individual liberties, seem to be indispensable to the preservation of a stable capitalism. (Fascism has not proved to be a lasting solution.) But in a society dominated by monopolies, petit bourgeois liberalism has completely ceased to correspond to economic and political reality. Sex is the only terrain where liberalism is still actively functioning. Furthermore, it can count on an immense ideological reserve—the complete and unconscious popular acceptance of opposing sexual models. The first decades of this century saw the development of a powerful culture of sex, whose most important ideologist is Sigmund Freud. Both the vanguard of the art world and, later, the mass media, incorporated into the social consciousness of the highly developed countries concepts such as "sexual-repression" and its counterpart "release from inhibition."

The theory that culture is the product of the sublimation of the sex instinct was given a scandalized but nonetheless warm welcome by the ideologues of the ruling class, who soon incorporated it into the bourgeois system of thought. That sex as the base of all culture and the therapeutic value of releasing inhibitions—concepts formulated by psychoanalysts—was promptly accepted and commercialized by class culture and the mass media. Sexual puritanism, which originally characterized bourgeois morality, was replaced by a call for "an end of inhibitions," for a rejection of the established norms.

Sex—cleverly manipulated through advertising, films, television and the press—impregnated the social consciousness of the developed countries. It is the last refuge of the myths of private initiative and individual sovereignty which, paradoxically, stem from puritan wedlock. The new liberty of women fulfilled the ideological function of an escape valve for neocapitalism.

Economic necessity has strengthened this alienation. The principal problem of contemporary capitalist economy is no longer to create the necessary conditions for the *production* of commodities but for the *sale* of these same commodities, the circulation of which is constantly threatening to slow down, preventing the earning of profits. The neocapitalist solution is the so-called consumer society in which advertising becomes the motive force of continuing economic expansion; light industry, aimed at the consumer, becomes its most dynamic sector. Demand no longer "exists" but is "created." Demand has become the ultimate product of radio, television, and mass publications which stimulate the continuous creation of new needs, guaranteeing a permanent condition of unsatisfied and inflated material wants.

The race for prestige is one of the characteristics of this society. Prestige is associated with the purchase and enjoyment of consumer goods, the establishment of social standards increasingly remote from the life of the exploited classes and the Third World. Competition between families and individuals is stimulated to the maximum, in order to guarantee the sales of neocapitalism.

While commodity relations pervade all areas of social life, men and women are increasingly subjected to the world of *things,* that is to say, of their own products. This new economic function of women in consumer society emphasizes their responsibilities as owners of their sex and as partners in family standing. Their function is, increasingly, that of purchasers; a great deal of advertising is focused on women, "dignifying" them in relation to men, stimulating them to buy goods which create a mystic sphere of masculine attraction and approval. Thus, women remain subordinate to men in a subtler, less barbarous way.

Romanticism emphasized the rights of woman over her sex (laying down a heavy smoke screen over the confiscation of her labor power within the framework of her voluntary surrender in marriage—no longer property but a continuing, legal object of exploitation). The rights of woman over herself were recognized by making her the owner of her sex. But like all property under capitalism, sex has the character of a commodity, and thus implies the unending search for buyers: women, in order to enter a marriage contract (i.e., *to sell themselves*), must become a permanent focus of sexual attraction. While the labor power of men is the commodity which they sell and with which they compete, the socially recognized value of women is their sex —and the mystique with which it is concealed. Sex competition is to women what competition for work is to men. If men move upward socially, acquiring a certain standing in the class structure through their work, women accomplish the same feat by a subtle use of sex. Even women in the labor market use the old weapons

of "enchantment," "beauty," "femininity," in order to advance economically and socially.

One of the products of sex competition (and one of its barometers), is a fluctuating, generally accepted fashion, which is nothing more than the normative expression of the sex market, analogous to the stock market. In addition, the increasingly rapid changes in fashion, standardization and mass production facilitated the the expansion of light industry.

The basic canons of beauty which govern the sex market are very far from being expressions of a spontaneous popular culture. They have a marked class character and their function is to accelerate production in light industry and especially to *infiltrate the consciousness of the exploited classes with the aesthetic and moral values of the ruling class.* The ideal woman, as presented by the mass media, literature, and popular songs, unquestionably belongs to the ruling class: slender, with velvety complexion, delicate, lacking any kind of muscular development. The male-female polarity created by the original division of labor is exaggerated to ridiculous extremes. Too much physical development resulting from manual work and sports; muscular arms; the broad, strong hands of a woman worker; a forehead wrinkled by study; all are systematically excluded from class culture and, consequently, not recommended for the woman who is prepared from earliest childhood for sex competition.

Not only the need to prevent stagnation in the circulation of commodities, but fundamentally the need to create a "no man's land," where the ideals of individualism and free exchange can survive (ideals which are the foundation of the bourgeois world), leads to the creation of a distorted culture of sex which in turn becomes an obsessive feature of neocapitalist popular ideology. Advertising tends to exaggerate sexual characteristics and functions to an intolerable degree. In this frenzied race of sex and profit, women become attractive commodities—objects of consumption for a masculine population eager for new experience. When women try to liberate themselves it proves difficult to escape the ideological rules of the games. Upon becoming aware that they are *objects*—i.e., that their human essence has been alienated by a dominant and uncontrollable power—they tend to project this condition on men. The "emancipated" woman begins to consider *them* as instruments of pleasure and play. A tragic war breaks out in which the sexes conquer one another, seeking escape from the tremendous pressures of monopoly-based society. Modern women find no rational explanation for their historical situation; not understanding that their oppression arises out of the division of labor, they adopt vindictive attitudes towards males.

The culture of class society has inculcated in women the notion that they can fulfill themselves within the narrow limits of sex; they still do not understand that the development of their true capabilities can come only from work. Therefore, they believe that the reasons for their oppression are to be found in biological reproduction, instead of social production. Thus, they will tend to rebel spontaneously against traditional patterns of sexual conduct; they will exchange the traditional husband for countless transitory encounters. Having been objects they will attempt to become sexual subjects, adopting authoritarian attitudes, living an imaginary independence which cannot lead to their fulfillment as human beings. Their enduring preoccupation with men continues; they revolve around men just as their grandmothers revolved around one man. Worried only about establishing their vindictive domination within the love relationship, they will postpone their integration into the struggle that will destroy the system which imprisons them. At last, exhausted by the ups and downs of this chronic warfare, they will surrender to the privatized home, where they will docilely proceed to reproduce the labor power of the ultimate conqueror.

Consumer society reaps fat benefits from this new stage in their lives, glorifying the role of the housewife through the mass media, and stimulating women to buy television sets, refrigerators, mixers and so on. In the last few years, advertising has led to the convergence of two ideals: the beautiful fashionable woman (*Be lovely! . . . Keep your husband!*), and the good housewife, firmly anchored in the kitchen. This woman suffers from a contradiction which can only be resolved by the acquisition of household articles, because she must provide a high level of consumption in the household, without ever appearing to be a worker. The obligation to do housework while looking like Jacqueline Kennedy, the conflict between the slave and the lady, is resolved in favor of light industry.

The working-class woman who cannot acquire consumer goods is no less a prisoner of the mass media than the middle-class woman. In consumer society there is no shelter, no refuge, that protects human beings from persistent ideological bombardment. . . .

Neocapitalism, which chains women to their condition as sex objects, offers them escape valves which channel their potential rebelliousness . . . and stamps them with well-defined ideological traits, which they will bring with them, even as they enter the struggle for the rights of women and for socialism. The left movements of the Western world have neglected to study these specific ideological traits. An analysis of them is, nevertheless, very necessary; the survival of these traits in socialism can severely block the development of proletarian consciousness.

These ideological traits manifest themselves as follows:

1. *Sexual Liberalism.* Sexual liberalism, the last stronghold of the traditional values of liberalism, is a contemporary ideological projection of the social division of labor between the public and domestic spheres. Accordingly, it maintains the right to existence of a *privatized morality* as opposed to a collective morality. It advocates the destruction of the family, without acknowledging its continuing status as the "basic economic unit of society," or that it cannot be abolished as long as class society exists.

   In political life, sexual liberalism focuses primarily on "the sexual liberation of woman" and underestimates the class struggle. Inspired by Wilhelm Reich, it has had a strong influence on some feminist and new left groups, which see human problems in the context of authoritarian sex relations and not in the class oppression from which it springs. Sexual liberation, as a feminist ideology, usually appears among students, professionals, and middle-class women, and is less common among urban and rural workers. When it survives under socialism it is both an expression of petit-bourgeois individualism and a "poor relation" of cultural neocolonialism.

2. *Female Economism.* In a consumer society,

women are usually encouraged to buy rather than to produce. Women, especially housewives, are the purchasers of 75 percent of all consumer goods. This phenomenon requires the elaboration of a whole policy and ideology of selling, inseparable from the dominant values of the ruling class; it tends to emphasize the original division of labor and the sexual roles which emerged from the latter, roles which are based on an exaggerated valuation of beauty, the maternal function of the housewife as well as rivalry between families to attain a higher social standing. The social existence of the housewife, *isolated in her small domestic sweatshop where she produces labor power,* determines her fundamentally individualist status. . . .

Competition among housewives has its concrete symbols. To achieve the social status recommended by the mass media, it is necessary to acquire certain consumer goods. Consumer-goods fetishism becomes a religion whose believers hasten the cycle of commodity circulation. The acceleration of these cycles depends on the creation of a specific social consciousness among women, which motivates them to consume goods totally unnecessary to the perpetuation of the species—from false eyelashes to face creams to electrical appliances (which do not solve the problem of the second workshift), to ideological and cultural goods such as women's magazines and films which strengthen the bonds that enslave them to the formidable mythology of sex. When this ideology of *female economism* is not rejected by national and social liberation struggles, it can become an invisible enemy of proletarian consciousness. On the economic level, it constantly hampers socialist planning: this leads to an overemphasis on light industry, subjecting it to the collective whim, obliging it to produce silk stockings for summertime use, false eyelashes, cosmetics and creams worthy of the court of Louis XIV, fashions and literature; it leads to a general emulation of consumer society. It also encourages the perpetuation of individual households as the economic unit of society.

Thus, if for neocapitalism the creation of a "feminine" social consciousness is a condition for survival, under socialism its total ex-

tinction is an immediate necessity for the development of the proletarian economy and ideology.

ROADS TO LIBERATION

If women think their situation in society is an optimal one . . . if women think their revolutionary function in society has been fulfilled, they are making a mistake. It seems to us that women must make a great effort to attain the place that they should really hold in society.

> Fidel Castro, Speech to Plenary Session of Federation of Cuban Women, December 1966

In the family (the man) is the bourgeois, and the wife represents the proletariat. In the industrial world, the specific character of the economic oppression burdening the proletariat is visible in all its sharpness only when all special legal privileges of the capitalist class have been abolished and complete legal equality of both classes established. The democratic republic does not do away with the opposition of the two classes: on the contrary, it provides the field on which the fight can be found out. And in the same way, the peculiar character of the supremacy of the husband over the wife in the modern family, the necessity of creating real social equality between them and the way to do it, will only be seen in the full light of day when both possess legally complete equality of rights. Then it will be plain that the first condition for the liberation of the wife is to bring the whole female sex back into public industry: and that, in turn, demands the abolition of the monogamous family as the economic unit of society.

> Frederick Engels, *The Origin of the Family, Private Property, and the State* (New York, International Publishers, 1942), pp. 65–66.

When a socialist revolution takes power, a sudden equalizing process takes place among members of its society, which is qualitatively different from the paltry gains made under capitalism: for the first time in history, women have complete legal equality; wage differentials are eliminated; prostitution and the double standard cease to exist; birth control is facilitated; a sustained effort is made to increase social services and to incorporate women into production. Taking the United States and the Soviet

Union as examples, we see that in the United States women constitute 7 percent of all doctors, 1 percent of all engineers and 3 percent of all lawyers, while in the Soviet Union the figures are 79 percent, 32 percent and 37 percent respectively.

For the first time in history women are considered to be human beings. From this moment on women—collectively and not in isolated groups—start the long march toward their total liberation. Engels foresaw that such circumstances would lead to a heightened awareness of the antagonism between the sexes which exists in class society. In the period of transition, a violent ideological struggle goes on among the masses of the underdeveloped countries, where male supremacy has been most brutal, and where—with some exceptions like Vietnam—mass integration of women has not taken place in the liberation movements, in armed struggle or in political leadership.

Sharp tensions arise within the family. The source of this conflict and the path toward its solution were pointed out by Engels in 1884:

> We are now approaching a social revolution in which the economic foundations of monogamy as they have existed hitherto will disappear just as surely as those of its complement—prostitution.
>
> . . . the position of men will be very much altered. But the position of women, of *all* women, also undergoes significant change. With the transfer of the means of production into common ownership, the single family ceases to be the economic unit of society. Private housekeeping is transformed into a social industry. The care and education of the children becomes a public affair. (*Origin of the Family*, p. 67)

Today, socialist practice demonstrates that marriage based on equality becomes possible only after the seizure of power by the proletariat. It will continue to be a real social necessity as long as competitive individualism—the legacy of earlier social systems—does not disappear. Its effective attainment is one of the most beautiful ideals of socialist men and women who struggle together for communism.

In 1919 Lenin confirmed Engel's analysis, pointing out that the first conquests of socialism revealed the true nature of the economic exploitation of women:

> . . . We really razed to the ground the infamous laws placing women in a position of inequality, restricting divorce and surrounding it with disgusting formalities, denying recognition to children born out of wedlock, enforcing a search for their fathers, etc., laws numerous survivals of which, to the shame of the bourgeoisie and of capitalism, are to be found in all civilized countries. We have a thousand times the right to be proud of what we have done in this field. But the more thoroughly we clear the ground of the lumber of the old, bourgeois laws and institutions, the clearer it is to us that we have only cleared the ground to build on, but are not yet building.
>
> Not withstanding all the laws emancipating women, she continues to be a *domestic slave,* because *petty housework* crushes, strangles, stultifies, and degrades her, chains her to the kitchen and nursery, and she wastes her labor on barbarously unproductive, petty, nerve-racking, stultifying and crushing drudgery. The real *emanicipation of women,* real communism, will begin only where and when an all-out struggle begins (led by the proletariat wielding the state power) against this petty housekeeping, or rather when its *wholesale transformation* into large-scale socialist economy begins." (*Collected Works,* Vol. 29, pp. 248–249)

Unfortunately, the revolutionary theory of women's role in the family has been little developed since Lenin. Scarce attention has been given to Engels' and Lenin's insistence on the role of the family in class society. This theoretical inertia has permitted the resurgence in left movements of, on the one hand, a romantic conception of the traditional family as a positive element in the construction of socialism and, on the other, its total negation, along with the theory of the abolition of the family. These conservative and utopian conclusions arise from a failure to analyze the following activities, which take place behind the facade of the monogamous family:

(a) biological reproduction;

(b) education and care of children, the sick, and the elderly;

(c) reproduction of labor power.

It is forgotten that the individual family will continue to be "the economic unit of society" as long as its economic functions are not collectivized. As the economic unit, *it is no more than a tiny, private, sweatshop for the production of labor power,* and clashes with the social economy created by the revolution—an economy no longer governed by private property and commodity relations. This contradiction within the relations of production, which is not only economic but also ideological, is a characteristic feature of the transition period.

It is neither the comradeship nor the positive psychological aspects of a couple's relations which are in contradiction with the construction of a classless society, but their private economic aspect, which is that of a small sweatshop where women's labor power is confiscated.

The roots of women's oppression can be found in:

(a) the original economic necessity of privately reproducing labor power;

(b) the division of labor between the sexes, which forces women to be responsible for invisible labor;

(c) the resulting development of a hidden ideology of sex which distorts our conception of male-female relations in a classless society . . . .

In the underdeveloped countries, limited economic resources make total socialization of domestic work impossible. But this should not prevent the creation of a morality in which men share housework, thus making it possible for their wives to hold outside jobs. Many partial solutions are possible, based on cooperation among neighbors, which do not require large expenditures by the state. But the application of these solutions requires a radical change in the everyday thinking of the people, which has been deeply permeated by individualism and male supremacy.

One of the most difficult problems facing the women's liberation movement today is the resistance, not only of men, but also of women themselves, to revolutionary change. Still bound to a culture evolved over the centuries of discrimination, women unconsciously cling to "traditional feminine values," that is, to the hidden ideology of sex. Under these conditions, unless the party intervenes vigorously, the first step toward raising women's consciousness

will drift toward limited forms of liberation; the narrowness holds a danger of hardening and reverting toward a sectarian, reactionary ideology.

The overestimation of sexual freedom as the only objective of feminine rebellion arises from the growth of consumer society and brings with it strong individualistic tensions. In practice it distracts women from such fundamental problems as the struggle to collectivize the second shift, eliminate the division of labor between the sexes, and to achieve full integration of women in the structures of proletarian power and the army. It frequently appears among intellectuals and students who have a position of relatively high status and do not face domestic problems; it also appears with great force in cultural milieux where individualistic traits persist. Advocating a private morality, it is opposed to the necessary universality of social values, essential to the proletarian ethic. Paradoxically, the women who reveal this ideological characteristic strengthen the vestiges of the old double standard by perpetuating the classic role of the mistress, even as they demand women's rights.

Female economism emphasizes both the housewife's purchasing function and maternal overprotection. As the initial process in the struggle against colonial backwardness, as the revindication of the economic importance of domestic work, as an answer to the most brutal discrimination, it usually presents, like sexual liberalism, positive aspects. But we must remember that both ideological currents were propagated by neocolonialism in its effort to stimulate artificial need.

The resurgence of female economism under socialism tends to reinforce the traditional division of labor between the sexes and perpetuate the home as the economic unit of society; it offers strong analogies with private artisanry in its privatizing effect on social consciousness. Female economism continues to cling to traditional status symbols, and exerts heavy pressure on light industry to produce unnecessary merchandise. In periods of shortages, it feeds the black market and is a magnificent conduit for the infiltration of imperialist values, avidly absorbing as it does all the echoes of fashion and middle-class life-styles, conveyed by the mass media of consumer society. It sanctifies the *eternal feminine* as a concept which *lies outside social classes,* instead of identifying it as nothing more or less than the product of the division of labor and class interests. It thus creates a special area, a kind of sanctuary the desecration of which would inflict endless evils on humanity, and in which the seeds of private property and competitive individualism survive, grow and multiply.

When female economism reasserts itself, despite the advances of proletarian culture, women take advantage of increased purchasing power and the newly created services, not by transforming themselves in a revolutionary way, not by total dedication to work and political activity, but by the acquisition of social status comparable to that of a housewife in consumer society. They tend to utilize services for their individual benefit and thereby reenter the consumer rat race. . . .

The consciousness required of women (especially women leaders) by the revolutionary process similar to that propounded by the Guinean revolutionary leader, Amilcar Cabral, for the petit bourgeoisie—in Africa the petit bourgeoisie plays a leading role in the independence struggle—namely, that *it must commit suicide as a class, through struggle and through merging with the proletariat.* Small producers, including housewives, are marginal, secondary classes, which lack the necessary authority to govern the country. The revolutionary process requires their assimilation into the basic working classes, which are the only ones able to stand up to imperialism. Thus, the class suicide of the housewife, her transformation into a proletarian, requires the elimination of the social traits acquired under capitalism.

The incorporation of women into production does not signify their total liberation. To the extent that housewives either become completely proletarian or perpetuate in part the ideological values of class society, we shall witness the advent of a revolutionary current in the social consciousness of women. The latter trend constitutes the best breeding ground for economic and political revisionism. Socialism is a transition stage between capitalism and a classless society, which cannot be built until we resolve existing contradiction between the need for invisible labor and the need to incorporate the neglected half of humanity into productive work and political life.

The private reproduction of labor power under socialism continues to be a cruel and unavoidable necessity. Official recognition of the second shift is an important step, but the socialization of housework through the expansion of services and social benefits is not so much a question of government policy as of economic development. As long as invisible labor persists, as long as the ideology of sex is not fought fiercely, traditional prejudices will survive—as evidenced by opposing sex models, female economism, and biological theories designed to justify the division of labor between the sexes.

It is not easy to distinguish reformist ideas of women's liberation from revolutionary ones because, among other reasons, their systematic formulation is lacking—all the more reason to try. One thing seems clear nonetheless: reformist ideas tend to perpetuate invisible work; revolutionary ideas reflect the need to incorporate women fully and definitively into the construction of a classless society.

REFORMIST IDEAS

It is relatively easy to proclaim the legal equality of women; it is very difficult to put it into revolutionary practice in the underdeveloped countries, where it implies the incorporation of women into social production and political action. These semiliterate women, hampered by a heritage of age-old discrimination and abuse, were trained in a class culture to exclusively reproduce labor power in the home; they were made into sex objects, into serfs, whose destiny was marriage. . . .

The pressure of female economism limits the integration of women to work requiring minimal physical effort at work centers located near the home. Women themselves sanction the perpetuation, under socialism, of the division of labor between the sexes which had taken shape under capitalism as a projection of their menial, domestic duties.

Certain pseudoscientific theories have been advanced, preventing women from taking jobs traditionally reserved for men. The practical basis for this is found in the second shift. It is not easy for women who perform difficult and exhausting work to bear the hours of invisible labor which await them at home. Reformist ideas appear when ideological concessions are made to the division of labor between the sexes and the invisible workshift—which tend to be accepted as permanent necessities.

The proposal to reduce the working day for married women has been offered as a solution. The anti-economic nature of such a measure is self-evident. Its reactionary content is less evident. At the least it would lead to:

1. an increment of individual wages at the expense of social benefits;

2. the weakening of the egalitarian position attained by women in the revolution, conferring on them a different legal status from that of men—a status that would sanction "biological determination," and condemn women to continue in the role of serfs who reproduce labor power; and

3. the strengthening of petit-bourgeois individualism. If the individual family were the economic unit of class society, a return to it through the reinforcement of invisible labor would inevitably lead to a reinforcement of the social consciousness of private property that still exists vestigially.

Excluded from heavy or dangerous work, alienated from their creative potential by the division of labor, women who gradually return to forms of invisible labor will not be fully transformed; they are stopped short and frozen into transitional patterns containing features of both past and future. Their integration into the proletariat is not complete, even if they work, for example, as lathe operators. It is widely known that even within socialist society small private producers continuously generate the social patterns of class society. Hence, we may assume the corrupting power of the presence of these invisible female artisans, semi-proletarians, semi-serfs, whose social condition prevents their transformation into full-fledged proletarians.

As long as labor power continues to be produced in thousands of domestic sweatshops, the influence of private property will not be eradicated from social consciousness, and the attempt to build a classless society and a new man and woman will necessarily remain incomplete. In this context, the correctness of Lenin's statement is even more evident: *the proletariat cannot attain its full liberation until women are fully liberated.*

REVOLUTIONARY IDEAS

Revolutionary ideas come into their own when the Party concentrates its efforts on the reeducation of women (and men), with the understanding that the abolition of private property, the integration of women into socialized work, and the creation of social services provide the necessary but not sufficient conditions for their liberation. Women's fate is intrinsically linked to the class struggle, carried on by the Party against the vices and culture of private property. Revolutionary advances by the mass of women seem to be made more easily in those areas where the social transformation of capitalism has not been completed, particularly in the vast peasant regions of Asia where patriarchal slavery was so brutal that women were still bought and sold like cattle. "Equal rights," marriage for love, and the values of consumer society were nonexistent. The subtle individualism that characterizes developed countries had not reached them, and a few traces of the old collectivism remained; the Marxist leadership understood the impossibility of a reformist solution. If they were going to incorporate women into production and defense they had to attempt the complete destruction of the patriarchal ideological superstructure. Women constitute the group that suffers the highest degree of distortion in class society. Though women in underdeveloped countries have performed feats of limitless heroism and sacrifice in the struggle against imperialism, they must overcome a deeply instilled ideological cowardice if, through internal struggle, they are to transform their servile condition.

The struggle of the revolutionary parties against ideas of inferiority in women is most delicate, for when women spontaneously break with their traditional insecurity, they are then subject to ultra-leftist deviations, similar to those which plagued slave and peasant rebellions in centuries past. Therefore, of fundamental importance is the assumption of leadership in the women's revolt, by revolutionary organizations, which must stimulate and channel, rather than stifle, or permit the movement to turn into female revanchism.

Revolutionary ideas reveal that the physical inferiority of women is not inevitable but is a historical product of the division of labor. A struggle to incorporate women into traditionally "male" jobs will reveal that, far from impairing their health, women will develop their body and mind. We must denounce domestic slavery and foster a social morality which provides for sharing of housework by men. These household tasks must be collectivized as far as possible. In practice, revolutionary ideas will destroy the inhibiting reflexes of exploited women. Keeping in mind that these are times of conditional peace, the mass of women must be prepared for participation in defense, and must be admitted to the armed forces. . . .

There is a tendency to impose rigid standards of sexual behavior, the validity of which is questionable on a long-term basis but which serves to eliminate the moral duality that used to stimulate in men what it brutally repressed in women. All the symbolism that contributed to the reification of women, as well as to class standards of beauty, must be destroyed, eliminating from the mass media the image of women as commodity. Women must be evaluated in terms of their role as workers, political leaders, or fighters.

The large-scale incorporation of women into the people's war is one of the most important achievements of revolutionary ideology, and is also the most effective measure for the total proletarianization of women, with all that that signifies for the destruction of traditional female taboos.

The best example can be found in the territories held by the National Liberation Forces of Vietnam, where the division of labor between the sexes in production and in warfare appears to have been reduced to a minimum. The incorporation of women into the Vietnamese people's war would not have been possible without the continuous effort of the NLF, which carries on a resolute struggle against sex discrimination in Vietnam. . . .

The military is the armed force of the class in power, exclusion from it on sexual grounds—with the corresponding implications for women's social consciousness—is logical in an oppressive society which systematically excludes women from positions of authority, but it is out of place in revolutionary armed forces, which represent the entire people.

Cuba is an exceptional case, where officer-training schools and command posts are being opened to women, even though Cuba is not at war. This helps to destroy the vestiges of male supremacy inherited from Spain, plantation slavery, and United States neocolonialism. Thus, it is an example of a frontal attack against sex discrimination during the early years of revolutionary transformation.

It would be too optimistic to expect that complete ideological proletarianization of women at this early stage of the transition period. It is a process which can be carried out only through a long and conscious struggle, and that is precisely why the lack of interest in a scientific theory of women's liberation—given its fundamental importance for the construction of a classless society—leaves the way open for a rebirth of reformism. If the condition of women continues to be ignored, it could lead, under adverse circumstances, to the stagnation of revolutionary ideology.

PART TWO

STERILIZATION

STERILIZATION: AN OVERVIEW

Adelaida R. Del Castillo

Exposure of the involuntary sterilization of Mexican women patients at the Los Angeles County Medical Center reveals the nature of covert assaults currently being perpetrated on the poor of this country and its ethnic minoritities. Their sterilization represents a direct violation of this country's most basic human and democratic rights, and has resulted in the total social and psychological disruption of victims' lives.[1]

Arguments by some would claim a major impetus behind these operations derives from profiteering motives on behalf of the medical profession, but such arguments fail to explain why victims are almost always indigent or members of minority groups. They fail to explain why the forced sterilization of black and poor white populations of the southern and northeastern regions of the United States parallels experiences in the Southwest where Indians and Mexicans are coerced or fooled into accepting sterilization as a necessary means of birth control.

The punitive use of forced sterilization against the economically and sociopolitically disadvantaged has a vivid history in this country, and is a direct outgrowth of eugenics.

Sterilization is an irreversible method of birth control performed surgically on either male or female. When performed on women, the operation normally involves the bilateral cutting, tying or removing of a small portion of the fallopian tubes blocking the passage of ovum into the uterus. This procedure is referred to as a tubal ligation.

Eugenics is the compulsory sterilization of persons with hereditary illnesses and differs from therapeutic sterilization in as much as the latter acts as a safeguard to the personal health or life of the individual.

The need for eugenic sterilization was proposed by Sir Francis Galton, Charles Darwin's cousin, in 1883 purporting the "biologically fit" should propagate while the "unfit" should not. Eventually, this came to imply the sterilization of the "criminally inclined" and the "socially unfit."

Now more recently, legislators, judges, and doctors throughout the country have unmistakenly advocated and mandated forced sterilization for other than eugenic purposes. The poor and ethnic minorities, by extension, have come to be seen as social misfits and an economic drain on the state.

Their sterilization has been advocated even though it violates a number of juridical precedents, statutory laws, and constitutional rights which protect the fundamentals of privacy and procreation.

These violations include a woman's right to choose when to terminate pregnancy, as established in *Roe v. Wade;*[2] the right to beget children, as in *Eisenstadt* v. *Baird;*[3] the parental right to procreation, as in *Griswold* v. *Connecticut;*[4] and the right to privacy, due process and the Equal Protection Clause guaranteed by the First, Fifth, Ninth, and Fourteenth Amendments.

LEGISLATION

The first sterilization bill introduced in the United States was proposed in the state of Michigan in 1897, but failed to be passed. That same year Dr. F. Hoyt Pilcher castrated forty-four boys and sterilized fourteen girls at the Kansas Institution for the Feebleminded. In 1905 Pennsylvania state passed a bill for the sterilization of clinically diagnosed idiots, but this bill was later vetoed by the governor. The state of Indiana, however, succeeded in passing a sterilization law in 1907 for males confined to institutions and diagnosed as idiots, imbecils, criminals, and rapists.[5] But, in 1921, the Indiana Supreme Court declared that law unconstitutional. By 1910 California, Connecticut, and Washington had adopted Sterilization measures of their own, and by 1920 fourteen other states had similar laws. In 1923 California was sterilizing "carnal abusers" of girls under ten years of age. However, by 1925 all such statutes seeking ratification were ruled unconstitutional by the courts except in the states of Virginia and Michigan.

In 1927 a precedent for compulsory sterilization was set by the United States Supreme Court in the case *Buck* v. *Bell.* This case involved Carrie Buck who had been committed to a state institution in Virginia, and had been diagnosed a feebleminded, moral delinquent because she was given to hallucinations and temper tantrums. Carrie's daughter had also been diagnosed as feebleminded and authorities feared Carrie would continue to bear "mentally defective" children if she were not sterilized before her release from the institution. The operation was said to be in the best interests of the patient, and society in general.

Although Carrie Buck contested Virginia's statute as a violation of her "right to bodily integrity and due process" the Supreme Court sanctioned the state's authority to sterilize. The opinion of the Court was expressed by Justice Holmes:

> We have seen more than once that the public welfare may call upon the best citizens for their lives. It would be strange if it could not call upon those who already sap the strength of the state for these lesser sacrifices, often not felt to be such by those concerned, in order to prevent our being swamped with incompetence. It is better for all the world, if instead of waiting to execute degenerate off-spring for crime, or to let them starve for their imbecility, society can prevent those who are manifestly unfit from continuing their kind. The principle that sustains compulsory vaccination is broad enough to cover cutting the fallopian tubes.[6]

By 1937 twenty more states had passed statutes similar to Virginia's. Today, twenty-six states have eugenic sterilization laws.

In 1953 sociologist J. E. Coogan published findings which revealed that the *Buck* v. *Bell* suit was chosen as a test case by the superintendent of the institution where Carrie Buck was interned. Neither Carrie nor her daughter were imbeciles, her daughter reportedly was very bright.[7]

The Supreme Court's decision, nonetheless, revealed an antipathy for those who "sap" the state and those considered biological and social inferiors. During the turn of the century, for example, sterilization was performed on "undesirable southern European" immigrants due to their "innate inferiority, poverty and illiteracy."[8] Descriptions similar to these continue in the portrayal of this country's poor.

During the post-World War II era criticisms against the poor increased, in particular against welfare costs in metropolitan areas where recipients were largely members of ethnic minorities.[9] Precedents for the sterilization of the mentally and physically ill (tuberculosis and venereal disease) involving prostitutes, criminals, and paupers had already been established. Attacks on welfare recipients seemed to be the next step.

In an article written for the *Saturday Evening Post* in 1950, Judge Jacob Panken expressed his disgust with the welfare system and described recipients as morally bankrupt, mentally backward, lazy, and without self-respect.[10] In 1961 the City Manager of Newburgh, New York, James Mitchell, was quoted in the *New*

York Times as saying that welfare agencies were guilty of subsidizing "crime, immorality, slums and a general pollution of social standards."[11] That same year a Union County grand jury claimed that a welfare family was one where "the fathers are deserters and the mothers are promiscuous."[12] In this manner impressions of welfare families as breeders of illegitimate children, who in turn increase the burden of public assistance, continued to be perpetrated. A 1965 Gallup Opinion Poll on welfare recipients showed respondants describing recipients as dishonest, lazy and lacking initiative; 27 percent felt unwed mothers should not be given aid and another 20 percent favored their sterilization.[13]

In 1957 North Carolina State Senator Wilbur M. Jolly introduced a bill to the state legislature calling for the amendment of North Carolina's eugenic sterilization statute to include giving birth out of wedlock as proof of a woman's feeblemindedness! His bill was proposed as remedial to the rising costs of welfare grants for illegitimate births under the Aid to Dependent Children program.[14] Senator Jolly's colleague, State Senator Luther Hamilton, was one who favored the measure because it would check against "breeding a race of bastards."[15] In the bill unwed mothers were described as "sexually delinquent."

Having failed to get this bill passed, Senator Jolly reintroduced a similar bill two years later, again seeking to penalize unwed mothers: "On the birth of a third illegitimate child the Eugenics Board . . . shall order the mother to show cause why sterilization should not be ordered."[16] Senator Jolly was especially concerned with North Carolina's black birthrate of which approximately 20 percent was out of wedlock.[17] Sterilization statutes would largely be used against black women. Senator Jolly could not get this second bill passed either.

Blacks were clearly the target in the sterilization legislation introduced by Mississippi State Representative David H. Glass in 1958, who noted that 7,000 black children compared to 200 white children had been born out of wedlock in 1957 alone. The bill died on the House calendar.[18]

In 1959 three grand juries in the state of Georgia recommended the sterilization of all mothers of illegitimate children. No legislation resulted.[19]

The late 1950s and early 1960s brought two bills before Delaware's General Assembly which would make welfare aid contingent on sterilization for mothers of two or more illegitimate children. The bills died in committee.[20]

In 1960 Senate Bill No. 91 passed the Maryland Senate by a vote of twenty-three to three which would have resulted in the sterilization of any woman convicted of more than two illegitimate births had the House of Delegates not defeated the bill.[21] This bill was also primarily intended for a black population.

A memorandum by William L. Rutherford, then a member of the Illinois Public Aid Commission, recommended in 1963 that Illinois' statutes on prostitution be amended to require all persons convicted of prostitution be sterilized. The term "prostitution" was defined as encompassing persons siring or giving birth to more than one illegitimate child; illegal abortion was to be considered as an illegitimate birth.[22] The recommendation was not adopted. That same year Iowa State Senator Howard Buck recommended that mothers on Aid to Families with Dependent Children be sterilized if they continued to have children out of wedlock.[23] No legislation resulted.

JURIDICAL MANDATES

If legislative attempts at sterilization of the poor proved ineffective, juridical mandates showed promise. In 1962 Judge Holland M. Gary, of the Muskingum County Probate Court in Ohio, sought to reduce the county's growing tax bills for public assistance by issuing sterilization mandates. In 1966 he forced Carolyn Wade to submit to sterilization on the basis of an affidavit filed by the County Child Welfare Board alleging that Wade was feebleminded according to Section 5125.24 of the Ohio Revised Code. A code which had been repealed in 1963.

Wade filed suit in 1971 and won. At issue, however, was not the fact she had been sterilized, but that there no longer existed a statute which sanctioned Judge Gary's sterilization mandates. The court noted: "There is no statute in Ohio which authorizes a judge to order sterilization for any purpose."[24]

In December 1963, Miguel Vega Andrade was convicted of non-support (his wife and children were on welfare) by the Pasadena Municipal Court in California. A year later he was granted probation after having consented to a vasectomy.[25] Similarly, after having convicted Victoria

Tapia and Marcos Palafox of welfare fraud in 1965, the Superior Court of Santa Barbara County granted both a reduced sentence and probation once they were sterilized.

In 1966 Nancy Hernandez, mother of two children, one illegitimate, was jailed by Judge Frank P. Kearny of Santa Barbara for refusing to accept a sterilization/probation proviso for a misdemeaner conviction. Admittingly, Judge Kearny failed to see anything "novel—legally, medically or sociologically" with the proviso. According to him, Mrs. Hernandez's "propensity to live an immoral life" made her a prime candidate for sterilization.[26]

MEDICAL AND ADMINISTRATIVE EXPEDIENCY

Dr. H. J. Stander noted in 1936 that medical practitioners used a double standard of consultation regarding sterilization: "If she is weak-minded or diseased and is liable to become a public charge, the operation is justifiable. In general, with pauper patients, it is our practice to effect sterilization at third (cesarean) section."[27] More currently, a 1972 survey on physician attitudes found that: "The obstetrician-gynecologists were the most punitive of the doctors surveyed, 94 percent favoring compulsory sterilization or witholding of welfare support for unwed mothers with three children."[28]

In 1969 the American College of Obstetricians and Gynecologists dropped recommended age and parity standards for female sterilization. In 1970 it withdrew its guidelines, recommending the signature of two or more doctors and a psychiatric consultation prior to sterilization. A year later the Department of Health, Education, and Welfare (HEW) expanded its birth control program to include sterilization. Federal support of family planning services was rapidly growing. By 1973 the amount of annual federal expenditures had sky-rocketed from $11 million to $149 million.[29] Although federal funding of birth control was now totaling 90 percent, abortion was not part of the program. Consequently, women on state aid, unable to afford an abortion, were given the alternative of a state-paid sterilization.

In Los Angeles the rate of sterilizations from 1968 to 1970, at the County Medical Center, rose by 450 percent while hysterectomies increased by 750 percent.[30] During this same period New York City's Mount Sinai Hospital increased its rate of sterilizations by 200 percent.[31]

In 1963 North Carolina's sterilization statute was amended to include sterilization for therapeutic purposes and in 1964 approximately 65 percent of all women sterilized in that state were black. Since then the North Carolina Eugenics Commission has refused to reveal the racial breakdown of individuals sterilized.[32]

The documentation of the involuntary sterilization of Mexican women in Los Angeles recounts how they were sterilized without their knowledge while in delivery or during abortions. Others were forced to sign sterilization consent forms by making abortion requests contingent on sterilization. In some cases, women in labor were promised pain relievers by hospital personnel once consent forms were signed. Spanish speaking women unable to read or understand English were deceived into signing sterilization forms presented to them as something else. Others were deceived into accepting sterilization which they were told was necessary after a set number of cesarean births.[33]

In April 1974, public pressure forced HEW's promulgation of federal regulations and guidelines establishing the parameters of informed consent to sterilization. However, a 1975 survey by the American Civil Liberties Union, of major hospitals around the country, indicates that "in the absence of any enforcement effort by HEW, the sterilization guidelines are being widely ignored, if not deliberately evaded."[34]

VOLUNTARY STERILIZATION: PUERTO RICO

The questionable use of sterilization as a birth control method for an oppressed people is best exemplified by its use in Puerto Rico. The island's birthrate had reached the unprecedented rate of 3 percent by 1947 causing the concern of U.S. authorities and the initiation of U.S. funded birth control studies.

Contraceptive sterilization practices among hospital patients reportedly began in San Juan, Puerto Rico in the early 1930s.[35] In 1937 the country's law was amended permitting the dissemination of materials and information on birth control. Three years later 7 percent of the island's women were sterilized. By 1954 this figure doubled to 16 percent and doubled again in 1965 when 34 percent of all married Puerto Rican women, ages 20 to 49, were sterilized.[36]

In 1969 a New York survey found 16 percent of all women interviewed were sterilized and of these, 95 percent were Puerto Rican. What is more, Puerto Rican women have expressed dismay with New York hospitals because sterilization is not readily available. These women return to the island for the operation. When asked, however, if they would recommend sterilization for others, one third of those sterilized said they would not.[37]

Prior to 1940 the most widely used contraceptive methods by low income Puerto Ricans was coitus interruptus and the condom. The question of whether alternative methods of birth control were equally encouraged prior to or during the introduction of sterilization is crucial and would certainly qualify what was termed the "voluntary" nature of sterilization practices in Puerto Rico.

An equally important influence on Puerto Rico's demand for sterilization is the emigration flow from Puerto Rico to the United States. American exploitation of the island's sugar, coffee, tobacco, and cotton crops precluded its industrial development causing vast unemployment and poverty, but most importantly providing a cheap labor force via emigration United States bound. American citizenship for Puerto Ricans helped to facilitate movement from one country to the other. By 1952 Puerto Rico's unemployment peaked at 16 percent.[38]

The post-World War II era saw 600,000 Puerto Ricans emigrate to the United States. This comprised 85 percent of the island's total emigration to this country.[39] Slumps in this country's economy, however, affected emigration flow. The economic depression of the mid-fifties, during the Eisenhower Administration, saw a significant reduction in Puerto Rican emigration falling suddenly from 31.7 percent in 1953 to 9.8 in 1954. Similarly, the depression of the 1930s had cut the island's emigration rate to half.

Studies conducted during the first half of the 1950s show that sterilization was the birth control method most popularized and most likely to be known before other methods of contraception among Puerto Rico's lower classes.[40] The impartiality of the studies, however, is questionable in as much as they seek to justify the mass sterilization of Puerto Ricans by depicting them as incorrigibly unreceptive to, and inept in handling other forms of birth control.

CONCLUSION

Currently, we are witnessing an accelerated campaign of aggression against Mexican people. Government authorities and the mass media hold them responsible for overflowing the job market, increasing the crime rate, and endangering public health. The medical profession, meanwhile, self-righteously feels no compunctions in executing and rationalizing the sterilization of the country's poor and its ethnic minorities.

Clearly, sterilization practices whether termed "voluntary" or "involuntary," take an abusive and punitive bias when its victims are indigent or non-white populations, or, when predominantly practiced on the oppressed. The impetus behind this abuse derives from the portrayal of victims as marginal human beings.

NOTES

1. For an elaboration of the issues and problems involved see Carlos G. Velez-I's "Se Me Acabó La Canción: An Ethnography of Non-consenting Sterlizations Among Mexican Women in Los Angeles.
2. *Roe v. Wade* 410 U.S. 113 (1973).
3. *Eisenstadt v. Baird* 405 U.S. 438 (1972).
4. *Griswold v. Connecticut* 381 U.S. 479 (1965).
5. James B. O'Hara and T. Howland Sanks, "Eugenic Sterilization," *The Georgetown Law Review,* Vol. 45 (1965), p. 22.
6. *Buck v. Bell,* 275 U.S. 200 at 207.
7. O'Hara, op. cit., p. 31.
8. Jack Slater, "Sterilization: Newest Threat to the Poor," *Ebony,* No. 28 (Oct. 1973) p. 156.
   Joseph L. Morrison, "Illegitimacy, Sterilization, and Racism: A North Carolina Case History," *The Social Service Review,* Vol. 39, No. 1 (Mar. 1965) p. 1.
10. Jacob Panken, "I Say Relief is Ruining Families," *Saturday Evening Post,* 223 (Sept. 30, 1950) p. 25.
11. A. H. Ruskin, "Newburgh's Lessons for the Nation," *New York Times,* Dec. 17, 1961, VI, p. 7.
12. "Relief Criticized in Union County," *New York Times,* Oct. 5, 1961, p. 41.
13. *Washington Post,* January 27, 1965 at 2A.
14. Morrison, op. cit., p. 1.
15. Ibid., p. 1.
16. Ibid., p. 2.
17. Slater, op. cit., p. 156.
18. Julius Paul, "The Return of Punitive Sterilization Proposals," *Law and Society Review,* Vol. 3, No. 77 (1968) p. 89.

19. Ibid., p. 81.

20. Ibid., p. 81 no. 4.

21. Ibid., p. 85.

22. Ibid., p. 81 n. 6.

23. Ibid., p. 82.

24. *Wade* v. *Bethesda Hospital,* 357 F. Supp. 671 (1971).

25. Paul, op. cit., p. 79 n. 3.

26. Paul, op. cit., p. 80 n. 3.

27. H. J. Stander, *Williams Obstetrics* (7th ed. C.D. Appleton-Century, 1936).

28. "Physician Attitudes: MDs Assume Poor Can't Remember to Take Pill," *1 Family Planning Digest* 3 (Jan., 1972).

29. "DHEW Five-Year Plan Report: Program Served 3.2 Million in FY 1973," *3 Family Planning Digest* (May 1974).

30. "Sterilization: Women Fit to be Tied," *Health Policy Advisory Center Bulletin,* Jan./Feb., 1975.

31. *Newsday,* January 2, 1974 at 4A.

32. Slater, op. cit., p. 152.

33. For an elaboration of some of these cases see Antonia Hernandez, "Chicanas and the Issue of Involuntary Sterilization: Reforms Needed to Protect Informed Consent," *Chicano Law Review,* Vol. 3:3 (1976). Also see Carlos G. Velez-I's article referred to above.

34. Elisa Krauss, "Hospital Survey of Sterilization Policies," *ACLU Reports,* 1975.

35. Harriet B. Presser, "The Role of Sterilization in Controlling Puerto Rican Fertility," *Population Studies,* Vol. 23, No. 3 (1969) pp. 343–361.

36. Ibid.

37. Susan C. Scrimshaw, "The Demand for Female Sterilization in Spanish Harlem: Experiences of Puerto Ricans in New York City" (mimeographed paper) 1970 and Susan C. Scrimshaw and Bernard Pasquariella, "Variables Associated with the Demand for Female Sterilization in Spanish Harlem," *Advances in Planned Parenthood,* Vol. VI (1971).

38. Stanley L. Friedlander, *Labor Migration and Economic Growth: A Case Study of Puerto Rico* (Cambridge, Mass.: The M.I.T. Press, 1965) p. 46.

39. Ibid., p. 49.

40. J. Mayone Stycos, "Female Sterilization in Puerto Rico," *Eugenics Quarterly,* Vol. 1 No. 2 (June 1954) p. 6. and "Birth Control in Puerto Rico," *Eugenics Quarterly,* Vol. 1 No. 3, (Sept. 1954) p. 180.

SE ME ACABÓ LA CANCIÓN: AN ETHNOGRAPHY OF NON-CONSENTING STERILIZATIONS AMONG MEXICAN WOMEN IN LOS ANGELES

Carlos G. Velez-I

INTRODUCTION

"Se me acabó la canción" is a phrase which was repeated quite frequently by one of ten Mexican women[1] who were sterilized without their consent between 1971 and 1974 in Los Angeles, California.[2] The phrase literally means, "my song is finished," but the connotations are far more important. From the point of view of the Mexican women "the song" is the melody of life which is inextricably linked to the ability to procreate children. This melody is the core of the social identity not only of the women, but interdependently it extends to Mexican males as well, in their ability to sire children.

The analysis of the social, cultural, and psychological effects of the forced termination of this melody is the focus of the ethnography of this work, but it is not the totality. For this is also an ethnography of the attempts to redress what for most human beings is a basic right. In addition, this is an explanation of the theories and techniques that were utilized to structure legal actions on the women's behalf, as well as their methodological implementation, and their efficacy in a court of law. But beyond this, through the use of theoretical constructs we will understand the genesis of negative differential treatment of working and non-working class Mexican people in the United States in analogous behavioral environments.* Lastly, however, it is also an ethnography of naïve applied anthropology.

BASIC ASSUMPTIONS

There are two primary assumptions that guide the following analysis, and they should be clearly stated. First, in the general area of "applied anthropology," in which this work may be placed, a built-in assumption can be perceived. As Bastide (1971) points out, much applied work depends on stratification models

Carlos G. Velez-I is Assistant Professor of Anthropology at the University of California, Los Angeles. Versions of this paper were presented before the International Congress of Anthropological and Ethnological Sciences, New Delhi, India, December 10–18, 1978 and at the post-congress of Applied and Action Anthropology, Calcutta, India, December 19–20, 1978 © 1980 by Carlos G. Velez-I

*See Note 3 for an explication of behavioral environments.

and focuses on the subordinate and super-ordinate relations between dominant and minority sectors. This work is not different from this traditional concern. However, opposed to Bastide's suggestion that in the intraethnic sphere most applied anthropologists yearn for the assimilation of minorities in plural socie-ties, I remain uncommitted to such a view. Sec-ond, much of the work in the United States con-cerning ethnic and racial relations has been, as Van den Berghe suggests: "the handmaiden(s) to the meliorative and reformists attempts of the well-intentioned liberal establishment..." (1970). It follows as a corollary that scholars should drop their pretenses of "objectivity," and state with as much precision as possible their position.

These two assumptions, then, must be con-sidered in order to understand clearly the his-torical conditions discussed, and the theoreti-cal constructs utilized. Certainly, the first bias is obvious in that I chose to serve in the capa-city of consulting cultural anthropologist in favor of the plaintiffs—the Mexican women who had been allegedly sterilized without their consent. I would not have served the defendants with equal conviction if I had been asked. There-fore, I certainly adhere to the applied anthropo-logical tradition in this manner. However, I drop the positivist credo of "objectivity" by stating that as a Mexican in the United States, I have experienced numerous behavioral environments in which I was the object of differential negative treatment because of my ethnic minority status, and I have witnessed the same treatment on other occasions. It follows, then, that this ex-perience filters and colors my selection of the theoretical constructs used in the analysis and conclusions derived in this study. Neverthe-less, I have attempted to keep within the bounds of the basic cannons of anthropological re-search. As will be shown, the course of events proved the theoretical constructs and hypothe-ses to be valid.

BASIC THEORETICAL AND METHODOLOGICAL CONCERNS

In order to appreciate the significance of the events analyzed here, it must be made clear that these occurred within a highly industrial-ized capitalist nation-state in which variance and heterogeneity of culture, rather than com-monality and replication organize behavior and behavioral environments.[3] Since class, ethni-city, socially defined racial groups, and special interest sectors form subcultures of various sorts within the nation-state, most complex societies are culturally plural by definition. Yet this diversity of culture is organized in the nation-state by a prism of behavioral expecta-tions which reflect a subcultural ideal in which economic and social values are the valid indi-cators of citizenship and nationality. In the United States this "subcultural prism" holds true. Citizenship, nationality, and ethnic iden-tity reflect the dominant ethnic group of Anglo-Saxon Americans.[4] It is indeed a curious para-dox of all nation-states that while pretending universalistic criteria for its citizens, in reality it distributes rights and duties according to a preconceived specific subcultural ethnic group ideal. That ideal often reflects the dominant ethnic group holding political and economic power, regardless of which "ism" the nation adheres to. Enloe (1973) suggests:

> If the group's ethnic identity is closely bound to the nation's identity it may not even appear to be an ethnic group. It will simply be the norm, the mainstream into which all minorities are submerged. Only when minorities [or oppressed majorities (numerical ones)] self-consciously assert the worth of their own cultures is the ethnicity of "invisible" ethnic communities exposed. Ukranian nationalism reveals the ethnic chauvinism of the Great Russians;[5] Turk-ish nomad's resistance to the Red Army reveals the ethnicity of the Han Chinese (1973, pp. 213–214).

In the United States it was not until the Chicano, Black and Indian power movements of the 1960s that the ethnicity of WASPs was re-vealed.[6] On the other hand, throughout Latin America there is little of the national subcul-tural prism that is invisible. The "mestizo" or "ladino" prism is the overt, explicit, national model and except for nations like Mexico that pay lip service to "indianism" (Indigenismo), most Latin American nations suffer a cultural ethnocentrism which seeks to assimilate or eradicate its indigenous populations. Brazil, Paraguay, and Venezuela have used particularly violent methods of implanting their national subcultural prism.

THE IDEOLOGY OF CULTURAL DIFFERENCES

For ethnic and racial minority groups revelation of the existence of such a prism leads to the understanding that an "ideology of cultural differences" has been used as the *raison d'etre* for the continued differential treatment of ethnic and racial minority groups. Kuper (1974) has suggested that the ideology of cultural differences is an elaborate rationalization. A dominant group, regardless of actual differences in culture, points to a subordinate group's inferior relationship with the dominant group as the aftermath of unresolvable differences in social organization, political systems, economic relations, religious and ideological beliefs and values, and certainly the expression of these differences in behavior. The thieving Mexican has been a rather traditional cultural characteristic associated with this ethnic group. As Paredes (1958) states in discussing the incessant conflicts between Mexicans and Anglos along the border frontier between Mexico and the United States:

> The picture of the Mexican as an inveterate thief, especially of horses and cattle, is of interest to the psychologist as well as the folklorist. The cattle industry of the Southwest had its origin in the Nueces-Rio Grande area, with the stock and the ranches of the Rio Grande rancheros. The "cattle barons" (Texans) built up their fortunes at the expense of the Border Mexican by means which were far from ethical. One notes that the white southerner took his slave women as concubines and then created an image of the male Negro as a sex fiend. In the same way he appears to have taken the Mexican's property and then made him out a thief (p. 20).

This ideology of cultural differences is used then to screen out other groups as too different from the subcultural prism to allow for access to resources unless they become "mainstream Americans" by acculturation and assimilation. Regardless of historical conditions and structural relations, the onus of undifferentiated access to resources lies in the hands of the ethnic minority. It may also be the case, however, that the ideology of cultural differences defines the ethnic minority as so different that only complete physical separation, as in South Africa, can be articulated as the national policy.

Such rationalizations are a contrast to the cross-cultural record. For the most part there are efficient conditions which have defined the quality of the relations between dominant ethnic national groups and subordinate ethnic national groups. Certainly as a point of departure, the Mexican ethnic minority in the United States, as is the case for many minorities in the New World, can trace their subordination to a war of conquest and other acts of violence. While violence as Wagley and Harris (1964) have pointed out, is not a universal characteristic for the rise of minority groups, the presence of violence ". . . in the process of birth of minority groups frequently provides an important key to understanding intergroup hostilities" (p. 252). Furthermore, the economic relegation of workers to subservient positions as sources of cheap labor in times of economic expansion of the nation-state may also generate subordinate minority relations between ethnic groups. Also the appearance of minority groups is always associated with the emergence or expansion of the nation-state so that cultural groups become overwhelmed by others who represent the national prism.

In addition to these elements which foster intergroup hostilities and subservient domination of one group by another, there also lie efficient conditions for a virulent sort of domination; that is, social racism which arises when two populations who differ phenotypically and culturally intersect in the aforementioned circumstances: conquest, violent confrontation, economic subservience, and nation-state expansion. The end result for the dominated population is differential negative treatment in most behavioral environments. When such conditions are coupled with an "ideology of cultural differences" and the national subcultural prism becomes economically, educationally, politically, and socially institutionalized, then clearly those who were annexed, conquered, enslaved, economically colonized, and materially denied will be placed in a structurally asymmetrical and subordinate status.

MEXICANS AND THE UNITED STATES: A HISTORICAL STRUCTURAL PRÉCIS

Recently, a number of stratification indices were used to rank ethnic and racial groups in the United States.[7] Of the fourteen groups mentioned the lowest four consistently retained that position during the twenty-year period (1950–1970) in which the data was collected. Significantly, these four groups are all ethnic or racial minorities who historically emerged from conquest (Mexicans, Indians), enslavement (Blacks), economic colonization (Mexicans, Indians, Puerto Ricans and Blacks), and annexation (Mexicans and Puerto Ricans). In addition, all four groups were to different degrees culturally and phenotypically distinct from the national subcultural prism. The other ten groups mentioned do not in fact comprise populations who have been colonized economically or were subjected to conquest or enslavement. Although other ethnic groups may differ phenotypically and culturally, intergroup hostility such as that between Japanese and Anglo-Saxons has been limited to extremely short periods, as during World War II.

Of all the ethnic populations in the United States, Mexicans and Indians have passed from conquest, annexation, purchase, and into economic colonization. For Mexicans, their subject population status is the result of having provided land and labor for 130 years to a national dominant subcultural group of Anglo-Saxons. As the aftermath of the "Texas War of Independence (1836)," the Mexican War of 1846, and the so-called Gadsen Purchase of 1853, the United States gained roughly half of Mexico and a population of 75,000 Mexicans. Thus through annexation, conquest, and the forced purchase of mineral-rich southern Arizona and the Mesilla Valley of southwestern New Mexico, the United States managed to acquire territory greater in extent than Germany and France combined (McWilliams 1968).[8] In addition, Mexican labor has been used, drawn, discarded, and repatriated by United States mining, agriculture, railroad, and heavy industrial corporate interests. Most recently the garment industry has been a particularly intensive user. For 130 years, depending on the state of economic conditions in the United States, such labor has

been both welcomed and expelled. It is clear from the Bracero programs[9] of the 1940s to the so-called twin-cities border projects,[10] that Mexicans have composed an extremely important segment of the cheap labor supply to various sorts of large corporate industrial interests.

Goldschmidt (1976, 1978) empirically shows that the correlation is extremely significant between the ownership of the means of production by large corporate industrial interests in agricultural contexts, and the ensuing size of lower-class populations. Thus ". . . as the proportion of product by the large (agribusiness) farm increases, the proportion of lower-class persons also increases" with a .76 statistical correlation. According to Goldschmidt the social structures of industrialized agricultural communities differ markedly from family farm communities, as his table illustrates.

It follows that use of the labor of an ethnic population by corporate modes of production has had very significant social structural implications for the communities in which they reside. For Mexicans who have always composed a large cheap labor force for corporately controlled industrial enterprises in either rural or urban contexts, community social structures largely reflect the agribusiness mode of production in which Mexicans are selected for the lowest sector of such a social structure.

When these various historical structural relations are combined with a largely chauvinistic national subcultural prism and "depigmented" phenotypic racist ideal, the probability of intergroup hostility and conflict remains very high.[11] Thus, basically a working-class and underclass ethnic minority population, Mexicans in the United States have received differential negative treatment in myriad behavioral environments.

THE DISTRIBUTION OF DIFFERENTIAL NEGATIVE TREATMENT IN BEHAVIORAL ENVIRONMENTS

A basic problem arises in the discussion of differential treatment of any minority population if only structural or historical arguments are articulated. Especially in a heterogeneous, complex, industrial state like the United States, differential negative treatment of its traditional

TABLE 1
Comparison Between a Family Farm and Agribusiness

Community in California

	Family Farm Town	Agri-business Town
Economic base is the same		
Total farm sales (millions)	$2.5	$2.4
Farm size is different		
Average farm size in acres	57	497
Farm size adjusted for productivity	87	285
Population characteristics differ		
Total population	7,400	6,200
Self-employed & white collars	970	240
Percent of labor force	51	19
Agricultural labor	550	800
Percent of labor force	51	65
Economic conditions differ		
Number of retail businesses	141	62
Total retail sales (millions)	$4.4	$2.4
Level of living (percent above combined mean)	70	30
Community affairs differ		
Number of civic organizations	21	7
Participation (members per 100 population)	42	29
Number of churches	15	9
Church attendance (percent)	72	59
Public parks	2	0
Civic affairs differ		
Participation in school activities (percent)	28	16
Newspapers (issues per week)	4	1
Local government (incorporation)	yes	no

SOURCE: W. Goldschmidt, *The Rural Foundation of the American Culture.* A Gregory Foundation Memorial Lecture. (Columbia, Missouri, 1976, p. 16.)

ethnic and racial minority groups is "distributed" according to the structure of the behavioral environments in which representatives of the dominant ethnic group intersect with subordinate populations. Thus it is simply just not valid that all Mexicans, in all circumstances, at all periods in history will receive negative treatment by Anglos and their representatives. Rather, there are specific behavioral environments that select for differential treatment where an "ideology of cultural differences" can be utilized as the *raison d'etre,* as the justification for the structurally asymmetrical relations that unfold in the course of social intercourse between Mexicans and Anglos.

The sort of behavioral environments that select for such treatment have their genesis in working-class or underclass environments, but not necessarily in the specific environments in which actual labor processes are carried out. Instead there is a higher probability that such differential treatment based on ethnicity will be expressed in behavioral environments that are characterized by high levels of paternalism and structural dependence. Thus the distribution of differential negative treatment can be predicted utilizing a probabilistic model in which various factors are identified as indicators of paternalism and dependence. Those behavioral environments, however which are characterized by competitive structural relations will not select for differential treatment of a population based on other than class factors. It may be the case, as it is with the Mexican population in which its male working force is made up of largely working-class and underclass sectors (82 percent),[12] that there is little respite from differential treatment since either competitive or paternalistic environments are the very basis of existence for the great majority of Mexicans.

Among those behavioral environments marked by paternalism and dependence are those in which groups and persons cannot make demands upon those who control services, resources, information or material goods. Such contexts require behavior patterns of extreme deference articulated through a routinized and elaborate etiquette. Thus, the use of titles of reference, indicating superior status will generate social distance and status differentials. In addition, expected responses within the environment will be "client"-like; that is, passivity rather than demands are the expected responses. Questioning of interaction or its quality will result in negative responses, sometimes in an argot available only to the "selected." The argot itself will be highly developed and in fact will mark the included from the excluded. Elaborate cultural rationalizations are in fact worked out as the only proper "institutionalized" method of communication. Furthermore, spatial separation ensures the relationship of dominance and subordination. There are spaces where only the "clients" are allowed to congregate, and others in which the paternal figures have access to the physical space of the client whenever they choose to move. Such physical segregation not only ensures boundaries but in fact accentuates the difference in roles between clients and paternal figures. Also there is a high probability that costumes and other attire will also mark the status difference between client and paternal figure so that there is little mistaking the two if a physically neutral space should happen to become availabe for social intercourse. In such contexts a "everybody knows their place" and despotism controls the quality of the social intercourse in such paternalistic behavioral environments.

Moreover, "clients" will be perceived as childish, immature, ignorant, and not informed of the specifics of the behavioral environment, a knowledge which is solely that of the paternal figures. The exclusive knowledge will be couched in a special argot available only to the specialist paternal figures who command the behavioral environments. Such artifacts are congruent with aristocratic, oligarchic, autocratic, or colonial political relations between clients and paternal figures which in turn will generate relations based on ascription and a priori definitions of statuses and roles. Such linguistic codes do ensure their maintenance. At no time during the life of the behavioral environment does the client become a paternal figure. Clients may "horizontally" change identity to other kinds of clients, but never vertically. However, paternal figures may acquire greater ascendancy within the boundaries of the behavioral environment. As a corollary, it follows that all paternalistic behavioral environments will be hierarchical and unequal. Social stratification of such behavioral environments is in fact castelike, and the behavior expected within each caste division will be homogeneous. The very institutional processes which allow entry into the upper-caste regions of the paternal systems are themselves so highly articulated that the homogeniety of the controlling paternal figures is almost assured.

Since the behavioral environment is hierarchical and oligarchic then it follows that value consensus is imposed and withdrawal of services, commodities, material goods, or information is the means by which value consensus is assured. Ideological conflict between social divisions is largely eliminated by the traditional etiquette and enforced value consensus. While conflict is endemic to this kind of structure because of the divergent social sectors which make up the paternalistic behavioral environments, there are few alternative choices for the subordinated clients since the information, resources, commodities, or material goods that are in the control of the paternal figures are valued and scarce to the subordinated clients. Thus scarcity makes value greater, a relationship which the paternal figure exploits in this type of context. The manipulation of value consensus is the fulcrum of control in a paternalistic behavioral environment.

These aspects of paternalistic behavioral environments will more than likely lead to differentiated negative treatment of a historically subordinated ethnic minority, especially those of working-class or underclass origin. Thus when Mexicans and Anglos have intersected in behavioral environments with paternalistic relations and characteristics, then Mexicans usually will suffer negative differential treatment and the liberal utilization of an "ideology of cultural differences" will form the *raison d'etre* for such differential treatment. The history of Mexicans in the United States is replete with countless examples.[13]

THE CASE IN POINT: STERILIZATION OF MEXICAN WOMEN IN LOS ANGELES

Twenty-four women have alleged that they did not or could not have given informed consent to sterilization procedures that were carried out during 1971 and 1974 at the "Medical Center," one of the major county hospitals in Los Angeles. Ten of the twenty-four women filed a civil action suit against the Medical Center in which the sterilizations were performed, and each has described the specific circumstances in which they occurred in affidavits and in Findings of Fact and Conclusions of Law.[14]

The evidence illustrates practices by the hospital staff (nurses and doctors) to pressure patients into signing consent forms during intensive labor stages by withholding medication, not soliciting consent for sterilization, or not informing the patients of the permanency of such procedures. In addition, some husbands were pressured to sign consent forms for their wives without their wives' knowledge. Even though there were no medical indications for such procedures to be performed, consent was obtained from the husbands after their wives had refused to sign the consent forms. There was even a recorded refusal by one woman to submit to sterilization, this appears on her medical chart at 5:00 a.m., and after having been given demoral, consent forms appear to have been signed by 6:28 a.m.—the time in which the surgical procedures were performed. One woman was falsely told that a tubal ligation was necessary because the State of California did not allow more than three Cesarian sections. Her third child was to be born in this manner as had her two previous children. According to her physician, conception of a fourth child had to be avoided since this one would also have to be delivered by C-section.

It is a remarkable fact that among the ten women, four did not learn of the sterilization procedures until after they had sought birth control devices. One woman did not become aware that such a procedure had been performed until four years later during a medical examination.

In each case the Medical Center reflects the basic characteristics of a paternalistic behavioral environment. In fact a stay in any hospital exposes an individual to a condition of passivity and impotence not often replicated easily in other environments, except perhaps in judicial contexts. Certainly, in each woman's case, the consent of sterilization was not informed due to the unusual pressures applied and the specific physical conditions in which most of the women were suffering. Furthermore, their lack of knowledge regarding the irreversibility of the procedures, the sedated condition of some of the women who did sign, and the total lack of written consent of three of the women, all point to unilateral, oligarchical, and paternalistic conditions within the behavioral environments in which they were a part.

THE HOSPITAL AS THE BEHAVIORAL ENVIRONMENT

Within the confines of the Medical Center relatively defenseless Mexican women were selected out for differential negative treatment and hostility exemplified by nonconsenting sterilizations. In part, such an abuse is greatest in public hospitals, such as the Medical Center in which the sterilizations of these women occurred, because these are institutions where the poor are regarded as practice cases for medical students. Interns gain status by the number of operations they perform, so it is unlikely that they would turn down the surgical opportunities which a dependently oppressed minority represents. According to one source, a doctor told a group of physicians training at a southern California county hospital as part of their entry into obstetrics:

I want you to ask every one of the girls if she wants her tubes tied, regardless of how old she is. Remember, every one who says yes to getting her tubes tied means two tubes (practice) for some resident or intern and less work for some poor son-of-a-bitch next year (Kennard 1974).

In addition, there is a general neo-malthusian ideology that permeates the medical profession. Dr. H. Curtis Wood, Jr., a medical consultant and past president of the Association for Voluntary Sterilization indicated this point of view:

People pollute, and too many people crowded too close together cause many of our social and economic problems. These in turn are aggravated by involuntary and irresponsible parenthood. As physicians, we have obligations to the society of which we are a part. The welfare mess, as it has been called, cries out for solutions, one of which is fertility control (1973).

At the Medical Center where the ten women were sterilized, Dr. Bernard Rosenfeld, coauthor of a Ralph Nader Health Research Group study on surgical sterilization and one-time OB/GYN resident at the Center stated:

Surgical teaching programs are having increasing difficulty in finding patients because they have traditionally had to rely upon the availability of indigents. With the increase of third party payments (insurance), the number of indigents has decreased, causing the Medical Center to resort to "selling" and various forms of coercing patients into consenting to surgery.

I estimate that while I was at the Medical Center, between 20 to 30 percent of the doctors pushed sterilization on women who either did not understand what was happening to them or who had not been given the facts regarding their options (Interview quoted in Siggins 1977).

Another "insider" also commented on the coercive practices at the Medical Center at the point in time in which the sterilizations of the ten women were taking place:

I saw various forms of actual physical abuse used to force women in labor to consent to sterilization. There were incidences of slapping by doctors and nurses. A syringe of pain-reliever would be shown to a woman in labor and she would be told "we will give you this and stop the pain if you will sign" (Benker press conference 1975).

Such abuses then point to a "neutralization" of the minority person as a human being and the objectification of the practice as a necessary one due to population rationalizations, surgical practice procedures for the interns, or for the "social good" of the patient. Whatever the genesis, they all point to differentiated negative treatment and, in each case, to an "ideology of cultural difference," as the core rationalization for such practices. Through sterilization the subcultural prism of the dominant group has articulated its power in the behavioral environment. In fact, this is an extension of cultural sterilization into the physical sphere.

ENTER THE ANTHROPOLOGIST: QUALITATIVE INDICATORS OF SUBCULTURAL RURAL STRATEGIES OF THE WOMEN

From November 1, 1977 through May 30, 1978, the field studies of these women and their families were designed to accurately gather data which would "place" them in relation to a heterogeneous Mexican population. The studies sought to establish the "subcultural strategies" which these women shared within the cultural boundaries of the Mexican/Chicano population in the southwestern United States. Using participant observation, unstructured interviews and questionnaires, it was determined that in fact the women shared subcultural rural Mexican strategies that were adaptive in urban contexts. These findings even surprised the lawyers who themselves had not quite known what to make of the reactions that these women had expressed in regard to the sterilizations.

The data showed that nine of the ten women were born in small rural communities such as rancherias or ejidos and had been socialized in such environments through the age of fourteen.[15] In Mexico, these women had fulfilled agricultural chores from milking cows to planting and sowing corn. The one woman who had not been born in a rural Mexican setting was born in Dallas, Texas, but had adopted equivalent strategies in Mexican barrios. We can infer that their socialization experiences from early ages were strictly divided according to sex. Also among other adaptive patterns, they learned high values on child bearing and strict divisions of labor.

In such social environments, fictive kinship, extended familial networks, and dense friendship networks assist emotional survival. In urban Los Angeles such extensive and intensive networks were generated by all of the women and their spouses. Thus compadrazgo relations were shared by all the women. All ten women had extensive fictive kinship ties for the four traditional occasions in which such ties are generated: baptism, confirmation, communion, and marriage. For some of the women who had four children, compadres and comadres alone numbered eighteen persons. Five of the ten women maintained extended generational ties so that a three-generational tier was valued and experienced.

In addition, the mean number of children in the women's families of orientation was 7.5 and in their spouses families of orientation it was 9.5. Thus not only were they from large families, but these consanguineal relatives could be regarded as possible network supports. Visitations between consanguines was intensive and Sundays were generally the days in which the gathering of both fictive, consanguineal, and ascending generational relations would meet for commensal activities or for the celebration of birthdays or feast days. Another means of network expansion was that generated through amistad (friendship). Their functions were not only primarily affectionate, but also material. The males assisted each other and reciprocated repair and construction work, the women visited and exchanged information, and in all, they formed borrowing and lending networks for household goods. In addition, all of the women and/or their spouses had participated with their families in tandas or revolving credit associations.

Such consanguineal, fictive, and amistad relationships were identified as rewarding or not, based on sentido familiar (familial sentiment). That is, persons who did not generally reciprocate in exchange relations within these various networks were considered to be lacking in sentido familiar. This sentido familiar had as its basis, however, two core elements as organizing principles: first, marriage and children mark adulthood and responsibility; and second, as a social corollary of the first principle, is the internalization of the social identity of una mujer and un hombre. For the women in the case, although having had ritual markers through quinceñera (debut) to announce the passage from adolescence to adulthood, in fact adulthood was defined once marriage had taken place and children had been procreated. Without such circumstances and regardless of statuses gathered in other contexts such as professional standing or educational achievement, a female was not considered privy to the councils of discussion among women on such topics as sex, behavior of men, or topics of seriousness such as death, and other aspects of the life cycle. It is interesting to note that as long as one of the female lawyers in this case was not married she in fact had no access to the discussions these women shared regarding their marital difficulties experienced as the aftermath of the sterilization procedures. It was not until the lawyer married that she gained access to their discussions.

While marriage marks entrance into adulthood, as a ritual it also legitimizes sexual intercourse for the specific purpose of propagating children. While all of the women were Roman Catholics, it was not only specific Church doctrine to which they pointed as the rationalization of this central principle. Rather, they adhered to a traditional belief that sexual relations were the mechanisms for bearing children and not for the distinct pleasure of the male and female. Thus, the potential for bearing children and concomitantly the potential for siring children were given expression in the belief that sexual relations were primarily for the propagation of progeny. This potentiality quotient is the main vehicle by which continuity of all relations can be assured through sentido familiar. As long as children were likely to be born, reciprocal relations were likely to be generated and the various social networks in which these women and their spouses participated could be assured of continuation.

The social corollary of the first organizing principle which defines adulthood through marriage and children is that the social identities of the women, and in part that of the males who were their spouses, were measured not just by the potential for bearing and siring children, but by their actual manifestation. The actual manifestation of childbearing for these women of this subcultural strategy was the means by which their adult status was reinforced and articulated within the domestic group. There these women received prestige and were recognized as valued adults because of the potential and ability to bear children, a potential and ability which was reinforced by the continued presence of small children in the household. To be una mujer was to have children. During the various network activities previously described the private domestic value of the women's social identity as una mujer was assured by the adult female members of those various networks. Constant references during social intercourse about the ages of the children of the women present, the short spacing between children in order to ensure maximal peer relations and caretaker roles available, and in fact the various household duties assigned to females during such network activities as cooking, serving, washing dishes, and feeding children contributed to a total domestic social identity.

For males, on the other hand, prestige among cohorts and within the network activities was indirectly associated with the potential for siring children. This potential took a slightly different political avenue for men because it was also used as the measure of political control over the female within the domestic household. Within the networks, a pregnant woman was the symbolic presentation of the male ability to control her social existence within the domestic household. Therefore, un hombre was able to control una mujer through impregnation. In addition, un hombre was assured continued existence through his progeny since they bore his name. They assured also the efficacy of the various social networks to which he belonged. As will be seen, for males this control of the female and of her continued social existence was one of the central social principles that was greatly compromised as the aftermath of sterilization.

For the most part, then, social identity of these women was closely associated to the domestic group, but more importantly to the potential for bearing children and the potential for their spouses to sire children as domestic group political leaders. Certainly, within the domestic group activities, such relations were expressed in the division of labor not only of the spouses but in the division of labor of their children. For the most part, male children had responsibilities distinct from that of female children with the latter primarily fulfilling caretaker household duties including feeding and caring of younger brothers and sisters. For the most part, male siblings were assigned protective roles regardless of age and tasks unassociated with the household. Gardening, collection of garbage, and permissive explorations were largely in the hands of male siblings. When asked at one point during the course of the work as to why none of the male children were observed participating in kitchen tasks, the general response from the women was that their husbands did not want them to be maricones (effeminates).

For the most part, then, such qualitative findings point to a subcultural rural Mexican strategy for both spouses since all husbands had been born in small towns in Mexico, except for one spouse who was born in rural Imperial Valley in California. Certainly the composition of their past networks had been very much in keeping with traditional means of support and help. They generated fictive kinship, amistad relations, maintained intragenerational solidarity, and planned for large numbers of children.

The socioeconomic characteristics do not point to such cultural systems and in fact the mean age of these women was 32.6 with a range of 24–39 at time of sterilization; a mean income of $9,500 per year which was the median family income for that of the total U.S. popula-

tion; a mean education of 8.5 years which is only .6 years below that of the median of Mexican females in the United States, and stable housing and employment characteristics. In no way could a "culture of poverty" be suggested as the core of behavioral principles.

QUANTITATIVE INDICATORS OF SUBCULTURAL RURAL STRATEGIES

The qualitative data however, would remain inconclusive unless the notion of subcultural rural strategies could be operationalized and control groups could be provided with instruments by which comparisons could be made. One central hypothesis generated was that the women in the case would more significantly express such strategies in their beliefs and values than two control groups that were randomly selected from two networks of Mexican and Chicana females who had not been sterilized. First, however, an instrument was devised which would elicit for or against responses of a rural sort; twenty-eight scales were responded to by nine of the women in the case, nine randomly-selected urban and rural Mexican-born married unsterilized females from a fifty-two person network, and eight randomly-selected urban U.S.-married unsterilized females from a thirty-seven person network. The instrument was derived from questionnaires previously constructed for equivalent purposes by Grebler, Guzman and Moore (1969), ethnographic statements by Madsen (1964), and Farris and Glenn's (1976) scales on familism. From the total twenty-eight scales, 61 percent were randomly selected for analysis and the responses (seventeen) all weighed equally.[16] Table 2 illustrates the mean response on rural strategies. Significantly, all the sterilized, rural Mexican females scored high. A rank order of percentages of these women reveals that no women scored under 71 percent, while four scored 94 percent or better. Among the unsterilized rural Mexican-born women one scored 100 percent, and the rest of the rural and urban women scored below that. Although scoring 30 percent below the sterilized rural Mexican women, more than half (seven) of these women were from urban Mexico which would account for higher negative responses. Nevertheless, the score of 56.4 percent is sufficiently high to insist upon the relation between rural

TABLE 2
Response on Rural Strategies

	All Sterilized Women	All Unsteriled Rural & Urban Mexican	All Unsteriled Urban Chicanas
Mean Responses: Rural Strategies	+ 14.6 — 2.3	+ 9.6 — 7.4	+ 4.9 —12.1
Percent for Rural Strategies	86.4	56.4	28.9

subcultural experience and positive responses to the rural scales, even from unsterilized urban and rural Mexican women. The further verification of the hypothesis however occurred in the analysis of the unsterilized urban Chicana women. Their mean score of 28.9 percent is again 30 percent less than that scored by the unsterilized rural and urban Mexican women. That is, the percentages of positive responses are reduced 30 percent by each of the control groups; so the less important the rural strategies to the group, the greater the increase in lower positive percentages. Thus, the negative response of the unsterile urban-rural Mexican women slightly more than doubled over the responses of the women in the case, and the Chicanas slightly less than doubled the negative responses to that of the unsterilized Mexican women. In comparison to the sterilized Mexican women, the Chicanas negative responses were quadrupled. One can suggest, then, that there is a strong relation between the degree of importance of subcultural rural strategies and the negative responses. The less the importance of the rural strategy, the greater the increases in negative responses. The greater the importance of the rural strategy, the fewer the decreases in positive responses.

An analysis of variance (ANOVA) confirms the hypothesis of significant differences between each of the three groups at α (Alpha) 0.05 (95 percent level of significance). In addition, analysis of variance between all three groups at α (Alpha) 0.01 (99 percent level of significance) show significant differences between sterilized Mexican women and unsterilized urban Chicanas. Furthermore, there are significant differences between the sterilized women and both groups of unsterilized Mexican/Chi-

cana women at the α (Alpha) 0.005 level as evidenced by a t-test comparison.

From these quantitative data, then, and in addition to the qualitative data which was presented in the previous section, the study concluded that the women who were sterilized had in fact shared subcultural rural strategies which contrasted significantly with those of the control groups. Within urban contexts such rural cultural and social systems fulfilled equivalent functions of self-help, and cooperation. The extensive networks of kin, friends, and ascending generational members, as well as the values and beliefs concerning *sentido familiar,* marriage and children all served as the basis for social living even within the urban environment. These social and cultural aspects served equivalent affective and material functions to those which were fulfilled in rural contexts. It is only within these cultural and social patterns that the effects of sterilization can then begin to be understood.

QUALITATIVE CONCLUSIONS OF THE STATE AND STRESS OF THE SUBCULTURAL SYSTEMS OF THE STERILIZED WOMEN

From the knowledge gained of the manner in which the social and cultural systems had worked before sterilization, it was then necessary to ascertain the "state" of the sociocultural systems after sterilization. On a social level, it was discovered that most of the women had gone through a process of social disengagement, beginning with the husband-wife dyadic relationship. Two of the husbands remained highly supportive of their spouses and no appreciable damage seemed to have resulted in their relationship. One of the two husbands, however, compensated for the loss of his wife's ability to procreate by showering her with gifts at most inopportune times. The other remained a saddened, but not bitter, male who counseled his wife and was extremely supportive of her. The other eight relationships suffered irreparable damage to different degrees. Three couples filed for divorce prior to the completion of the judicial procedures on July 7, 1978. The other five relationships were marked largely by jealousy, suspicion, and in two cases—physical violence and abuse. Jealousy and suspicion arose in three of the husbands due to the change they perceived in their political control over their wives' sexuality. Basically they feared that their wives would avail themselves of the sterile state, or that other males would make overtures toward their wives once their sterile state was revealed. In this regard, their wives' social identity had changed from respectable woman to possible whore.

The relationships between mothers and children for eight of ten women shifted as well. Physical punishment of children had increased to the point that in at least five of the cases, children sought to remove themselves from their mother's presence at every opportunity. Children themselves had begun to express anger to their own siblings so that sibling conflict had also increased. Aggression between mothers and their children and between siblings shifted the qualitative relationship from affection and nurturance to that of fear and violent reaction.

In all cases fictive and *amistad* relations suffered and visitations which germinated such relations decreased dramatically. Saints days, parties, fiestas, and Sunday exchanges have been largely avoided by all the women through withdrawal from fictive and amistad relations. For the most part, the women agreed that it was less painful to withdraw from these relationships than to answer questions regarding either the sterilizations or the reason why more children have not been sired, since the last born were, by this time, at least four years old. To inquiries about future pregnancies the retort that they were "guarding against pregnancies" was short-ranged. Such questions were exceedingly painful since, of the ten women, five had already chosen names for their future progeny. For the most part these were names of paternal or maternal grandparents.

Consanguineal relations were also affected. Six of the women did not share the fact that they had been sterilized with immediate siblings, and in three of the cases with their own mothers. This denial, of course, could only take place if social relations were themselves withdrawn by the women in order to avoid the topic altogether. In addition, this also meant that their spouses' consanguineal relatives were also avoided so that this provided another source of conflict between husbands and wives.

Such conflict became so endemic that in three of the relationships, the husbands lost their employment, two became alcoholics, and one left the family and has not been seen for four years from the date of the sterilization.

The degree of cultural disruption has been immense. The basis of social identity and self-image has been largely eliminated for all of the women. In the place of the culturally constituted social definition of self, a substitution of what can be termed the "Mula (Mule) Syndrome" has been generated. The mula syndrome refers to the cultural redefinition of the women as "unnatural," "insufficient," or "incomplete women" for they are no longer of domestic value. One woman expressed her situation: "I can no longer be a companion to my husband." Cultural symbols of self-worth were negated and in their place symbols of self-deprecation and self-blame took hold. Of course, these led to feelings of guilt, shame, worthlessness and self-blame. They blame themselves for what has occurred and are blamed in part by some of the husbands for not resisting sterilization, they then turn in anger against themselves. This situation has been expressed in acutely vivid dream content. Thus, one woman dreamt she found herself traveling to Mexico without her children and upon arrival becoming embarrassed when asked by relatives where they are. Another has nightmares in which her children have been stolen, killed and eaten by unidentified figures. Others have dreamt of finding themselves alone with dead persons, or totally alone and lost without their children or husband, while others recall seeing their children drowning in lakes.

The sense of personality loss, and worthlessness, all part of the grief reaction to the sterilization procedures, led to acute depression. For each woman her sense of continuity with the past had been fractured, her sense of self-worth had been shattered, self-blame had been internalized, and a new social identity of impotence had been generated. Each woman in fact is now stigmatized. The sterilization procedures stand as visible and permanent marks of humiliation which they can never remove. The greater the effort at denial, the greater the anger and self-hate generated. The greater the anger and self-hate, the greater the necessity of expression upon themselves or upon others. The greater the expression, the greater the increase in conflict, social disengagement and cultural disruption.

RURAL STRATEGY, CULTURAL DISRUPTION, AND PREDICTIVE DEPRESSION

From the qualitative analysis presented of the effects of sterilization, a hypothesis was developed. The greater the importance of the rural strategy had been among the women's sociocultural systems, the higher the probability of deeper depression as the aftermath of cultural disruption. This hypothesis was based on the notion that although beliefs do not define actual behavior, they were nevertheless central to the personality of individuals and had been extremely important in assessing the moral worth of others and assessing themselves. This is not a causal argument. It suggests that if the subcultural systems which the women had shared, including their spouses, were such that few alternatives for social identity were available after their disruption, or if the spouses in their reaction upheld the core values of such social identity by denying alternative rewarding roles for their wives, then more than likely the depression for the women would be concomitantly high.

From observed contexts and knowledge of the environments of each woman, each was ranked according to what had been the degree of importance of such strategies to their entire sociocultural systems prior to sterilization. Thus each woman was ranked according to the following system and given a score (see tables 3 and 4).

TABLE 3

Degree of Importance of Rural Strategy		
(VH)	Very High	— 16 – 17
(H)	High	— 14 – 15
(M)	Medium	— 12 – 13
(L)	Low	— 10 – 11
(VL)	Very Low	— 8 – 9

My qualitative judgment was the following:

TABLE 4

Woman	Degree of Importance of Rural Strategy	Score
Madrigal	VH	16 – 17
Bienavides	VH	16 – 17
Figueroa	H	14 – 15
Hurtado	H	14 – 15
Hernandez	H	14 – 15
Rivera	H	14 – 15
Hermosillo	H	14 – 15
Acosta	M	12 – 13
Orozco	M	12 – 13

A second set of scores was quantitatively derived from the rural strategies questionnaire. In turn these scores were compared to the qualitatively derived ranking. This comparison appears in table 5.

For each matched score a numerical value of two points was allowed, for each error of one interval a score of one point, and for errors of more than one interval zero points. In summing the numerical values of accurate versus inaccurate scores according to the process above, it was possible to predict a degree of importance of the rural strategies with a total score of thirteen out of eighteen possible points for an accuracy of 72 percent.

TABLE 5

Woman	Qualitative Judgment	Quantitative Score from Questionnaire
Madrigal	VH: 16–17	VH: 16
Bienavides	VH: 16–17	M: 12
Figueroa	H: 14–15	VH: 16
Hurtado	H: 14–15	VH: 17
Hernandez	H: 14–15	H: 15
Rivera	H: 14–15	H: 15
Hermosillo	H: 14–15	VH: 16
Acosta	M: 12–13	M: 13
Orozco	M: 12–13	M: 12

Then the qualitative judgments and the quantitative comparisons were combined for a new ranking by order of *depression* according to the degree of the importance of rural strategies exhibited in the sociocultural systems of which the women had been a part and their responses on the questionnaires. The following are the ranked estimates according to the degree of depression on a scale of one to ten with one the highest, ten the lowest (see table 6).

TABLE 6

Woman	Degree of Depression
Madrigal	1
Figueroa	2
Hernandez	3
Acosta	4
Hurtado	5
Bienavides	6
Rivera	7
Hermosillo	8
Orozco	9
no respondent	10

The next step for verification was to ask the consulting psychiatrist on the case, Dr. Terry Kuper, to provide his ranked estimates according to the degree of depression, as well as for the female attorney's judgment of the degree of depression according to her best knowledge. The psychiatrist had been working on the case for three years prior to my request and the lawyer for four years. His opinion would provide a professional perspective, her's a popular one. At no time had we spoken concerning the degree of depression suffered by each woman, but unfortunately at this time the psychiatrist was only able to provide me with the top and bottom two, since he had no immediate access to his records when this information was solicited. Therefore, his ranking is incomplete (see table 7).

From the ranked data appearing above, the major hypothesis of the relation between the rupture of traditional rural beliefs and their sociocultural systems and degrees of depression is verified by the independent ranking of the psychiatrist who has agreed with extreme accuracy with the anthropologist. The popular

TABLE 7

Woman	Degree of Depression Velez-I	Kuper	Lawyer
Madrigal	1	2	1
Figueroa	2	1	3
Hernandez	3	0	4
Acosta	4	0	2
Hurtado	5	0	6
Bienavides	6	0	7
Rivera	7	0	5
Hermosillo	8	8	9
Orozco	9	9	8

judgment of the lawyer was slightly off in ranking the second most depressed person but was in complete agreement with both psychiatrist and anthropologist concerning the bottom two. All of these steps were necessary to present to a court of law, as an empirically sound judgment, the effects of sterilization on the sociocultural systems of the women and the relationship between the disruptions of those systems and the generation of acute depression and its distribution. The greater the importance of rural strategies had been among the women, the higher the probability of deeper depression as the aftermath of cultural disruption and social fracturing of networks.

These findings and the verified hypotheses were then presented in a court of law as part of the evidence in behalf of a law suit which these women had filed in federal court. As will be seen, it is ironic that the very evidence used to illustrate the damages done to the social and cultural systems of these women, was in fact partially used by the court to rationalize a decision against them. The court processes and the final decision, however, do verify the theoretical position this work assumed: that in paternalistic behavioral environments, Mexicans would be treated negatively. The court is one such behavioral environment.

MADRIGAL V. QUILLIGAN: THE TRIAL AS A BEHAVIORAL ENVIRONMENT

On May 31, 1978, a civil suit for damages began in District Court for the Central District of California. The complaint was entitled

"Dolores Madrigal et al., Plaintiff v. *E.J. Quilligan et al."* The action was brought against Dr. E.J. Quilligan, chairman of Medical Center's Department of Obstetrics and Gynecology, and eleven other doctors on behalf of the ten women. In order to appreciate the final outcome of the suit, however, we should recall the central contention that "paternalistic behavioral environments" foster differential treatment of Mexicans when the efficient conditions are present. The trial will be treated as such a behavioral environment and the efficient conditions articulated.

The courtroom was very much like most in that spaces were defined in proper domains for the judge, the plaintiffs' attorneys and the defendants' attorneys. Since the trial was a nonjury type the focus of all the attention by the attorneys on both sides was on the judge. Neither the trial per se nor the judicial arguments will be detailed since both are much beyond the scope of this work. Instead, the contrasts within the confines of the trial will be addressed in order to understand the behavioral environment within the total context of the social question involved.

These contrasts were most immediately apparent in the attorneys. The plaintiffs' two Mexican lawyers were from a local poverty legal center. One of the lawyers was a thirty-five year old male who had graduated in the top of his class a few years previously. He was legally blind from a childhood disease so that the enormously thick glasses he wore accentuated and distorted his dark brown eyes. For the most part, this soft-spoken, medium-sized, and slightly pudgy man, shuffled as he moved between the plaintiffs' table and the podium that sat squarely in the middle of the room facing the judge's panelled bench. The other lawyer was a recently graduated Mexican woman, and like the other lawyer, had been working on the case for four years. Dark, thin, and well-dressed, the young female lawyer moved assertively between the plaintiffs' table and the podium. She spoke in a clear, clipped and slightly-accented diction. They differed little from the ten plaintiffs in court, except for variance in quality of dress.

In opposition, the defendants' lawyers were the best that money could buy. Both the male and female lawyer were from one of the more prestigious Beverly Hills law firms and both seemed quite relaxed in their roles in the courtroom. She moved assertively and quickly from the defendants' table even though she was about thirty pounds overweight. Well dressed, articulate, and quite polysyllabic, this unattractive Anglo woman did not in fact actually present any of the defendants nor did she cross-examine witnesses. Instead she largely was responsible for making legal motions, registering legal requests, and seemed to assist her partner. He was like his fair counterpart, fiftyish, well groomed, articulate and quite polysyllabic without the stuttering that seemed to mark the presentations of the plaintiffs' lawyers. Both in hue and in presentation of themselves, there were obvious contrasts which seemed to divide the courtroom into the Mexican side and the Anglo side. The judge seemed to sit in the middle, or so it seemed.

The judge, the Honorable Jesse W. Curtis, a white-haired seventy year old person, seemed like the stereotype of the paternalistic figure commanding the courtroom. Firm-jawed, angular faced, with piercing blue eyes set beneath profuse eyebrows that moved in unison in mostly frowns, this Nixon-appointee to the federal bench was known by reputation as a conservative judge who lived aboard his yacht in Newport Beach, one of the most prestigious areas in southern California. He and the defendants' lawyers were obvious analogues and stark contrasts to the plaintiffs and their lawyers. The judge did not in fact sit in the middle.

For two and a half weeks the plaintiffs' lawyers presented evidence that under duress, after hours of being in labor and under medication, the plaintiffs could not have given informed consent. Dr. Don Sloan, an internationally known gynecologist and obstetrician, testified that given the circumstances surrounding the sterilization procedures, none of the women could have provided informed consent. Each woman in turn provided their testimony in Spanish, in which they detailed the contexts of their sterilization. A handwriting expert examined the signatures of those women who had signed consent forms and concluded that in fact each woman had been suffering great distress and stress at the time. Dr. Terry Kuper presented his evidence of the sterilization procedures on each woman and concluded that to different degrees each woman had suffered irreparable psychological damage and that long periods of psychotherapy would have to be undertaken by each one. I offered the data discovered in this work in much the same manner and development, except initially the judge was not going to permit my testimony. When Judge Curtis was made aware of my impending testimony, he remarked from the bench that he did not see what an anthropologist was going to say that would have any bearing on damages and that if I was getting paid, that my testimony would not be worth a "plugged nickle." He concluded that after all "We all know that Mexicans love their families." Nevertheless, I was able to present the data contained and except for minor cross-examination, no opposing expert was presented to refute my testimony. Of interest to note, however, were the concluding questions that Judge Curtis addressed to me which would be of significance in the final opinion.

After having concluded my testimony, the Judge asked me how long I had spent on the case. I answered that I had spent 450 hours of time between field work, creation of the instrument, selecting the control groups, and ascertaining what the effects had been on the women's sociocultural systems. He then asked me if I would have undertaken the study in any other manner. I responded that I would not have since ". . . as an anthropologist to have done otherwise would not have been worth a hill of beans." He repeated the same question again, slightly rephrased, and I answered that professional ethics would have prevented me to come to the conclusions that I did unless I rigorously followed the methodology I had used. The Judge thanked me and I stepped down.

The defense presented no rebuttal of expert witnesses and did not cross-examine the plaintiffs. Instead they called each one of the doctors in question and from the plaintiffs' medical files commented on the medical procedures contained. At no time did any of the doctors recall any of the women but they all asserted that their "custom and practice" was not to perform a sterilization unless a woman had consented and understood what she was doing. When cross-examined as to whether they spoke Spanish well enough to detail the procedures, they responded generally that they knew enough "obstetrics Spanish" to get them by. When pressed for details about the individual women,

they all answered that they could not recall them as patients since there were so many.

The final decision was handed down June 30, before Judge Curtis left for a lengthy Scandinavian vacation. It stated rather succinctly that the judgment was entered for the defendants. The women lost, but the judge's rationalization is interesting and informative because it in fact verifies the theoretical position which underlies this exposition—that in paternalistic environments in which Mexicans are differentially treated in a negative manner, the "ideology of cultural differences" will be used as a rationalization for the structural and asymmetrical characteristics of the environments.

The Judge's remarks are as follows:

Communication Breakdown
This case is essentially the result of a breakdown in communications between the patients and the doctors. All plaintiffs are Spanish speaking women whose ability to understand and speak English is limited. This fact is generally understood by the staff at the Medical Center and most members have acquired enough familiarity with the language to get by. There is also an interpreter available whose services are used when thought to be necessary. But even with these precautions misunderstandings are bound to occur. Furthermore, the cultural background of these particular women has contributed to the problem in a subtle but significant way. According to the plaintiff's anthropological expert, they are members of a traditional Mexican rural subculture, a relatively narrow spectrum of Mexican people living in this country whose lifestyle and cultural background derives from the lifestyle and culture of small rural communities in Mexico. He further testified that a cultural trait which is very prominent with this group is an extreme dependence upon family. Most come from large families and wish to have large families for their own comfort and support. Furthermore, the status of a woman and her husband within that group depends largely upon the woman's ability to produce children. If for any reason she cannot, she is considered an incomplete woman and is apt to suffer a disruption of her relationship with her family and husband. When faced with a decision of whether or not to be sterilized, the decision process is a much more traumatic event with her than it would be with a typical patient and, consequently, she would require greater explanation, more patient advice, and greater care in interpreting her consent than persons not members of such a subculture would require.

But this need for such deliberate treatment is not readily apparent. The anthropological expert testified that he would not have known that these women possessed these traits had he not conducted tests and a study which required some 450 hours of time. He further stated that a determination by him based upon any less time would not have been worth "beans." It is not surprising therefore that the staff of a busy metropolitan hospital which has neither the time nor the staff to make such esoteric studies would be unaware of these atypical cultural traits.

It is against this backdrop therefore that we must analyze the conduct of the doctors who treated the plaintiffs in this case.

Doctors' Custom and Practice

Since these operations occurred between 1971 and 1974 and were performed by the doctors operating in a busy obstetrics ward, it is not surprising that none of the doctors have any independent recollection of the events leading up to the operations. They all testified, however, that it was their custom and practice not to suggest a sterilization unless a patient asked for it or there were medical complications which would require the doctor, in the exercise of prudent medical procedures, to make such suggestion. They further testified that it was their practice when a patient requested sterilization to explain its irreversible result and they stated that they would not perform the operation unless they were certain in their own mind that the patient understood the nature of the operation and was requesting the procedure. The weight to be given to such testimony and the inferences to be drawn therefrom will be determined in the light of all the testimony relating to each doctor's conduct.[17]

The Judge's final opinion also excluded the testimony by the handwriting expert, the psychiatrist on the case, and refuted the testimony by Dr. Sloan, the gynecologist and obstetrician, by saying that his statements "... completely defy common sense." Why they do so, he did not explain. His conclusion, however, is quite enlightening in that he admits that in fact all of the women had suffered. He states:

This case had not been an easy one to try for it has involved social, emotional and cultural considerations of great complexity. There is no doubt that these women have suffered severe emotional and physical stress because of these operations. One can sympathize with them for their inability to communicate clearly, but one can hardly blame the doctors for relying on these indicia of consent which appeared to be unequivocal on their face and which are in constant use in the Medical Center.

Let judgment be entered for the defendants.

Jesse W. Curtis
Senior United States
District Judge (19)

CONCLUSIONS

First it must be obvious that within paternalistic institutionalized behavioral environments, Mexicans have a high probability of being negatively treated. Certainly the medical sterilizations and the legal judgments uphold this fact. Regardless of the overwhelming evidence to the contrary, the judge disregarded evidence and testimony presented and chose instead to consider the "custom and practice" of the doctors, rather than following rules of evidence.

Second, his misuse of the anthropological data in which he identified the women as belonging to a "relatively narrow spectrum of Mexican people" was not presented as empirical evidence. Instead this commentary was used to illustrate the "atypicality of their cultural traits." In other words, the women were so culturally different that the doctors could not have known that the sterilizations would have affected them in so adverse a manner. This belief removes the legal and moral responsibility for their actions. The "ideology of cultural differences" then is used as the very basis for an unjust and detrimental decision against a group of largely defenseless Mexican women. After all, how could the doctors have been aware that the sterilizations would have such an effect on Mexican women since the hospital in which these operations were carried out is in the middle of the largest Mexican barrio outside Mexico City. The judge legitimized the doctors' actions and his action against the women by noting that the doctors were too busy to note these cultural differences and even more importantly, they were so different that the doctors could not have known the effects of sterilizations unless they had carried out studies similar to the one I carried out in the case.

Third, all the work which went into the presentation of this material is still very much in the "meliorative and reformists attempts" of the well-intentioned liberal establishment. I too blundered and in fact was responsible for providing the judge with exactly the ammunition he needed to utilize the "ideology of cultural differences." Ironically, while fairly objective empirical findings of effect were presented which were too overwhelming to ignore on the record, the judge's only recourse was to utilize the data against the women since it could not be refuted.

Fourth, and last, all of the activities which make up this work occurred within the confines of an industrial capitalist state in which the diversity of culture is organized and controlled by a national prism which reflects a dominant ethnic group of Anglo-Saxon Americans. Both the sterilization of the physical ability of a group of ethnic minority women to procreate, and the resultant cultural sterilization of the same group of women were in fact provided legitimization by the court. The decision reinforces that national prism and ensures the superordinate ethnic group of Anglo-Saxon Americans continued domination by whatever means.

As one woman so astutely observed: Se me acabó la canción.

NOTES

1. On November 1, 1977, I met with two attorneys to discuss the effects of alleged unconsented sterilization procedures that had been conducted on ten Mexican women in Los Angeles, California. I had received a telephone call earlier from one of the lawyers who represented a civil suit against a major metropolitan hospital in Los Angeles for allegedly permitting sterilization procedures to be conducted on non-consenting Chicano women. Both lawyers presented the case from the perspective that ten "Chicanas" had been sterilized without their consent. They then asked for my assessment of the possible cultural and social ramifications of such practices on the ten women.

   I replied that I could not offer an informed judgment without analyzing the case and the women. However, I felt able to venture an opinion, an educated one at best. I suggested that quite variable responses could be expected dependent on the behavioral contexts in which these women had been a part, their cultural histories, and their present support networks. Furthermore, at that time, I postulated, and it must be emphasized that it was merely a postulate, the following. If the women had been born in Mexico in rural contexts or in the United States in equivalent circumstances, then sterilization could have severe psychocultural and social results even beyond those expected of other women in the United States. Also, I suggested that the degree of damage could vary with the background of the women. Thus, if the women were urban Chicanas and

part of lower-class sectors, then their reaction could also be severe, but perhaps their social beings may not be as importantly related to the potential for bearing children. In either context, the severity of a nonconsenting sterilization on the women would be dependent on a variety of exogenous and endogenous variables including class, ethnic maintenance, social networks, work experience, and the psychological well-being of each woman prior to the sterilization procedure.

   The lawyers then asked me if I would be willing to serve as a consultant on the case in order to test out the postulates that I had suggested. I explained that I could not entertain any a priori conclusions in regard to the women, but that I would be willing to undertake a basic field study of the individuals involved and the circumstances of their sterilization. From the data I would submit an informed opinion of the effects, if any, of the surgery. Consequently, I agreed to serve as a consulting cultural anthropologist for their clients, with the stipulation that whatever conclusions I reached would have to be validated by empirical findings.

2. I use the term "Chicana" to designate U.S.-born women of Mexican heritage who are socialized within industrially-structured population centers in either agricultural or urban contexts. Cultural specifics from language to belief systems are "distributed" according to class and occupational sectors. "Mexican" is the term I use to designate Mexican-born persons who are socialized within rural or urban contexts and in a possible variety of structural settings from industrial to small village "close corporate" communities. Cultural specifics from language to belief systems are "distributed" according to class and occupational sectors. The differences between populations will be both cultural and structural; however, similarities will also be reflective of cultural specifics arising from equivalent structural conditions. The term "working class" Mexican denotes little specifically and assumes a homogeniety of experiences that is ahistorical in content.

3. Theodore Schwartz (1971) states that the behavioral environment is the environment as conceived by the member of a society. It includes those physical features which are culturally relevant, as well as all culturally recognized beings and forces and their relation to man. One might term the study of cultural constructs of the behavioral environment "phenomenological ecology." If we take "environment" as the objective or real situation in which a people live, "ecology" would be the culturally mediated relation between man and environment.

   In addition, however, I characterize behavioral environments as temporal and spatial extensions of culturally constituted constructs. Thus, a "working area" is an extension of constructs upon the environment and "becomes" a working area when time, space, social relations, artifacts, goals, and values all intersect from the extensions provided by living beings who form and shape the specificity of the working area. I use the word "extensions" as projected information bits which carry the constructs containing the specifics of the working area(s). While the extensions carrying the cultural constructs may be partially "congealed," as physical artifacts these become active only within a socially stimulated context. A factory may contain all the congealed data within its machinery to function automatically, but only an extended cultural construct(s) and its social context provide it with temporal and spatial "life."

I utilize the concept of behavioral environment as an important construct which may be fruitful in designating those situations that promote negative differential treatment. Some environments can be considered "paternalistic" when the cultural constructs demand extreme deference articulated through a routinized and elaborate etiquette, titles of reference and superiority, a specialized argot or jargon, differentiated costumes and attire, allocated physical spaces, and segregated activities. Social relations are based on dependence asymmetry, social distance, and ascribed status differentials without vertical mobility for the client population. "Clients" are perceived as immature, childish, ignorant, and underdeveloped so that the controlling figures in the environment have political control over them and economic access which commands the allocation of valued resources, services, material goods, or information. Enforcement is based on the withdrawal or threatened withdrawal of such resources so that ultimately the roles fulfilled by "clients" vis-à-vis their "patrons" are based on coercive support. (For an elaboration of the differences between coercive and legitimate support see the discussion by Marc J. Swartz in his "Introduction" to *Local-Level Politics*, Chicago, Aldine, 1968.)

Yet, "competitive behavioral environments" in comparison to paternalistic ones are marked by factors of achievement, affective neutrality, mobility, rational legitimate support, and are legalistic, representative, and "earned." The relations between participants, although hierarchical are not passive-dependent but active-interdependent. These may be asymmetrical, but all concerned here expect change and development through participation. Competition is designated within boundaries and conflict is defined and agreed to within parameters that do not threaten the relations between members in the environments. There is a general value consensus without coercion, and resources are allocated to those who can best meet the goals of the behavioral environment. Both "paternalistic" and "competitive" models are polar types and operationalization is still to be developed.

The basic notions of paternalistic and competitive relations are owed to Pierre Van den Berghe's two fine basic works in ethnic and race relations: *Race and Racism*, (New York: John Wiley & Sons, 1967) and *Race and Ethnicity*, (New York: Basic Books, 1970). In these two works, the author uses the characteristics of paternalism and competition as independent and dependent societal variables which mark the nature of the relations between dominant and subordinate groups within a developmental polar model. I contend that, regardless of larger societal developments, paternalistic and competitive behavioral environments will coexist in even the most "competitive industrialized" social contexts. In the most rational of institutionalized bureaucratic contexts, paternalistic factors may very well mark most relations between participants.

4. See Charles Wagley and Marvin Harris, *Minorities in the New World,* (New York and London: Columbia University Press, 1964) and Richard M. Burkey, *Ethnic and Racial Groups,* (Menlo Park, Calif.: Cummings Press, 1978) for a discussion of the relation between nationality, ethnicity, and citizenship.

5. From the Soviet perspective, ethnic chauvinism of the Great Russians does not exist. Y. Bromley (1978) explains that Soviet culture, not Russian culture, is the prism of the Soviet Union and that the Soviet Union is not a nation-state but a state of collected nationalities and minorities integrated to develop a new historic entity—the Soviet people. The Russian language, for example, is the *lingua franca* necessary for socialist construction, the requirements of the national economy, and the growth of towns with multiethnic and multilingual populations (p. 24). For Bromley, the adherence to an internationalist socialist perspective has resulted in a cultural syncretism of all nationalities into a Soviet culture which has a single socialist content. "Thus, not merely a national but a whole Soviet culture takes shape in the course of the mutual influence and mutual enrichment of the intellectual cultures of the peoples of the USSR and the assimilation of the achievements of world culture" (p. 25). This ideological belief is most interesting in light of the agitation of ethnic minorities such as Soviet Jews in the Soviet Union.

6. Ibid.

7. See Burkey, *Ethnic and Racial Groups* for the fourteen groups which were stratified according to four indices, pp. 300–400.

8. See Rodolfo Acuña, *Occupied America: The Chicano's Struggle Toward Liberation,* (San Francisco: Canfield Press, 1972) in which Acuña states that as a matter of historical record the chief negotiator for the United States in fact threatened his Mexican counterparts with the ultimatum that if Mexico did not accept the terms offered, the United States would take the territory under negotiation.

9. The Bracero program for contract labor was initiated in 1942 in the United States to fill manpower shortages generated by World War II. The program was resumed in 1951 with the enactment of Public Law 78. Recent hysteria concerning the undocumented worker of Mexican descent in the United States has generated calls for the reinstitutionalization of such a program in order to stem what is seen as a "brown tide" of humanity spilling into the United States. Yet as David Weber pointed out in a recent article (*Los Angeles Times,* January 14, 1979), Mexican documented and undocumented workers have a long historical cultural tie to the Southwest and contribute immensely economically, socially, and developmentally to the United States. See also Mauricio Mazon "Illegal Alien Surrogates: A Psychohistorical Interpretation of Group Stereotypes in Time of Economic Stress," *Aztlán: International Journal of Chicano Studies Research*, 1975, Vol. 6, No. 2, pp. 305–324.

10. The twin-cities programs are joint capital intensive projects in which light industry is created in Mexico for the express purpose of using cheap Mexican labor in a border area and then shipping the assembled product to the United States for sale. The Nogales Sonora-Arizona and El Paso-Cd. Juarez cities are among the most notable examples.

11. See Wagley and Harris, *Minorities in the New World* for the efficient and necessary conditions for inter-group conflict and its maintenance.

12. See *A Study of Selected Socio-Economic Characteristics of Ethnic Minorities Based on the 1970 Census: Volume I: Americans of Spanish Origin.* Department of Health Education and Welfare (Office of Special Concerns: July, 1974).

13. See Tomás Almaguer "Toward the Study of Chicano Colonialism," *Aztlán,* 1971, Vol. 2, No. 1, Spring, pp. 7-21, and also his "Historical Notes on Chicano Oppression: The Dialectics of Racial and Class Domination in North America," *Aztlán,* 1974, Vol. 5, Nos. 1 and 2, pp. 27-56. Carey McWilliams' *North From Mexico,* (New York: Greenwood Press, 1968, originally 1949) is the seminal work on the differential treatment of Mexicans and the historical antecedents to continued intergroup conflict. David J. Weber's *Foreigners in Their Native Land* also details the historical events comprising intergroup conflicts. For union and labor struggles, the issue of *Aztlán* devoted to labor history (1975, Vol. 6, No. 2, pp. 137-324) is the best yet written on the topic.

14. See "Findings of Facts and Conclusions of Law," filed by Los Angeles Center for Law and Justice (May 31, 1978:1-78), and also "Affidavit" by Maria Figueroa (June 18, 1975), "Affidavit" by Georgina Hernandez (June 15, 1975), "Affidavit" by Consuelo Hermosillo (June 18, 1975), "Affidavit" by Estela Benavides (June 18, 1975), "Affidavit" by Rebecca Figueroa (June 18, 1975), and "Affidavit" by Guadalupe Acosta (June 18, 1975). Also see Antonia Hernandez "Chicanas and the Issue of Involuntary Sterilization: Reforms Needed to Protect Informed Consent," *Chicano Law Review* (1976, Vol. 3, pp. 3-37).

15. Rancherias are small agricultural settlements in which the population density of the residential area is equal to the area used for subsistence. Ejidos are communal lands assigned to a community by the Mexican federal government.

16. The selected scales solicited information of social identity, traditional beliefs of witchcraft and medicine, sex roles, acceptance of outside agency or control, and familism.

17. See Judge Jesse W. Curtis "Opinion," (No. CV 75-2057-JWC, United States Federal Court, June 30, 1978, pp. 1-19).

REFERENCES

1975   Acosta, G. Affidavit, June 18.

1974   Acuña, Rodolfo. *Occupied America: The Chicano's Struggle Toward Liberation.* San Francisco: Canfield Press.

1974   Almaguer, Tomás. "Historical Notes on Chicano Oppression: The Dialectics of Racial and Class Domination in North America." *Aztlán: Chicano Journal of the Social Sciences and the Arts* 5:27-56.

1971   _____. "Toward the Study of Chicano Colonialism." *Aztlán: Chicano Journal of the Social Sciences and the Arts* 2:7-21.

1975   *Aztlán: International Journal of Chicano Studies Research* 6:137-324.

1973   Bastide, Roger. *Applied Anthropology.* New York: Harper and Row. Originally published in French by Payot, 1971.

1975   Benavides, E. Affidavit, June 18.

1975   Benker, Karen. Statement made before a press conference at the Greater Los Angeles Press Club, December 6.

1977   Briggs Jr., Vernon M. et al. *The Chicano Worker.* Austin and London: The University of Texas Press.

1978   Bromley, Yulian. "Cultural Aspects of Ethnic Processes in the USSR." *Soviet Studies in Ethnography* 72:16-26.

1978   Burkey, Richard M. *Ethnic and Racial Groups.* Menlo Park, California: Cummings Press.

1978   Curtis, Jesse W. Opinion, June 30, No. CV 75-2057-JWC: 1-19.

1973   Enloe, Cynthia. *Ethnic Conflict and Political Development.* Boston: Little, Brown and Company.

1976   Farris, Buford E., and Norval D. Glenn. "Fatalism and Familism Among Anglos and Mexican Americans in San Antonio." *Sociology and Social Research* 60:395-402.

1975   Figueroa, R. Affidavit, June 18.

1973   Gaylin, Willard. "Editorial: The Patient's Bill of Rights." *Saturday Review of Science* Vol. 22.

1947   Goldschmidt, Walter. *As You Sow.* New York: Harcourt, Brace and Company.

1976   _____. *The Rural Foundation of the American Culture.* A Gregory Foundation Memorial Lecture. Columbia, Missouri.

1970   Grebler, Leo, Joan W. Moore, and Ralph C. Guzman. *The Mexican American People: The Nation's Second Largest Minority.* New York: The Free Press, A Division of the Macmillan Company.

1975   Hermosillo, G. Affidavit, June 18.

1976   Hernandez, Antonia. "Chicanas and the Issues of Involuntary Sterilization: Reforms Needed to Protect Informed Consent." *Chicano Law Review* 3: 3-37.

1978   Hernandez, Antonia, and Charles D. Nabarrete. Findings of Fact and Conclusions of Law, *Dolores Madrigal et al., Plaintiffs* v. *E.J. Quilligan et al.,* United States District Court, June 2: No. CV 75-2057-EC.

1975   Hernandez, G. Affidavit, June 15.

1974   Kennard, Gail. "Sterilization Abuse." *Essence,* October: 66 ff.

1974   Kuper, Leo. *Race, Class and Power: Ideology and Revolutionary Change in Plural Societies.* London: Gerald Duckworth & Company Limited.

1964   Madsen, William. *Mexican Americans of South Texas.* New York: Holt, Rinehart and Winston, Inc.

1975   Mazón, Mauricio. "Illegal Alien Surrogates: A Psychohistorical Interpretation of Group Stereotyping in Time of Economic Stress." *Aztlán: International Journal of Chicano Studies Research.* 6: 305-324.

1949/   McWilliams, Carey. *North From Mexico.* New
1968 rpt York: Greenwood Press.

1974   Office of Special Concerns. *A Study of Selected Socio-Economic Characteristics of Ethnic Minorities Based on the 1970 Census: Vol. 1: Americans of Spanish Origin.* Department of Health, Education and Welfare, July.

1958 Paredes, Américo. *With His Pistol in His hand: A Border Ballad and His Hero.* Austin and London: University of Texas Press.

1971 Schwartz, Theodore. "A Glossary of Terms for Culture and Personality." Mimeographed. University of California, San Diego.

1977 Siggins, Richard V. "Coerced Sterilization: A National Civil Conspiracy to Commit Genocide Upon the Poor?" Unpublished manuscript. Loyola University, School of Law, Los Angeles.

1968 Swartz, Marc J. "Introduction." In Marc J. Swartz (Ed.), *Local-Level Politics.* Chicago, Illinois: Aldine.

1970 Van den Berghe, Pierre, ed. *Race and Ethnicity.* New York: Basic Books.

1967 _____. *Race and Racism: A Comparative Perspective.* New York: John Wiley and Sons.

1958/ Wagley, Charles, and Marvin Harris. *Minorities in*
1964 rpt *the New World.* New York and London: Columbia University Press.

1973 Weber, David J., ed. *Foreigners in Their Native Land.* Albuquerque: University of New Mexico Press.

1979 _____. "Mexico, So Far From God, So Near the U.S. and Now So Rich." *Los Angeles Times,* Part 5, January 14: 2.

1973 Wood, Jr., H. Curtis. "Statement of Address." *Contemporary OB/GYN.* January. Quoted in Kennard "Sterilization Abuse," *Essence,* October: 86.

PART THREE

LABOR ACTIVITY

CAPITAL'S FLIGHT: THE APPAREL INDUSTRY MOVES SOUTH

NACLA Report on the Americas

CAPITAL ON THE MOVE: AN OVERVIEW

The American economy has expanded at an unprecedented rate since World War II. Within the United States, however, economic growth has proceeded unevenly. Investment and employment have risen consistently and dramatically in some regions, while declining precipitously in others. Regional growth patterns indicate that a wholesale movement of capital has occurred in the post-war period, reversing the economic fortunes of entire geographic regions.

The Northeast region, stretching from Maine to the Delaware border, was once the industrial heartland of the United States. Today, it is the most serious casualty of changes in the geographic pattern of capital accumulation. It has the highest unemployment rate in the nation, the highest rate of business failure, and the slowest rate of population growth. Per capita income is rising more slowly there than in any other region of the United States.[1]

The South, on the other hand, once the most backward sector of the U.S. economy, has been the major beneficiary of economic expansion in the post-war period. Personal income, jobs, markets, and population are all growing faster than the national average. Industries such as rubber, auto, textiles, petro-chemicals, and electrical parts are all expanding southward. And at least forty of *Fortune's* top-ranked industrial firms have fled the Northeast in the last ten years, to set up shop in the South.[2]

Between 1960 and 1975, the Northeast suffered a net loss of 400,000 jobs in the manufacturing sector alone—a decline of 9 percent in New England and 13.7 percent in the Mid-Atlantic states. In the same period, manufacturing employment rose by 43.3 and 67.3 percent in the Southeast and Southwest, respectively.[3] By 1974, for the first time in U.S. history, manufacturing jobs in the South outnumbered those in the Northeast (see chart A). Between 1969 and 1974, total non-agricultural employment rose by approximately 20 percent in the South, compared to only 7.1 percent in New England and 1.8 percent in the Mid-Atlantic states.[4]

The outflow of capital and jobs from the Northeast has eroded the tax bases of state and city governments, driving many to the brink of bankruptcy. State and local taxes in the Northeast were already 20.6 percent higher than the national average in 1975.[5] The alternative to raising them still further has been to drastically diminish the quantity and quality of essential

Reprinted from *NACLA Report on the Americas* formerly *NACLA's Latin America and Empire Report* (Oakland, California), March, 1977, Vol. 11, No. 3, pp. 2–9. Reprinted with permission of North American Congress on Latin America.
© 1977 by NACLA

social services. In the southern states, on the contrary, state tax revenues have grown at a faster rate than the average for all fifty states in every fiscal year since 1970–71.[6] No southern city is bordering on fiscal crisis.

The movement of capital from North to South began in the post-war period of rapid economic expansion. Today, in the midst of a severe recession, it shows no signs of abatement. According to a study conducted by the *National Journal,* the movement of investment, jobs and population to the South began to accelerate "with unprecedented speed" around 1970. "Within the past five years, the shift appears to have achieved a critical mass, with grave implications for 'older' America."[7] Estimates indicate that between now and 1990, manufacturing employment will rise more slowly in the Northeast than in any other region of the United States: 2.7 percent in New England and 7.7 percent in the Mid-Atlantic. Employment in the Southeast and Southwest will increase by 30.6 and 31.8 percent respectively.[8]

Highlighted by the fiscal crisis of New York City, the economic crisis of the entire Northeast has attracted the attention of business, government and labor. In a special report, *Business Week* recently compared the current situation to the American Civil War, predicting that "the second war between the states will take the form of political and economic maneuver. But the conflict can nonetheless be bitter and divisive, because it will be a struggle for income, jobs, people, and capital."[9]

Indeed, inter-regional rivalry is intensifying as a result of capital's flight to the South. In 1976, seven governors from the Northeast formed a coalition to save "the aging industrial belt" from economic extinction. A Congressional caucus from the Northeast region had already been formed a year earlier. Both groups charge that federal tax and spending policies reveal a pattern of regional favoritism toward the South. They are demanding a greater share of federal expenditures on national defense, transportation and social services for the Northeast. In the words of one legislative aid, "if we don't do something soon, the federal government is going to have to start an Appalachian Regional Commission for the Northeast."[10]

Labor has been particularly hard hit by the flight of capital to the South. The abundance of low-wage, nonunion labor in the South has attracted many industries: In 1970, wages in the South were 20 percent lower than the national average and only 15 percent of its work force was unionized.[11] In North Carolina, the most industrialized state of the South, only 9.8 percent of the labor force belonged to unions in 1974—compared to 45.4 percent in New York and similar percentages in most northeastern states.[12]

The massive movement of capital to the South has put heavy pressure on workers in the North to accept wage cuts, forfeit benefits, and tolerate speedups, retrenchment, and automation as a means toward saving their jobs. Employers in the Northeast now take the threat of shutdowns along to the bargaining table as the ultimate weapon in their battle to keep labor costs down.

Even labor's essential ability to organize itself has been called into question by capital's flight to the nonunion South. Union membership, as a proportion of the total nonagricultural labor force in the United States, has declined steadily over the past few decades, from 31.5 percent in 1950 to 26.7 percent in 1972.[13] Longtime bastions of antiunionism in the South—such as textile giant J.P. Stevens—remain unorganized. Traditionally unionized sectors of U.S. industry are moving South and fighting tooth and nail against unionization in their relocated plants. According to the *New York Times,* "General Motors has successfully blocked the establishment of union shops in two of its six southern plants, a move that has drawn considerable attention from other companies contemplating a move Southward." [14] General Electric and Westinghouse, also expanding in the South, are less than 50 percent unionized.[15]

Today, the platform of every insurgent candidate for union office stresses the need to "organize the unorganized" as a matter of survival for the labor movement as a whole. The South is the target area of every major campaign.

Capital's movement from the Northeast to the South has altered fundamentally the terms of labor's struggle with capital over wages, working conditions and unionization. These changes in the relations between capital and labor, as well as the complex causes of capital's movement, have yet to be examined in a serious and systematic manner.

Over the past few years, a considerable

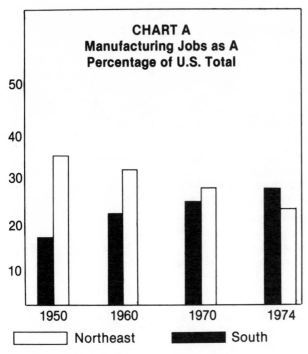

**CHART A
Manufacturing Jobs as A
Percentage of U.S. Total**

50

40

30

20

10

1950   1960   1970   1974

☐ Northeast   ■ South

SOURCE: *Handbook of Labor Statistics*, 1975.

amount of study has been devoted to the question of capital movements abroad and their effect on the domestic economy. Yet the geographic restructuring of capital within U.S. borders has received only superficial treatment. Some theories refer to this new configuration as a struggle for economic (and political) hegemony between "old" capital and "new" capital. Others more prosaically call it a confrontation between "yankees" and "cowboys," representing northern and southern capital.[16] Theories of sunbelt supremacy have been woven to explain the rise of political figures from the South and the presumed demise of the "Eastern Establishment."

What these theories ignore is that capital is a mobile force, bound neither by regional nor national frontiers. Indeed, the history of world capitalist development is precisely a history of capital pushing beyond regional and national borders, invading new markets and internationalizing production. Hence, to counterpose old capital to new, northern to southern, is to obscure the basic movement taking place in the pattern of capital accumulation. Inter-regional differences that tend to attract capital or expel it have been largely ignored. And the crucial impact of capital's movement on the conditions of labor's existence have not been examined.

A CASE STUDY

The apparel industry,* producing clothes and accessories for men, women and children, provides a clear illustration of capital's mobility and its effect on the working class. In the post-war period, thousands of jobs in the apparel sector have been exported abroad; domestic production has dramatically shifted its geographic locus. The needle trades have steadily abandoned their birthplace—the large industrial cities of the Northeast and Midwest—in favor of the rural South. The reasons for this exodus and its effects on the working class, particularly in the Northeast and the South are the subject of this *Report.*

THE NEEDLE TRADE

Understanding the geographic movement of capital in any given branch of production requires some understanding of that industry's basic structure and activities. What does the industry produce? How is it produced and by whom? What are the social and economic relationships that govern both the production and circulation of its products?

The answer to the first question already reveals the complex nature of the industry under study. The output of the apparel industry includes a very wide variety of products, broadly grouped as men's and boys' clothing, women's and children's apparel, and miscellaneous textile products.** Literally hundreds of different products, multiplied by as many different styles, are produced by the industry each year. On the whole, each production unit tends to specialize in a particular product-line (dresses, suits, shirts, etc.), although the range of styles produced by a single shop may be very large. Major sub-divisions of the apparel industry and

---

*Apparel is the generic term for a branch of production that incorporates both the ladies' garment industry and the men's and boys' clothing industry.

**For statistical purposes, this study follows the Department of Commerce definition of the apparel industry, corresponding to the standard industrial classification (SIC) number 23. Major group 23 includes "establishments producing clothing and fabricating products by cutting and sewing purchased woven or knit fabrics and related materials such as leather, rubberized fabrics, plastics and fur." Three- and four-digit SIC numbers referred to in the text correspond to sub-groupings within the industry classified according to product.

their relative size in terms of employment are listed in table 1 below.

The heterogeneous nature of the industry's output, and the tendency for firms to specialize, make it necessary to supplement our discussion of the industry's general structure with distinctions among its different branches. Nonetheless, certain generalizations can be made concerning the technology of apparel production, its organizational structure, markets and labor force, that are valid for the industry as a whole.

TECHNOLOGY

Technological developments in the twentieth century have revolutionized production in many branches of industry. Productivity has soared, while millions of workers have been replaced by sophisticated, multi-purpose machines. The production of steel, chemicals and textiles, to name only a few examples, bears little resemblance today to the techniques of half a century ago. Apparel production has undergone important changes as well, through the introduction of new machinery and improvements on existing techniques. But the pace and scope of changes in the means of production have been much less dramatic than in most other industries.

The sewing machine invented by Elias Howe in 1846 is still the centerpiece of apparel production, although it has since been streamlined and greatly speeded up. A variety of attachments have been introduced—needle positioners, automatic threat cutters, pleaters, hemmers—that reduce working time and simplify many tasks. Specialized machines can now make button holes and sew on buttons automatically, in split seconds. And recently, sewing machines have been developed that can guide fabric while it is being sewn and require an operator only to load and unload.

In the cutting room, advanced production techniques have been borrowed from sheet-metal and boiler-shop techniques: die-cutting to replace hand-cutting, and pattern-grading equipment to produce different size copies of a master pattern.[17] Laser beams, suspended above the cutting table, follow a computer program and make it possible to cut many hundreds of layers of fabric in a very short period of time.

TABLE 1
Major Sub-Divisions of the Apparel Industry, by Employment in 1972

Industry Group	Group No.	No. of Employ.	% of Total Employment
Total Group:			
Apparel and other finished products made from fabrics and similar materials	23	1,369,000	100%
Sub-Divisions:			
Men's, youths' and boys' suits, coats and overcoats	231	125,000	9.1
Men's, youths' and boys' furnishings, work clothing and allied garments	232	363,000	26.5
Women's, misses' & juniors' outerwear	233	433,000	31.6
Women's, misses', children's & infants' undergarments	234	105,000	7.7
Hats, caps, and millinery	235	15,000	1.1
Girls', children's and infants' outerwear	236	75,000	5.5
Fur goods	237	5,000	0.4
Miscellaneous apparel and accessories	238	62,000	4.5
Miscellaneous fabricated textile products	239	186,000	13.4

SOURCE: U.S. Bureau of the Census, *Census of Manufacturers,* 1972, General Summary, MC 72(1)–1.

Despite this impressive array of new machines and techniques, the degree of mechanization in the apparel industry as a whole is still very low relative to manufacturing as a whole. The most advanced machines on the market are found in only a small number of shops, while most of the operations involved in cutting, sewing, pressing and packing are still performed on manually operated, single-purpose machines.[18] According to a recent study conducted by the Fashion Institute of Technology, semi-automatic machines represent only a fraction of the twenty-odd million industrial sewing machines currently in use.[19]

While important differences exist between branches of the industry, apparel production on the whole is a highly labor-intensive process. In 1971, capital invested per worker amounted to little over $9,000—about half the ratio for textile production and less than one-quarter the ratio for all manufacturing.[20] The development and introduction of new techniques has been severely inhibited by the nature of the production process, the materials worked on, and the demand for the apparel industry's products.[21]

Limits to Technical Change

Much to the dismay of industry engineers, the basic raw materials of apparel production are difficult for humans to handle and even more problematic for machines. Whether silk, cotton or polyester, a piece of fabric is limp and stretchable; it curls and flaps and attracts static electricity. Unlike a steel bar, it cannot preserve its own shape and must be guided carefully through successive operations. The fact that garments must conform to the curves of the human body multiplies these operations and renders them more complex. Frequently, machines are found to be inadequate to the task.

Even when technical obstacles are overcome, conditions in the industry are not conducive to rapid mechanization. In any industry, large investments in fixed capital can return their cost only when applied to a large volume of production. In the apparel sector, long production rungs are the rare exception. More than a dozen different styles of a particular item—blouses, for example—may be produced in a single small shop. Furthermore, these styles change frequently and abruptly, since what consumers will buy is extremely unpredictable.

Many shops, for example, staked their fate on the Nehru jacket, Edsel of the needle trades, and many faced bankruptcy when it became just a passing fad. Without frequent shifts in fashion, the apparel industry would contract significantly. Yet the manufacturer who is uncertain of future business prospects will think more than twice about investing in expensive machinery. Short production runs and a high rate of business failure in the apparel industry make mechanization a risky and often uneconomical endeavor.

Some sectors of the industry are less vulnerable than others to frequent shifts in fashion. Those producing standardized, casual types of clothing tend to be more highly mechanized: jeans, sport shirts, underwear and trousers in the men's wear branches, and skirts, pants, underwear and nightwear in ladies' apparel. Significantly, sportswear production has enjoyed the highest growth rate in the industry since World War II. Suburban living, more leisure time and a more youthful population have fostered a huge leap in demand for casual, practical clothes, while the demand for formal apparel (suits, coats, dresses) has steadily declined.

The most sophisticated sewing and cutting machines then are found in only the largest shops and generally in those producing volume products such as sportswear. For the industry as a whole, mechanization is proceeding at a slow and irregular pace. Automation of apparel production remains a capitalist's dream, while present-day shops continue to operate on the basis of simple technology and labor-intensive methods.

EASY ENTRY

In the case of auto production, steel or chemicals, one would be hard put to name more than a handful of major American producers. There is no equivalent, however, to G.M. or U.S. Steel in the needle trades. In fact, apparel is often referred to as the last enclave of "pure competition" in American industry. The fact that capital requirements are low crowds the industry with a very large number of producers, both small and large, and keeps competition fierce.

In 1974, it was estimated that a beginning capital of $50,000 would suffice to set up shop in the apparel industry. Often, even less is needed since machines can be leased or paid for in installments. In 1972, there were 24,438 establishments in the United States competing for a slice of the market for apparel goods. The average size of an establishment is very small. Roughly half the plants in the industry employed fewer than 20 workers, while only 14 per cent employed 100 or more.[22]

Clearly, giants do exist within the industry. Levi-Strauss, for example, the largest producer of jeans and work clothing, operates over 100 plants in the United States and abroad, and recorded sales of over $1 billion in 1975. Manhattan Industries employs over 8,000 workers in plants producing many types of men's and women's clothing.[23] Large conglomerates, such as Gulf and Western, General Mills and Consolidated Foods, have been "picking up pieces of the rag trade" to diversify their holdings.[24] Our major point, however, is that small, garage-size shops exist alongside large-scale enterprises in each and every branch of the industry (see table 2). The sales of the industry's four largest companies account for only 5 per cent of total industry sales—compared to 80 percent for the four largest firms operating in the automotive industry.[25]

The process of centralization, or the absorption of many small capitals by a few large capitals, is considerably slower in the apparel industry than in most other branches of production. Moreover, while large firms may be getting larger, most analysts predict a lasting role for the small enterprise that can "turn on a dime" with frequent shifts in fashion.

CONTRACTING

Easy entry, as the result of low capital requirements, is reinforced by the organizational structure of the apparel industry. Not all firms engage in all stages of production and, hence, not all require the same capital outlays. Rather, the industry is divided into three types of establishments, each performing a different set of functions.

Only the "inside shops," or *manufacturers,* perform the full range of production functions: designing, purchasing fabric, cutting, sewing and selling the finished product. The apparel *jobber,* on the other hand, buys fabric, designs garments and later sells them—but does not actually manufacture them. The jobber has a showroom and usually a cutting room, but sends the pieces to "outside shops," or *contractors,* to be sewn. It should be noted that many establishments employ more than one mode of operation. Some manufacturers accept contract work when production in their plants is slow, or contract out work when there's more than they can handle.

Since the early decades of the industry's development, the jobber-contracting system has added flexibility to an industry where uncertainty reigns, by minimizing the unused plant capacity of all concerned.[26] When orders rise, for example, the jobber can find additional contractors to fill them, without being left with idle machines when business is slow. The contractor, in turn, is not dependent upon orders from any one jobber.

INTERNATIONAL COMPETITION

The competitive structure of apparel production is by no means limited to the domestic arena. The industry's simple technology makes it easy and inexpensive to set up shop in virtually any part of the world. Furthermore, the separation of entrepreneurial functions from production tasks, under the jobber-contracting system, facilitates the export of certain stages of production abroad, while maintaining close ties to the domestic market.

From insignificant levels in the pre-war period, apparel imports rose slowly in the 1950s and rapidly throughout the 1960s and 70s. Between 1961 and 1975, imports measured in square yards required for manufacture rose by 555 per cent, and by 736 per cent measured in dollar value.[27] Today, one of every four garments sold in the United States is imported, up from one in twenty just a decade ago.[28]

Virtually all branches of the industry are affected by imports. In women's and children's apparel, the extent of import penetration rose from 3.8 per cent in 1961 to 23.1 per cent in 1974.[29] Imports of men's suits have gone from 2 per cent of domestic production in 1968 to

TABLE 2
Distribution of Plants According to Industry Group, by Number of Employees, 1972 (%)

SIC #	Total # of establ.	1 – 19 employees	20 – 99 employees	100 + employees
23	24,438	50.0	35.7	14.3
231	856	33.4	28.4	38.2
232	2,787	28.2	31.9	39.8
233	9,526	41.2	48.6	10.2
234	1,002	32.4	36.5	31.0
235	496	64.9	28.2	6.9
236	1,061	31.8	48.2	20.0
237	797	94.0	5.9	.1
238	1,302	47.8	40.0	12.1
239	6,611	73.5	21.0	5.5

SOURCE: U.S. Bureau of the Census, *Census of Manufacturers, 1972,* Subject Series: General Summary, MC 72(1)–1.

over 18 per cent in 1975. Forty per cent of men's sport coats were imported in 1975 and 36.8 per cent of men's trousers.[30]

The major sources of imports have remained relatively constant since the 1960s, with the largest suppliers located in the Far East. In 1975, Hong Kong, Taiwan, South Korea and Japan accounted for nearly two-thirds of all apparel imports to the United States. Other regions, however, and particularly Latin America and the Caribbean, are rapidly expanding their output.

In the apparel industry, competition from abroad takes many forms. A large percentage of imports are produced by indigenous firms selling directly to U.S. retailers. An equally important source, however, is the growing number of U.S. firms setting up production facilities abroad, in order to re-export apparel to the United States. Some U.S. firms have established subsidiaries abroad to carry out all stages of production, from cutting to finishing. A more common practice, however, is that of exporting only certain stages of production in order to take advantage of lenient tariff laws.

Changes in U.S. tariff legislation in the 1960s have led to the rapid proliferation of contracting operations abroad, i.e. to the internationalization of relationships described earlier between domestic manufacturers or jobbers, and outside contracting shops. In particular, Item 807.00, added to the Tariff Schedules of the United States (TSUS) in 1963, provides that American-made articles may be assembled abroad in whole or in part, and returned to the United States with duty paid solely on the value-added by foreign labor. For the apparel industry, Item 807.00 has fostered the practice of performing only design and cutting operations in the United States, and sending out fabric to be sewn into finished goods abroad. Contracting operations abroad may be owned by indigenous capitalists or by U.S. firms.

Apparel produced under the provisions of Item 807.00 represent a rising percentage of total U.S. apparel imports: from 0.3 per cent in 1965 to 10.2 per cent in 1975.[31] In 1965, 807.00 imports came from only nine countries. Today, assembly operations are spread over thirty-six countries. Mexico,* Central America and the

*For a much fuller account of assembly operations in the northern border region of Mexico, see *NACLA's Report: Hit and Run: U.S. Runaway Shops on the Mexican Border* (Vol. IX, No. 5, July-August 1975).

Caribbean countries are favored sites—only a short jet flight from Miami, Dallas, or Los Angeles, cities that have become major cutting center for firms operating under 807.00 provisions.

THE LABOR FORCE

As seen in the preceding sections, mechanization in the apparel industry is still at an incipient stage. Second perhaps only to baseballs, apparel requires the most labor-intensive process of production. Let us examine then the nature of this labor force—totalling over a million workers—and the conditions of their employment.

The apparel industry currently accounts for about 8 per cent of total employment in the manufacturing sector as a whole. Employment has risen substantially in the post-war period, from 819,000 in 1940 to approximately 1.2 million in 1974.[32] Employment is highly seasonal, however, involving temporary lay-offs or part-time schedules for many workers during the slow seasons. Workers in the industry average only forty weeks of work per year.

As an employer, the apparel industry has several distinguishing traits: (1) it has the highest concentration of semi-skilled jobs of any manufacturing industry. Operatives make up 80 per cent of employment, compared to 45 per cent for manufacturing as a whole. (2) Apparel is the largest industrial employer of women. One out of every five women employed in manufacturing belong to the apparel work force, and four out of every five apparel workers are women. (3) Apparel is a major employer of minority workers and particularly non-white women. In New York City, for example, non-white workers made up 49.7 per cent of the work force in 1969. That percentage has risen still higher in the past few years.

Add up these traits—unskilled, female, non-white or poor-white—and you have the cheapest, most exploited pool of labor to be found in the United States. Chinese women in Los Angeles, Latin and Chinese women in New York, Chicanas in the Southwest, black and poor white women in the South.

WOMEN'S WORK

More than 80 percent of all apparel workers today are women. For the great majority, their wage is their only source of income, and 56 per cent of these women support families. Nevertheless, the pervasive myth that women "don't have to work," that their earnings are only incidental to a stable family income, provides a convenient rationale for their super-exploitation: women can be laid-off when business gets slow, and they can be relegated to the lowest-paying job categories.

According to a Labor Department study, "the apparel industry is seasonal in nature and subject to cyclical swings, and women provide a flexible source of labor supply." Within the industry, women are invariably found in the sewing room, as operatives, handsewers or finishers, while the higher-paid cutters, graders, markers and hand pressers are predominatly male. In the shirt industry, for example, where nine out of ten workers are female, women earned forty-two cents an hour less than male workers in 1971. A study of shops producing trousers showed that women averaged $2.59 an hour in 1974, while men averaged $2.95.

DE-SKILLING THE LABOR FORCE

The composition of the apparel industry's work force has changed dramatically over the past few decades, in terms of sex, race and skill levels. Workers in the original sweatshops were typically recent European immigrants, highly skilled in the trade of tailoring. Many more men were employed by the industry than is currently the case. Apparel was predominantly a craft industry, reliant upon experienced workers that had mastered all the intricate operations involved in producing a single garment. Indeed, it was no coincidence that New York City—port of entry for successive waves of immigrants—became the original center of apparel production in the United States.

Reliance on the availability of skilled craft labor, however, is expensive and risky for the capitalist. A limited source of skilled labor can die with age not be replenished without cost to the capitalist. Skilled laborers may band together to demand higher wages, in the knowledge that untrained labor cannot readily take their place. Hence, the dynamic of capitalism is to continuously reduce the skill requirements of the work force and thereby cheapen the worker. The work force must be rendered

homogeneous and unskilled. No worker must be irreplaceable. All must be interchangeable. The less skill that is required for a particular task, the larger the pool of workers than can potentially perform it.

With the development of capitalist production, therefore, "every step in the labor process is divorced, as far as possible, from special knowledge and training and reduced to simple labor." In most industries, homogenization of the labor force goes hand in hand with the introduction of new technology. Machinery tends to disassociate the labor process from the particular skills of the workers—to the extreme of requiring merely the pushing of a button or turning of a switch. In apparel, skills have been gradually diluted both by newer production techniques and by the minute subdivision of labor. Technical improvements on the sewing machine, special attachments and specialized machines have simplified many tasks. Changes in the organization of production have played an equally important role in changing the industry's demand for labor, from skilled to predominantly unskilled.

In virtually all sectors of the industry today, excluding high-fashion and highly-tailored clothing, the task of producing an entire garment has been broken down into many simplified operations, which are distributed among different workers. Far less skill and training is required to learn one operation and do it repeatedly, under the section system, than to master the production of an entire garment. Today, one worker may do nothing but sew straight seams, another sew in zippers, another sleeves, etc. According to the ILGWU, "After elementary instruction in the handling of a sewing machine—and it requires very little time—the rest of the learning process consists of a progressive and relatively rapid acquisition of maximum operating speed."

Cutting, marking and grading are operations that still require a great deal of skill and experience. It is no coincidence then that the most intense efforts at mechanization are related to precisely these tasks.

Trends in the post-war period have accelerated the industry's switch to section work and unskilled labor. Not all types of garments can be broken down to the same extent. As a rule, practical, less stylized garments lend themselves better to a greater subdivision of tasks.

The post-war boom in demand for casual, more standardized products, and the concurrent decline in demand for formal apparel, permitted the expansion of section work and the employment of less skilled, industrially less experienced labor.

Today, apparel pays lower wages than any other major industry group in the United States. While average hourly earnings in manufacturing as a whole were $4.40 in 1974, they were a meager $2.99 in the apparel sector. Considered on a yearly basis, earnings in the apparel industry are even lower, due to the seasonality of employment.

Payment by piece-rate also distinguishes apparel from most other branches of industry. Nearly 80 percent of apparel workers are paid on a piece-rate basis, while time rates generally apply only to machine repair personnel, cutters, janitors and work distributors.

ORGANIZED LABOR

The organization of the labor force grew up mirroring the original basic division of the industry into men's and boys' wear, and women's and children's wear. Men's and boys' wear was generally made up of relatively larger shops and a more skilled labor force; women's and children's wear was characterized by smaller shops and less industry stability, due in part to greater changes in style. In recent years distinctions between these product lines have blurred, with implications for labor which we will explore later.

Obstacles to organizing unions in the needle trades have always been very great. Decentralization, still relatively characteristic of the industry today, historically meant that workers in the many scattered tenement shops were extremely isolated from each other. This was overcome somewhat in the larger, mass-production shops that were developing alongside the earlier form. Vicious conditions of exploitation in both the tenements and the newer factories provided little opportunity for developing organization, although contributing to an urgent sense of need for it. Finally, the vast majority of workers were newly arrived immigrants, thus additionally divided by different languages and customs.

What many of these workers had on their side, however, was a militant, class-conscious,

often explicitly socialist, tradition brought with them from Europe. It was out of this tradition, and the conditions of intense exploitation, that a series of long and violent strikes occurred in the beginning of the century— strikes that exposed the myth that women and immigrants could not be organized.

At the turn of the century two unions existed, both affiliated with the American Federation of Labor and both poorly equipped to organize workers in the needle trades. One was the United Garment Workers (UGW), begun in 1891 as a craft union of mainly native-born males—highly skilled custom tailors and cutters organized in the men's clothing and overall shops. The UGW's inherent weakness was this craft orientation, which threw up roadblocks to organizing the increasingly large numbers of unskilled, women and immigrants. The other union was the International Ladies Garment Workers Union (ILGWU), founded in 1900 in the newly developing women's wear industry. It was initially neither strong nor large enough to even be recognized by employers. According to its own historians, "In its first decade the ILG made little difference. Strikes, often brief but bloody, left a trail of defeats." There was even talk of disbanding.

However, major changes were in the offing. After a series of strikes in the men's wear industry, which the UGW did its best to sabotage, the tensions over craft versus industrial unionism and the question of organizing immigrant workers were at the breaking point. At the UGW convention in 1914, the split finally came when many of the militant delegates representing the new work force were not allowed to be seated. In response, more than two-thirds of the UGW members left to form the Amalgamated Clothing Workers of America (ACWA), a union committed to industrial organization, which soon eclipsed its predecessor.

The ILGWU was also radically transformed by a series of strikes. In 1909 a walkout of women workers sparked a general strike in the shirtwaist industry. Although the strike did not win official union recognition, the shirtwaist local grew from 100 to 10,000 during the four-month strike period. The industrial character and viability of the organization was clearly set, but it took a general strike of 60,000 cloakmakers in the following year for the union to finally win recognition from the manufacturers.

The negotiations to settle this strike became historic, innovating a function for the union as the stabilizer in a chaotic industry and giving first expression to a strategy that both the ILGWU and the ACW were to pursue in the decades that followed.

Present Status

Representing a non-strategic sector, the number of workers organized was and remains the basis of the unions' strength. Currently, the ILGWU claims to represent approximately 376,750 workers, 99 per cent of whom are apparel workers. It is one of the richest unions in the country with total assets of slightly over $147 million.

Until recently, the ACWA, with its primary representation in men's and boys' wear, claimed a membership of approximately 350,000, about a one quarter of whom worked outside of the clothing industry proper, for example as laundry or xerox workers. In June 1976, the ACWA merged with the Textile Workers Union of America (TWUA) to form the Amalgamated Clothing and Textile Workers Union (ACTWU). With a combined membership of approximately 500,000, the ACTWU is one of the fifteen largest unions in the country.

The UGW still exists although it now is perhaps more significant as a convenient peddler of a union label than as an organizer of workers. It still maintains jurisdictional cloudiness with the ACWA, but its present membership is quite small (less than 25,000), mostly employed in the work clothes industry.

NOTES

1. *New York Times,* November 11, 1976.
2. See, for example, Kirkpatrick Sale, *Power Shift: The Rise of the Southern Rim and Its Challenge to the Eastern Establishment* (New York: Random House, 1975).
3. *National Journal,* June 26, 1976, p. 885.
4. Ibid.
5. Ibid., p. 886.
6. *Congressional Record,* June 15, 1976, p. E3388.
7. *National Journal,* op. cit., p. 885.
8. *Business Week,* May 17, 1976.
9. Ibid.
10. *National Journal,* op. cit., p. 891.
11. *Business Week,* May 17, 1976.
12. Bureau of Labor Statistics.
13. U.S. Department of Labor, Bureau of Labor Statistics, *Handbook of Labor Statistics,* 1975 (Bulletin 1865).
14. *New York Times,* November 17, 1976.
15. *Business Week,* May 17, 1976.
16. The most noted proponents of this thesis are Kirkpatrick Sale, Carl Oglesby and William Domhoff. See for example, Sale, *Power Shift,* Oglesby's articles in *Ramparts* and *Boston Phoenix,* 1971–77, and Domhoff. *Fat Cats and Democrats* (New Jersey: Prentice Hall, 1972).
17. Harry Braverman, *Labor and Monopoly Capital* (New York: Monthly Review Press, 1974), p. 211.
18. U.S. Department of Labor, Bureau of Labor Statistics, *Labor in the Textile and Apparel Industries* (Bulletin 1635) (Washington, D.C.: U.S. Government Printing Office, 1969), p. 35.
19. New York City Planning Commission, "Critical Issues," *Plan for New York City,* Vol. 1.
20. *Wall Street Journal,* October 18, 1976.
21. *Labor in the Textile and Apparel Industries,* op. cit., p. 27.
22. U.S. Department of Labor, Bureau of Labor Statistics, *Industry Wage Survey: Men's and Boys' Shirts (Except Work Shirts) and Nightwear,* October, 1971 (Bulletin 1794), (Washington, D.C.: U.S. Government Printing Office), 1973, p. 3.
23. U.S. Department of Labor, Bureau of Labor Statistics, *Industry Wage Survey: Men's and Boys' Separate Trousers,* June 1974 (Bulletin 1906), (U.S. Government Printing Office), 1976, p. 2.
24. Braverman, op. cit., p. 82.
25. ILGWU, *The Domestic Women's and Children's Apparel Industry,* op cit., p. 30.
26. Eloy Ricardo Mestre, "The Growth of the Apparel Industry in Southeast Georgia" (Ph.D. Dissertation, New School for Social Research), 1969.
27. *Handbook of Labor Statistics,* 1975.
28. *Justice,* (ILGWU), Vol. LVII, No. 9-10, May 1-15, 1975, p. 10.
29. Irving Howe, *The World of Our Fathers,* (New York: Harcourt Brace Jovanovich), 1976, p. 300.
30. ILGWU, 1975 *Financial Report,* p. 15.
31. *Wall Street Journal,* October 18, 1976.
32. Estimates of UGW membership made by U. S. Department of Labor, Bureau of Labor Statistics, Washington, D.C. office, October, 1976.

SILICON VALLEY: PARADISE OR PARADOX?

Alan Bernstein
Bob DeGrasse
Rachel Grossman
Chris Paine
Lenny Siegel

INTRODUCTION

The "Fruit Bowl of America," fertile Santa Clara Valley, has come of age. Suburbs, shopping centers, freeways and industrial parks are marching through the orchards that until recently produced half the world's prunes and a bounty of apricots, cherries and walnuts.
— Living in Santa Clara County,
Bank of America

Within the past twenty-five years, Santa Clara County has developed from a peaceful valley of orchards and canneries into a suburban metropolis of sprawling towns and a center of high technology industries. The county has changed rapidly, but the coming of age brings problems as well as maturity. Growth and development has brought prosperity to many people, but has also spurred severe urban problems and accelerated environmental decay. The image of industrial parks marching through orchards is appropriate, for local corporations have become a center of the war industry. The expansion of industry has also

introduced new hazards for people working in high technology firms.

Santa Clara County, which opens out from the southern end of the San Francisco Bay, is one of the fastest growing regions in the United States. Population, now 1,200,000, has nearly doubled since 1960. Economic development as well as population growth has been concentrated in the northwest part of the county, extending from Palo Alto in the north, to San Jose, the county seat and population center. In 1956, San Jose covered twenty-two square miles. Today it spreads over 140 square miles of surrounding land. The southern towns of Morgan Hill and Gilroy, while still predominantly rural and agricultural, may soon become "bedroom communities" housing workers employed in North County cities.

Santa Clara County is one of the most affluent counties in the nation, having a strong economic base in the electronics industry and a median family income of $18,500 in 1976. Wealthier residents enjoy the elegant homes and tree-lined streets of Palo Alto, as well as the rural luxury of Los Altos Hills. The area has a pleasant climate all year long, and a beautiful landscape of foothills and plains.

Prosperity and growth have flowed directly from the expansion of high technology industries in Santa Clara County. Originally spawned

Reprinted from *Silicon Valley: Paradise or Paradox? (The Impact of High Technology Industry on Santa Clara County).* Published by the Pacific Studies Center, Mountain View, California. © 1977. Reproduced with permission of the Pacific Studies Center.

by Stanford University's Engineering Department, the industry is composed of hundreds of firms located mainly in Palo Alto, Mountain View, Santa Clara, and Sunnyvale. Manufacturers specialize in state-of-the-art innovations in semiconductors (the building blocks of computers), and military, medical, and consumer electronics.

Local high technology industries are generally touted as the key to a future technological paradise as well as the guarantor of prosperity. This article will examine other aspects of the industry not usually dealt with in the laudatory feature stories in business journals and newspapers.

Approximately 200,000 people are directly or indirectly dependent on the industry for jobs, according to the Employment Development Department. High technology firms employ many scientists, engineers and managers who enjoy a high standard of living. On the other hand, the large number of blue-collar workers in the industry, often non-white women, face comparatively low wages, frequently unhealthy working conditions and periodic layoffs.

The rapid expansion of industrial parks and electronics plants has accelerated the process of urban sprawl, covering the old orchards with low-density factories and tracts. Because industry has chosen to concentrate in the northwest county, and cities provided more land for industry than housing, many employees, particularly lower income workers, are unable to find housing near their jobs. This has created a housing shortage and has also helped to drive up housing costs. The housing and employment pattern has increased commuting, and heavy traffic flows snarl local

THE CITIES OF
SANTA CLARA COUNTY

highways and roads. Increased automobile use has intensified local pollution problems.

The imbalance of housing and jobs also affects the distribution of taxes and services in the county. Northern cities have a good industrial tax base, plus the benefit of not having to provide services to the employees of corporations who live elsewhere. Cities to the south however, lacking a lucrative tax base, are given the additional burden of providing services to the workers of North County firms.

Most residents of Santa Clara County are familiar with the problems they face: pollution, housing, taxes, job security, local over-dependence on military spending, etc. Solutions to these problems are seen very specifically: enact stricter legislation, build more housing, organize a union. Issues are addressed as isolated problems and the result is a patchwork of individual and inadequate solutions. By demonstrating that these problems have common origins in the development of high technology industries, we hope to aid the process of finding integrated solutions approaching these problems as part of a unified process.

The questions underlying these issues concern the fundamental distribution of power in our society; in this case business being left alone to make decisions which have socially harmful consequences. This study is not simply meant as an exercise of finger-pointing at business, for individual city governments, through short-sighted and self-interested policies, as well as educational institutions, played crucial roles in the formation of these problems. However, it is only by challenging unquestioned business prerogatives and asserting the public right to control processes which shape how we live and work that we can ever achieve more than partial and temporary solutions to the problems which we face.

IMPACT ON LABOR

Satellites, computer memory disks, light emitting diodes, kidney dialysis machines . . . this list of ultra sophisticated products continuously grows in the annals of Santa Clara County electronics firms. This industry is proud of these technical achievements. However, in focusing on these technological breakthroughs, one can not forget the thousands of workers who have planned, blueprinted, and assembled these products.

Approximately 200,000, or one third of the work force, are directly or indirectly involved in the electronics industry in Santa Clara County. The State Employment Development Department (EDD) totals these figures from the hundreds of electronics companies, chemical manufacturers, computer programming services, employment agencies and other local businesses that are directly tied into the electronics industry.

Over 120,000 people are employed in the 175 major electronics companies alone. This figure diverges from other EDD surveys that peg local electronics employment at approximately 85,000.

These electronics companies constitute a major industrial center. However, their elegant industrial parks camouflage the many serious problems that workers face on a day to day basis. These workers deal with some of the most dangerous health and safety conditions in the United States. Workers constantly face the threat of forced overtime or layoffs due to the rapid fluctuations in market demand. Large portions of the workforce are employed in low paying, low skill assembly line jobs. Workers are becoming increasingly divorced from the results of their labor as a result of increased automation and specialization. Workers suffer these and other problems in isolation, as they are virtually unorganized in the Santa Clara County area.

COMPOSITION

Eighty-five percent of the production workers are women and 50% of those are third world. They are promoted very slowly, although affirmative action is helping that now. An Hawaiian woman is supervisor. There is only one woman engineer in the whole place. And almost all of the electronics technicians are men. So its pretty blatant discrimination. — assembly line worker in a Santa Clara semiconductor firm.

Large portions of the electronics workforce are involved in direct production activities, despite the industry emphasis on research and development activities locally. Nearly 50 percent of the workers in the semiconductor branch are actually on the assembly line. Five local semiconductor plants with a total workforce of 2,837, employ 1,106 assemblers and 434 technicans. Another survey of four electronics equipment manufacturers found 1,039 assemblers and 701 technicians out of a total of 3,369 employees. (See table 1 and chart 1.)

There are distinct patterns of racial and sexual discrimination in the electronics workforce. There are 704 white males out of a total of 811 professional and management staff in the five semiconductor plants. Men also predominate in the categories of technicians and craftsmen, 327 out of 434. Clericals consist mainly of women, 322 out of a total of 389, 84 percent (283) of these are white. The overwhelming majority of assemblers are women, *1,054 of of 1,106.* Of these women, 54 percent (555) are minorities, mainly Spanish speaking and Filipino Americans. (See chart 2.)

Wages and salaries for these different categories vary dramatically. Starting wages for assemblers begin at the legal minimum wage of $2.50/hour. Technicians earn entry level wages of $3.50–$5.00/hour. Engineers start at salaries ranging from $12,000 to $35,000 a year.

We work with acids, one woman was asked when she was hired if she knew anything about acids. She said "no," the supervisor said, "Good then you won't be scared by them." Also its crowded and things aren't organized. Just recently a bottle marked acetone was filled with waste acid, and a woman poured and it all started steaming and the vapors are very dangerous to breathe in and are caustic. We work with solvents too which are dangerous. I get headaches from all this as do other people. —an assembly line worker at Siliconix, Santa Clara

Since I've been at Lockheed, I've been laid off a total of five times in nine years, for a total of three years. Layoffs are real severe problems, to people who are married, people who have house payments, families to bring up. —a machinist at Lockheed, Sunnyvale

These two workers have raised some of the many serious issues workers in the electronics industry have to face, dangerous health and safety conditions, constant cycles of hiring and firing, stressful and pressured jobs, unorganized work places.

TABLE 1
Semiconductor Industry:
Survey of Five Plants

	Total	Professionals & Managers	Technicians & Craftspeople	Clericals	Assemblers
Total	2,837	811	434	389	1,106
Male	1,282	786	327	67	52
Female	1,555	25	107	322	1,054
Minority Total	796	91	83	51	571
Male	168	82	58	12	16
Female	628	9	25	39	555
Black Total	89	5	10	5	69
Male	16	3	9	1	3
Female	73	2	1	4	66
Spanish Speaking Total	417	24	45	30	318
Male	70	21	28	8	13
Female	347	3	17	22	305
Asian Total	279	60	28	16	175
Male	80	56	21	3	0
Female	199	4	7	13	175
Am. Ind. Total	3	2	0	0	1
Male	2	2	0	0	0
Female	1	0	0	0	1

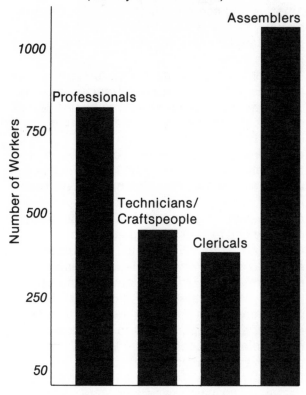

CHART 1
Semiconductor Industry
Occupations by Category
(Survey of Five Plants)

Health and safety problems are immediate to every worker's life. The industrial and scientific instruments industry is the first most dangerous and the electrical instruments industry is third most dangerous for workers in terms of exposure to carcinogenic substances according to the National Institute of Occupational Safety and Health (NIOSH).

Electronics production work, particularly in the semiconductor industry, is a series of sophisticated chemical reactions. Workers use a number of solvents, acids, fiberglass materials and gases from the initial fabrication of a silicon "chip" through the final assembly and testing phases.

Workers complain of physical problems after using these chemicals, ranging from nausea, headaches, dizziness, skin rashes, respiratory problems to liver and kidney problems. Researchers are very concerned about the long term carcinogenic (cancer-causing) effects of these chemicals, particularly the possible connection between TCE and breast cancer. TCE has been proven to cause breast cancer in test animals. Other suspected carcinogens include benzene and chloroform.

The industry will not openly acknowledge that these health and safety hazards are a problem or even its responsibility to worry about. Workers have reported harassment by management if they complain about the safety conditions. It is difficult for workers to prove that health problems are job related. There are federal and state regulatory agencies, the Occupational Safety and Health Administration (OSHA) and Cal OSHA which have regulations about many chemicals but are too bureaucratic and slow, according to workers. Also workers report becoming ill even when air levels of specific chemicals are within OSHA standards. At one California plant women complained of nausea and dizziness after using TCE in amounts one-half those of the OSHA maximum.

The relative infancy of the electronics industry and the constant innovation in production processes also contributes to dangerous

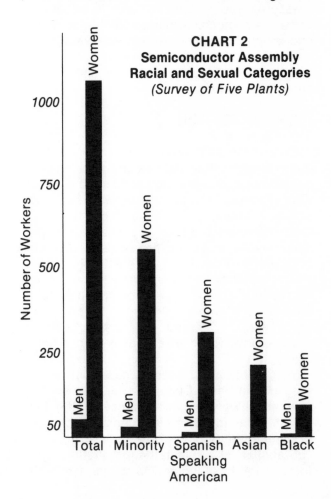

CHART 2
Semiconductor Assembly
Racial and Sexual Categories
(Survey of Five Plants)

health and safety conditions. Because of intense competition, companies develop new production techniques rather than research health and safety.

Companies bear the responsibility of providing the safest possible conditions and informing their workers about dangerous chemicals. According to workers, the companies are not fulfilling this responsibility. Several assemblers at a small semiconductor plant reported that despite the publicity about the dangers of TCE over the past several years, their employer has just installed vents in the past six months.

Workers must deal with other serious problems besides the dangerous chemicals. Workers often experience eye strain, after peering through a microscope for hours at a time. Workers also report of migraine headaches, ulcers, high blood pressure, and dependency on amphetamines, because of the intense pressure to increase production. Since companies have not fulfilled their responsibility, pressure by organized workers is needed to force the companies to provide optimal health and safety conditions—adequate ventilation, protective clothing, decreased production pressures, and worker controlled health and safety committees.

ORGANIZATION

One of the paradoxes of the local electronics industry is that despite the poor working conditions, very few companies have union organizations. Those companies that have unions are generally the established large systems firms such as Lockheed and Westinghouse rather than the newer semiconductor companies. Since the local electronics industry is generally an open shop, workers are inexperienced with the potential benefits of unionizing. Company attempts to put down any unionizing efforts and their threats to move production overseas also hinder union organizing.

The electronics industry has built up its presence in Santa Clara County, after shifting from the highly unionized areas of the East Coast. It has found the unorganized workforce of Santa Clara County to suit its needs.

Statistics show that the production workforce in the local industry is primarily minority

and women. Many of these women come from farm labor backgrounds and consider these factory jobs to be a step up. Many workers are recent immigrants from Asia and Latin America and can only find assembly jobs. The majority of these workers who are women are particularly vulnerable as many are raising families alone.

The transiency of assembly line work also prevents unionizing efforts from developing. The frequent fluctuations in production levels mean that workers are constantly being hired and laid off. Companies often have a policy of maintaining a temporary workforce on the assembly line to avoid paying the legally required fringe benefits. Companies reportedly use the excuse of decreased production levels as a means of laying off workers suspected of being active in organizing attempts.

The Western Electronics Manufacturers Association (WEMA) provides companies with many resources to fight any unionizing attempts. WEMA maintains close surveillance on any union campaigns. It also provides seminars for executives on how to keep unions out of the plants. Recently, at one such seminar, executives simulated a unionizing drive in order to better understand and control potential union drives in their plants.

INTERNATIONALIZATION

The electronics industry creates a tangible bond between Santa Clara County and many other countries, particularly those of Asia and Latin America. While the industry is primarily headquartered in Santa Clara County, it literally spans the globe with production, warehousing, administrative and sales facilities. Lester Hogan, Vice-Chairman of the Board of Directors of Fairchild Camera and Instrument Co. of Mountain View explained, "Because of this international structuring, the U.S. semiconductor industry has been able to compete, and in fact dominate world markets."

The history of this internationalization process has been a quest for ever cheaper production costs. In this technically competitive industry, the main means of cutting production costs has been to cut labor costs. Companies have gone overseas in order to pay wages a fraction of those in the U.S. These corporations have paid wages in Asia ranging from $90.00

(U.S.) a month in Taiwan, to $43.20 in Malaysia, to approximately $30.00 a month in Indonesia for assembly work.

Fairchild serves as an example of this international frontier breaking. It currently operates facilities in at least eighteen countries, at least ten of which have production facilities. Fairchild was the first U.S. electronics corporation to begin assembly operations in Asia, when it set up a factory in Hong Kong in 1963. It followed this with a plant in Korea in 1965/66, in Singapore in 1968, in Indonesia in 1973/74. When Fairchild set up its Hong Kong plant it was primarily interested in setting up a system in which "the advanced countries would concentrate on the high-technology work and managing and the poor countries would mainly do the manual work." according to Hogan. Fairchild has recently moved a major warehousing facility to Singapore in order to have greater access to markets in Asia and Europe.

Asian governments have invited these corporations in with the hopes of gaining technological expertise, increasing foreign exchange and soaking up some of the large pool of Asian unemployed. However, these societies have received negligible benefits if any, from these corporations. First, the corporations bring only the lowest level technology to Asia, that of the assembly and warehousing operations. These corporations have a strict policy of retaining research and development in their U.S. installations; to keep the research closely synchronized with top level policy decisions and to protect the vital technology from competitors.

The electronics firms only make a minor contribution because they do not integrate their activities into the Asian economies. They bring the components to Asia and then re-export them immediately to the U.S. for final testing.

Finally, these companies do not alleviate the terrible unemployment problems in the Asian societies. They offer only the lowest paying, low skill jobs and retrench workers as frequently as in the California plants. Fairchild in Singapore, for example, fired almost half of its 3,600 employees in response to a recession in the semiconductor market in 1974 and 1975.

These companies also bring dubious benefits from the point of view of an Asian assembly line worker. These workers are almost exclusively women between the ages of sixteen and twenty-five. Many of these workers support their families with these incomes. In Korea, young women are required to have nearly perfect vision to get an assembly job. However, within the first year of employment, 87.5 percent have severe eye problems including chronic conjunctivitis, nearsightedness, and astigmatism, according to one study.

These Korean workers receive inadequate wages. Workers at Signetics earn $98.00 (U.S.) a month despite the Korean government's statistics that a family of five needs at least $200 a month minimum income, causing great hardship for women financially responsible for their families.

These workers are thrust into alien cultural and social settings with these jobs in foreign owned factories. They are often required to live in factory dormitories, cut off from their communities. In Penang, Malaysia, the electronics companies sell cosmetics, provide beauty classes, and play continuous rock music in the factories. They even sponsor "Miss Intel" or "Miss National Semiconductor" beauty contests. These young Malay workers are so barraged with media that they respond with attempts to assimilate the Western ideals of beauty—they often spend a substantial part of their already meager salaries of fifty cents a day on cosmetics and other products in the hopes of appearing like the women pictured in the advertising. Tragically, these young Malay women are then sometimes branded as "loose women" by their conservative communities.

Government labor policies in these Asian countries are very attentive to the needs of the employers. Most of these governments prohibit or severely regulate labor unions, and ban strikes. The South Korean government enacted laws purportedly to eliminate lengthy labor disputes. In practice, the government steps in to "solve" any labor disputes with police troops. Korean workers have no right to organize, to bargain collectively, to strike. Knowing that striking was illegal, Korean workers at Signetics staged a five-day hunger strike and sit-in demonstration in the company cafeteria to gain higher wages. They won an increase from U.S. $80.00 to $98.00 a month. Despite two repressive government policies, these workers found that organized action was successful.

Assembly Plants With Parent Companies in Santa Clara County

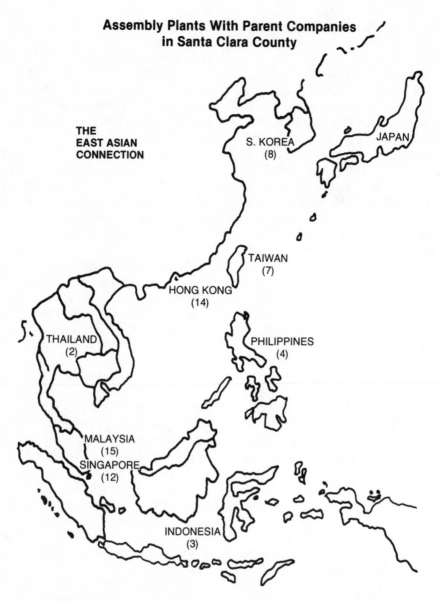

THE
EAST ASIAN
CONNECTION

S. KOREA
(8)

JAPAN

TAIWAN
(7)

HONG KONG
(14)

PHILIPPINES
(4)

THAILAND
(2)

MALAYSIA
(15)

SINGAPORE
(12)

INDONESIA
(3)

The situation of the Korean workers points out the common problems Asian and American labor face. Essentially, they are on different sections of the same assembly line. Workers experience the same dangerous health and safety conditions, the same repression of unionizing attempts, the same inadequate wages, and the same lack of control.

The companies and established labor unions in the U.S. have undermined this potential unity. The unions have launched a "buy American" campaign and are urging Congress to restrict imports of foreign assembled products. They have blamed Asian, Latin American, and other workers for the job cut-backs and other problems American labor is facing.

But these transnational electronics corporations make the decisions to move to Asia, and to Latin America. These corporations rather than foreign workers bear the responsibility for cutbacks in American jobs.

This high technology owes much to the thousands of workers who labor here and abroad. However, it has consistently ignored the welfare and needs of these workers. Conditions will not improve until these assemblers, technicians, and engineers organize to form health and safety committees, unions and communication links with co-workers in other countries.

LOS ANGELES GARMENT DISTRICT SEWS A CLOAK OF SHAME

Lisa Schlein

The California Mart, where Los Angeles' clothing manufacturers display their lines to buyers, is a burgeoning, three-building complex connected by circular corridors. Buyers move on high-speed escalators past the stained-glass galleria and soft color-coordinated walls throughout the thirteen story citadel of wealth and well-being.

A two-million square foot symbol of Southern California's growing prominence in the garment industry, Cal Mart dwarfs the shabbier tenement-like buildings in the surrounding ten-block area of downtown Los Angeles where the clothes on display in the Cal Mart are sewn.

The other side of the Cal Mart is found two blocks down Main Street—past the $1.50-and-up skid row hotels, the bars, taco stands, adult book stores, pawnshops and small retailers. There, hand-written signs solicit "operadoras con experiencia en maquina de una aguja" (experienced single-needle machine operators).

While New York still leads the country in menswear manufacture, California is now the largest producer of ladies' sportswear in the United States, with most of that in the Los Angeles Area. The California Department of

Industrial Relations reports, for instance, that 78,000 of the state's garment workers are employed in Los Angeles' more than 3,000 firms.

Most of the Los Angeles garment industry is not unionized. Union shops guarantee machine operators fringe benefits, a minimum wage of $3.00 an hour and piece work rates which should assure the average worker an hourly wage of $3.60. In nonunion shops it is not uncommon for operators to work ten or twelve hours a day for $1.00 to $1.50 an hour. Piece work rates are set very low and there's no guaranteed minimum. Fringe benefits are not generally provided.

Attempts to organize garment workers, or even regulate abuses, are frustrated by the dispersion of production. Only a few processes may actually occur in the plants of main manufacturers, with the rest subcontracted or sent out as homework.

The contracting system has always existed. However, in the early days of Los Angeles garment industry, it was not widespread. Many shops at that time handled all aspects of garment production under one roof. Not until the late 1960s did the process of contracting out begin to accelerate. Within the last ten years, the practice has overwhelmed the industry. Mario Vazquez, an organizer for the International Ladies Garment Workers Union

Lisa Schlein is a free lance writer and radio journalist. This article appeared in the *Los Angeles Times,* March 5, 1978. Reprinted with permission of the author.

(ILGWU), says "there seems to be a correlation between the increased migration of Latin American workers and the dispersion of the industry. Because," Vazquez continues, "this migration created a pool of workers that could be exploited."

Investigations in 1976 by the California State Labor Commissioner uncovered 622 legal violations at 271 garment firms in the Los Angeles area. Most of the offenses were against the industrial homework laws and involved the illegal manufacture of wearing apparel in private homes. Eight thousand illegally produced garments were confiscated.

Other violations included substandard working conditions, failure to pay the minimum wage, failure to keep adequate time and pay records, or failure to provide workers' compensation coverage.

Labor Commissioner James Quillin says that 98.5 percent of the firms visited were "either in violation of the labor code or the industrial welfare commission orders. This is an incredibly high percentage."

Criminal charges were filed against fifteen firms. "This is probably the first time the City Attorney's office in Los Angeles has vigorously prosecuted employers for violations in the labor code and the industrial welfare commission orders," says Quillin.

To date, ten firms have been convicted of permitting or negligently allowing illegal homework in the city of Los Angeles. Fines of $250 to $1,250 have been handed down, and some firms have been placed on summary probation.

"Tokenism," says Vazquez, "All they're doing is slapping their wrists at the most."

Vazquez has received complaints from "people who are forced to work all night and are locked in the building until the work is finished." He has documented lists of violations involving unsanitary conditions, lack of bathroom facilities and drinking water, overheating, sexual abuses of female workers, blackmail by employers of "illegal aliens," physical beatings, fake payroll deductions and lack of ventilation that results in a high concentration of cotton dust particles in the air.

Years of exposure to cotton dust can cause byssinosis, (brown lung disease) in garment workers. Dr. James Dahlgren, director of ambulatory care at Cedars-Sinai Medical Center, says byssinosis is similar to the black lung disease suffered by coal miners. "There's a chemical in the cotton fibre which has been shown to cause a narrowing of the lung areas. It can give rise to an asthma-like syndrome and over many years of exposure can chronically give rise to lung damage. By then the effects are irreversible," says Dahlgren.

Industrial homework, as defined in the California State Labor Code (section 2650), is work done in a home—"any room, apartment, or other premises . . . used in whole or in part as a place of dwelling." This also includes "outbuildings such as garages or sheds."

Industrial homework involving the manufacture of garments refers to large-scale production that is "not for the personal use of the employer or member of his family." Home designing and tailoring by a neighborhood seamstress does not fall into this category.

Apparel homework is forbidden in California. Cutthroat competition in the garment industry would invariably lead to extensive exploitation of homeworkers, says Assistant State Labor Commissioner Beatrice Christensen. "People who do homework are more exploitable because their work options are limited."

Conditions in the sweatshops are difficult to control; in illegal homework they are impossible to control. "Homeworkers are cheated in every possible way," says Vazquez. "They are paid cash. There is no record of the time or the hours they work. They are not given unemployment, social security or disability protection. Employers take taxes away from their pay. Since wages are paid in cash, however, those tax deductions are never actually turned in to the government. So, it's a federal fraud that's being committed and it's also a fraud against the state."

Labor Commissioner Quillin's "sweep" of the Los Angeles garment industry eighteen months ago revealed that illegal homework was rampant. Estimates of the number of workers involved run into the thousands. Quillin's investigators turned up mini-factories that operated all hours of the day or night. The quarters no longer resembled homes because every room was used for storing material and hanging garments. Quillin says the investigators found "homes with eight or nine machines in the living quarters, and garages equipped with a dozen or more machines."

Homework laws have been on the books for a long time but have largely been ignored. Assembly Bill 353, for instance, which went into effect on January 1, 1976, provides tighter controls over industrial homework and severe penalties for repeated infractions by manufacturers. However, California State Labor Commissioner Colleen Logan laments the lack of state funds which severely restricts enforcement of those laws and the failure of the garment industry to do enough self-policing.

In an effort to overcome the problems of minimal funding, Labor Commissioner Quillin put together a proposal for federal funding and as a result will be able to assign forty-five people to enforce labor and industrial welfare laws. A twelve-person task force began working the garment district March 2, 1978.

But another enforcement problem exists according to Blanca Hadar, the deputy city attorney who has been handling garment industry prosecutions. "A very common business approach is that the manufacturer uses contractors and it is these contractors who come in contact with the industrial homeworker. So the manufacturer is usually at least once removed from the industrial homeworker and this makes for more difficult prosecution."

Bernard Brown, president of the Coalition of Apparel Industries in California, acknowledges that homework is going on. But he feels that most contractors are legitimate and concerned about their image. "There's pressure on a contractor to come up with the best price because of the competition. This pressure forces the contractor to do something illegal once in a while; but I think the overall percentage of abuses in the Los Angeles garment industry is very low. With illegal aliens it's a greater amount, but with minimum wages it's a very, very small problem."

"Illegal aliens"—or undocumented workers as Mexican American activists prefer to call them—are the backbone of the garment industry. They are also, as Joseph Dernetz, deputy district director of the Immigration and Naturalization Service (INS), says "the most vulnerable people around for purposes of exploitation. We receive numerous complaints that unemployment compensation, withholding taxes and other wage deductions are not being paid to the government. Other complaints indicate that employers are getting kickbacks

from illegal alien's for hiring them. Many complaints indicate that an alien's neighbors and friends are inclined to blackmail him under the threat of reporting him to the Immigration Service."

But most garment industry workers find themselves in a no-win position. On one hand, recent raids by the INS on garment factories have led the ILGWU to file suit alleging that the practices and policies of INS agents violate constitutional law. The suit also said that only persons of Latin American descent or with Spanish surnames were questioned extensively about their status in this country.

On the other hand, employers, often justify poor working conditions by claiming to be protecting workers from the INS.

Teresa, a former undocumented worker in her mid-thirties worked for six months as a single-needle machine operator in a small nonunion shop. "My fellow workers told me that once, before I came to work in that shop, the INS came by and the employer forbade the women to go outside," she recalls. "Now, he uses that as a pretext not to give them any breaks. He keeps the doors closed. Once, one of the machines started short-circuiting and a fire started and all the windows and doors were closed. I demanded to know why he didn't keep the doors open. He said he did that to protect the workers from the Immigration, so no one would know they were inside working."

Labor unions have traditionally favored tough immigration laws, claiming that alien workers take jobs away from American citizens and depress wages and working conditions with their low demands. In an historic departure from this position the ILGWU decided early in 1975 to organize workers without regard to their immigrant status.

Mario Vazquez considers this a realistic position based on the high percentage (at least 80 percent by his reckoning) of undocumented workers. He points out that in the 1940s and 1950s, the union had over 20,000 members. Now, due to runaway shops, union membership is about 7,000.

The decline in union membership must be attributed in large part to the changing composition of workers and a lost tradition of unionization. The original Los Angeles garment workers and union leaders were transplanted

New Yorkers with European roots. They came replete with the tradition of socialist ideas and a strong regard for unions. As the labor force changed in favor of Latin American workers, the union lost much of its force. Its effort to communicate and organize among people who could not relate to unions became frustrated, leading to the present situation.

At present, all that's needed to go into the garment business is a seller's permit, issued free of charge by the State Board of Equalization, and a city business license, which costs about twenty dollars. The ILGWU has proposed legislation that would require applicants to take a test before they could be licensed. Also required would be stiff security bonds to insure compliance with labor laws and regulating authorities on health, building codes, electrical wiring and occupational safety.

"Upgrading the image" of the garment industry, as suggested by industry representatives, is good public relations but hardly sufficient to eliminate the abuses which abound. Stronger legislation regulating industry practices must be enacted and enforced, and should constitute a comprehensive, humane government policy toward undocumented workers. Until their rights as workers are considered, they will remain underground people exploited by an industry which feeds upon their fear.

If such steps are not taken, the Los Angeles garment industry will continue to produce the latest fashions—under the most primitive conditions.

WOMEN AT FARAH: AN UNFINISHED STORY

Laurie Coyle
Gail Hershatter
Emily Honig

INTRODUCTION

When four thousand garment workers at Farah Manufacturing Company in El Paso, Texas went out on strike for the right to be represented by a union, many observers characterized the conflict as "a classic organizing battle."[1] The two-year strike, which began in May 1972 and was settled in March 1974, was similar in many ways to earlier, bloodier labor wars.

There was a virulently antiunion employer, Willie Farah, who swore in the time-honored manner that he would rather be dead than union. There was a company which paid low wages, pressured its employees to work faster and faster, consistently ignored health and safety conditions, and swiftly fired all those who complained. There was a local power structure which

harassed the strikers with police dogs and anti-picket ordinances, denied them public aid whenever possible, and smothered their strike and boycott activities with press silence for as long as it could. There were strikebreakers, and sporadic violence was directed at the striking workers. On the side of the strikers there was a union, the Amalgamated Clothing Workers of America, which mustered national support for the strikers and organized a boycott of Farah pants. There was support from organized workers and sympathizers throughout the United States. Finally, there was a victory—an end to the strike and a union contract.

However, any account of the Farah strike which focuses exclusively on its "classic" characteristics misses most of the issues which make it an important and unfinished story. The Farah strikers were virtually all Chicanas. They were on strike in a town whose economy is profoundly affected by proximity to the Mexican border, in a period when border tensions were on the rise. They were workers in an industry plagued by instability and runaway shops. They were represented by a national union committed to "organize the unorganized," but which often resorted to tactics which undermined efforts to build a strong, democratic local union at Farah.

Perhaps, most important, 85 percent of the strikers were women. Their experiences during

Laurie Coyle is a teacher at Mission Head Start in San Francisco. Gail Hershatter and Emily Honig are graduate students in the Department of History at Stanford University.

The authors wish to thank the real authors of this oral history—the women workers at Farah who generously shared their lives and opinions with three outsiders. Many of them asked to remain anonymous because they still live and work in El Paso, Texas. (Palo Alto, California, March 1978) © 1979 by Laurie Coyle, Gail Hershatter, and Emily Honig.

and since the strike changed the way they looked at themselves—as Chicanas, as wives, and as workers—and the way they looked at their fellow workers, their supervisors, their families, and their community.

The account which follows does not focus on Willie Farah's flamboyant antiunion capers. Instead, it attempts to explore the effect of the strike on the women who initiated and sustained it. This article is based on extensive interviews (approximately seventy hours) conducted during the summer of 1977. In these interviews the women described their working conditions, events leading to the strike, the strike itself, the development of the union, and their lives as Mexican American women in the Southwest. In an effort to accurately place the Farah strike in perspective, this article also deals with the social and economic context in which the strike took place. The account appears here primarily as it was told by the Farah strikers themselves —eloquently, sometimes angrily, and always with humor.

BEFORE THE STRIKE

The history of the Farah Manufacturing Company exemplifies the myth and reality of the American success story. Unlike many other Southwest garment plants that ran away from the unionized Northeast, Farah got its start in El Paso. During the depression, Mansour Farah, a Lebanese immigrant, arrived in El Paso and set up a tiny shop on the South Side. Farah, together with his wife and two sons, James and Willie, and a half-dozen Mexican seamstresses, began to turn out the chambray shirts and denim pants that were the uniform of the working West.

When Mansour died in 1937, James was twenty-one and Willie only eighteen, but they were well on the way to becoming kingpins of the needle trade. Winning government contracts for military pants during the war mobilization effort enabled the company to expand, and it emerged from World War II in the top ranks of the garment industry. In the postwar period, the rapid expansion of the garment industry transformed the South into the largest apparel-producing region of the United States. The Farah brothers shifted production to meet the growing demands of the consumer trade, and sold their product to the major chain stores, J.C. Penneys,

Sears, and Montgomery Ward for retail under the store names. In 1950, the Farah brothers began marketing pants under their own name, and built a loyal and growing clientele in men's casual and dress slacks. The company expanded until it employed 9,500 workers in Texas and New Mexico.[2] Before the strike, it was the second largest employer in El Paso.

Farah's major role in developing El Paso's industry and expanding the employment ranks made the family prominent in town. At least among some sectors of the population, Farah had the reputation of being a generous boss who lavished bonuses on his workers, gave them turkey at Thanksgiving, bankrolled an elaborate party each Christmas, and provided health care and refreshments on the job. The company's hourly wages, however low they were, seemed generous in comparison to the piece rates which were standard in the garment world. Farah was the only garment plant in El Paso that would hire the inexperienced. In a town where the overwhelming number of unskilled Chicanas had to find work in retail or as domestic servants, many women considered themselves fortunate to work at Farah.

After the sudden death of James Farah in 1964, Willie undertook a major expansion of the company, constructing or acquiring a plant in Belgium, in Hong Kong, and five in El Paso— the Gateway, Paisano, Northwest, Clark Street and Third Street plants. Within ten years, from 1960 to 1970, Farah's share of the market for men's casual and dress slacks rose from 3.3 percent to 11 percent.[3] In 1967, the company went public and qualified for the New York Stock Exchange. The booming growth, new capital investment, and increased planning and control of marketing resulted in major changes within the plant, including increased pressure on workers to produce more, higher quotas, and greater impersonality on the job.

WORKING CONDITIONS

Many workers felt that the expansion ruined what had been warm relations between management and employees. One woman remarked on the changes:

In 1960, there were only two plants. They had time for you. But it started growing and they didn't give a damn about you, your health, or anything. They just kept pushing.

While some workers saw these changes as significant departures from happier days, many felt that the public image of Farah as one big happy family had never accorded with the reality on the shop floor. Willie ran his business like a classic patron, conducting unannounced plant inspections and instructing women in how best to do their jobs. The most minute aspects of production, down to a seamstress's technique for turning corners, were matters of near fanatical personal concern for Farah. His overbearing presence led many workers to feel that he assumed responsibility for work problems.

In fact, he would shower the workers with promises of liberal pay raises which never materialized. One woman who began working in 1953 recollected:

I used to tell my kids, work hard and your boss will love you and treat you well. So years and years passed, and though I was one of the fastest seamstresses, nothing was repaid, neither to me nor to the other workers. One day before the organizing drive began, I met Willie Farah and I asked him why he worked us so hard and never gave us a raise. He told me to come along to the office, and when we got there he said, "Listen, I don't know a thing about what happens to the workers on the floor. If it will make you happy, I will go myself to your supervisor and check to see if you are getting your due." Well, great, I thought, being sure of the quality of my work. Time went on and nothing happened. Seven months passed and no Willie. I asked, what happened, Willie doesn't want to give me my due?

For many, wages were never raised above the legal minimum, and workers were often misled to believe that legislated increases in the minimum wage were raises granted by management. Wages remained low under the quota system; since pay increases were based upon higher and higher production rates, workers' wages continually lagged behind spiralling quotas. Women were pitted against one another in the scramble to meet management demands and protect their jobs. As one women observed:

They would threaten to fire you if you didn't make a quota. They would go to a worker and say, "This girl is making very high quotas. It's easy, and I don't know why you can't do it. And if you can't do it, we'll have to fire you." So this girl would work really fast and if she got it up

higher, they'd go to the other people and say, "She's making more. You'll get a ten cent raise if you make a higher quota than she." They would make people compete against each other. No one would gain a thing—the girl with the highest quota would make a dime, but a month later the minimum wage would come up. I knew a girl who'd been there for sixteen years, and they fired her, and another who was there for sixteen years and still making the minimum.

In the garment industry where labor comprises a major portion of a firm's expenditures, southwestern companies like Farah keep their competitive edge over unionized plants in the Northeast by these cutthroat pay practices.

Many women who were pretty and willing to date their supervisors received preferential treatment. One seamstress, who had worked on a particular job operation for twenty years, received less than the attractive young woman who had begun the operation only a year before. The less favored women were subjected to constant harassment:

Every day they would come around to your machine to see how much you'd make. If you didn't make your [quota of] 300, they would hurl things at us, yell at us like, "You don't do nothing, you don't do your job, I'm gonna fire you." Embarrass me in front of all those guys pressing seams next to me. I was so embarrassed, but I said nothing. I got to the point where I dreaded going to work.

Rather than hire Chicanos who had worked on the shop floor, it was standard practice for the company to hire Anglo males as supervisors. Their treatment of Chicana workers was frequently hostile and racist. Women were humiliated for speaking Spanish. When they could not understand a supervisor's orders, he would snap his fingers, hurl insults, bang the machines and push them. One worker remembered that:

In my department, the cafeteria, there was a supervisor . . . This man didn't like Latinos—he had a very brusque manner when talking to us. He wasn't a supervisor; he was an interrogator! He would talk to me in English, which I can't speak, and insist upon it, even though he knew I didn't understand. The others would tell me what he said—things that offended, hurt me. But I couldn't defend myself.

Workers who challenged arbitrary decisions were dismissed on the spot. "When I was just learning to sew," a striker remembered, "I made a mistake on three pieces and the supervisor threw them in my face."

> I couldn't say anything, being new there. But an old man who worked with the seamstresses defended me, saying that I wasn't trained yet and there was no reason to throw them at me because everyone made mistakes at the start. They fired him for that, because he wasn't supposed to meddle in those things. He'd been there for fifteen years.

All of these racist and abusive practices played a role in helping to control the work force.

Health problems in the plant were numerous. Some workers contracted bronchitis from working directly under huge air conditioners, while others suffered from a lack of ventilation. The pressure to produce was so great that women were reluctant to take time to go to the bathroom or get drinks of water. As a result, many workers developed serious kidney and bladder infections after several years of work. Equipment was faulty and safety devices were inadequate. Needles often snapped off machines and pierced the fingers and eyes of the seamstresses. Company negligence resulted in many accidents; such negligence was reflected in the care received by workers at the plant clinic:

> One time I felt sick. I knew I wasn't pregnant. He [the doctor] gave me a checkup, checked my blood and said I was pregnant. I *knew* I wasn't pregnant. "Yes, you are." Two weeks later I got really sick. You know what it was? It was my appendix, about to erupt. I went to [the] emergency [room] . . .

> Once, a needle broke on my little finger. The nurse said there was nothing wrong with it. I said it hurt, but she just put a tape on it. The next day it was *that* big. The nurse was very mean—didn't know how to get along with people. I went to the clinic downstairs. I said, "Look, I cut my finger yesterday. I feel something in it." They took some X-rays. I had the needle point stuck in my bone. They should have taken X-rays or told the supervisor to go check the needle to see if it was complete.

Several workers were fired after having been injured on the job. Others had their injuries and illnesses misdiagnosed and were sent back to work without proper treatment, sometimes with serious consequences:

> I saw several times people fainting . . . There was this time the doctor told this guy there was nothing wrong with him and kept giving him pain killers. In the afternoon, he was the guy who did cleanup and sweeping, he just bent over—he couldn't stand the pain anymore. They took him to the hospital and at the hospital he went into a coma. He was in a coma and they couldn't operate on him. I think it was his gall bladder.

The doctors were not only incompetent, but they were also unsympathetic and insensitive to workers' feelings. Many workers felt that the company doctors and nurses were there primarily to keep them at their machines, rather than to provide them with health care:

> The plant doctor gave the same medicine to everyone in the factory and sent you back to work. I remember I'd been working there for three years and had heard a lot of stories about what was going on. I never went there. I took my own aspirins to work.
>
> One day I was really sick and wanted to go home. I could hardly walk. I was almost fainting and had chills. But I walked to the clinic, and the first thing the nurse told me (she got my chart—it wasn't mine, it belonged to somebody else and had my *name.* She didn't see my badge), and said to the other nurse, "I think somebody just doesn't want to work." It kind of made me feel bad because I'd never stepped into the office before. So I told her it wasn't my chart, that I'd never been in before, and she said, "Oh, I don't know." When I went in to see the doctor he didn't even tell me what was wrong with me, he was already writing the prescription. So I said, "Doctor, I want to go home." And he answered, "Why didn't you tell me that in the first place?" as if I were wasting his time.
>
> When I walked out of their clinic I was sicker than when I walked in, because I thought they thought I was a pretender. After three years of not being sick.

If people had to go outside for additional medical care, the company would not assume financial responsibility.

In addition to "free medical care," company benefits included bus transportation to and from work and Christmas presents and bonuses.

Since company expenditures for these "extras" were paid for in part by the interest on workers' savings in a company-controlled acount, the "benefits" were more illusory than real. Real benefits such as maternity and sick leave, seniority, and a pension plan were absent from the company package. Women who took maternity leaves without compensation returned to the factory to find that they had been switched to new operations and that their wages had been cut. Pregnant women underwent substantial hardships in order to avoid the consequences of these practices. One woman recalled:

When I was pregnant with my youngest, I was working there and my husband was also working there. But what he was making wasn't enough . . . I worked up to the eighth month. And let me tell you, it was pretty bad because they take no consideration; even if you're pregnant you still have to do the same thing, the same quota. They don't even take you down [from the machine] to rest your legs. If you're standing up you have to stand all day. Then after the baby is born you just take a month off, and that's it. You have to go back to work. If you didn't go back to work *exactly* a month after, you would just lose your whole seniority. That was another reason we decided we needed a union and we should organize.

The denial of maternity benefits caused a great deal of anger among the workers, the majority of whom were women.

Few Farah workers ever retired from the company. Usually workers were shoved out just before retirement age, so that Farah was not obliged to pay their pensions. Older workers were frequently the lowest paid and the least likely to be promoted despite their extensive work experience. Instead, they were expected to work long hours at the most demanding operations. Their health ruined by this ordeal, many workers quit prematurely. Farah absorbed new employees continually, and had little consideration for the needs of aging workers. Many women were bitter about the treatment of the older workers, and realized that their "benefits" were only guaranteed by their own wits, resilience, and ability to make the grade:

They could keep their turkey. We didn't need their cake. We needed better conditions, better

safety. Only the favorite people there could talk. Especially the older people were the people they tried to get rid of so they wouldn't reach retirement. They had a retirement plan, but only two people have reached it—the nurse and one other. At the Coliseum, there were twenty people who were going to retire [after twenty years of work]. They never did retire. They [the company] changed their quota and got them out.

The factory conditions described by women workers were by no means unique to Farah. Exploitation, low wages, no security, and minimal employer liability were the lot of working people whether they grew up in El Paso's barrios or across the Rio Grande in El Paso's sister-city, Juarez.

FAMILY BACKGROUND: MEXICO AND EL PASO

The border economy affected the lives of women at Farah even before they entered the work force, shaping their family backgrounds and presenting them with enormous obstacles when they tried to act on their own behalf.

Since the Spanish Conquest, El Paso has served as a major passageway for commerce and migration between north and south. The 1848 U.S. acquisition of the entire Mexican territory north of the Rio Grande River established an artificial division of a land that was one, geographically, economically, and culturally. This allowed for the increased penetration of both sides of the new border by U.S. capital. In the early twentieth century, the railroad drew large numbers of campesinos to the El Paso region from the interior of Mexico to lay the basis for agribusiness and industrial expansion in the area.

The boundaries policed by the border patrol scarcely disguise the historic integration and interdependency of the Mexico-Texas region. The border itself is marked by the Rio Grande River, which is a mere thirty feet wide and four feet deep on the outskirts of El Paso and Juarez. Today, more than ever, the United States economy depends on cheap labor from the Mexican side of the river to harvest its seasonal crops, replenish its industrial work force, and maintain profits in its labor-intensive industries.

The close cooperation of authorities on both sides of the border, as well as the special privileges granted to twin plants, allows for the optimum flow of labor and goods between El Paso and Juarez. The state of Texas has protected these privileges by establishing the right-to-work law. This law stipulates that no worker in a plant be required to join a union, and furthermore that *all* workers, whether they are union members or not, are entitled to the benefits provided by a union contract. Collective bargaining efforts have frequently been undermined by this law, and El Paso remains a largely nonunion town.

The availability of unorganized workers on the El Paso side, many of whom are Mexican nationals without rights of permanent residence, and many others who are unskilled Chicanos, has created an ideal situation for companies investing in labor-intensive operations such as electronics and garments. El Paso has become the last frontier of U.S. industry on the move south and out of the United States. "Runaways?" asked one Farah worker incredulously. "Industries in El Paso don't need to move. They have the advantage that they can get people from Juarez to work for less."

The United States government participates actively in depressing wages by manipulating the migrant work force to meet the needs of industry. The issuance of green cards, which are temporary permits for Mexicans to work in the U.S., guarantees business an abundant supply of labor which can be curtailed or expanded when necessary. In addition, the H-2 program of the U.S. Department of Labor allows an individual employer to bring in a specified number of workers from Mexico if he can prove that a labor shortage exists. This program has been used to strikebreak in the cotton industry in the South, and more recently, against union strikers in Texas. The Immigration and Naturalization Service (INS) also plays a role in regulating the presence of Mexican workers without documents. It allows them to enter during critical harvest periods or when there are labor disputes, and at the same time deports those undocumented workers who have joined strikes. "The INS knows that there are illegals," one Farah worker complained,

> . . . because when they need them, they send them in by the hundreds to the U.S. When they

need them they look the other way. But when they don't need them, they get them out of there *fast*. They *know* they're there.

Even in normal times, and particularly in the last eight years with unemployment on the rise, there is intense competition for jobs in the El Paso area. The complexity of the El Paso labor market has the built-in potential for conflicts among United States-born Mexicans and Mexican nationals with or without documents. Employers in El Paso use the competition for jobs to create and exacerbate conflict among these groups whenever labor troubles arise.

Many Farah strikers maintained close ties with friends and family in Juarez. Women who had extensive personal contact with life in Mexico, either because their parents had crossed the Rio Grande or because they themselves had grown up there and come to the United States as adults, tended to see the Mexicans and Chicanos as one people. When they looked at the undocumented workers of today, they saw the experiences of their own parents. "I was born over there and raised here," one striker recalled.

> I was seven when we came here. I remember, when we were living in Juarez my father had to come back and forth every fifteen days. He used to live on a farm in the U.S. I don't have any grudges against wetbacks. I do support the Texas farmworkers. If they want to sign up the whole border I don't mind. I understand how it is over there. I understand what it is to have a father as a wetback. I understand what people are trying to do with the border situation.

Many workers at Farah, as children, took part in the pilgrimage north to find work. Some of their families crossed the border illegally. "My father was a laborer," one woman recollected. "There was no work in Mexico. My parents were having a picnic one day, and zoom—they came across." Families contracted to work seasonally, harvesting cotton and pecans. Some never intended to make the United States their home, but they became permanent residents when they found that the money they earned during temporary work visits to the United States could not sustain them when they returned to the increasingly constricted economy of rural Mexico.

Other women at Farah came north as adults to seek work. Even when they succeeded in finding a stable job, the relocation entailed severe hardships and demanded major readjustments. Most of the women had grown up in the poverty-stricken rural areas of northern Mexico. They had almost no formal education, and many married very early in life. While the daily struggle to survive prepared them for the grinding labor of the factory, nothing in their backgrounds had prepared them to assume roles traditionally restricted to male heads-of-household: to leave the home, enter the industrial work force, and, for some, become the major breadwinner of the family. That the move was a radical departure from their upbringing can best be understood from the childhood recollections of the women who experienced these changes. "My childhood?" a striker reminisced:

I was born in a village where they mine silver, Cusinichi. My father worked there, as did his father and his grandfather. It was a company town. The company was American and there was a union. My family helped build the union. My father wanted to have schools, to have benefits. My father spoke to me often about how the company was very rich and that we were all making the company rich and it was just that the company give us a part for our children. My father talked a lot about this, and sometimes they would throw him out of the mine. After great fights, my father would be back in the mine.

He was a product of his times. He thought that only men should go to school, that we women should only learn to write. Men are the ones who support the family, and so the women don't need anything more.

My father named me after his mother, and even though I had two brothers and three sisters, I was my father's favorite. I was the only child until age four, when my brother arrived. Everything was for me. They took me to work, to the mines, to visit my father. He had a little office where they kept records of people injured on the job, etc. And they also took me to the paymaster. In those days they paid cash. I went everywhere with my father and uncles, to union meetings where everyone didn't stop talking shouting and discussing their problems. A child learns when it is born. When a child begins to breathe a child begins to learn.

Thus I spent all my time with my father and uncles, but when I'd learned to read and write at nine years, I was not sent to school any more. "No, Papa," I began to cry and shout. When he saw me sitting with a long face and asked me

why, I said, "Why can't I go to school anymore?" So he said to go ahead. So they cut my hair and I went. I finished elementary.

Afterwards, I would look up at the mountains, so high. The mines were in the mountains. What more is there? I was dying to know. What's beyond the mountains? What are the people like? Of course my father wouldn't consider my leaving home. He wanted me to get married and have children.

One day my cousin went to the city of Chihuahua. When he returned, I asked him, "What is it like there?" Oh, the buildings are tall, very tall, and the streets—some of them are paved." Here they were made of dirt. "Imagine! The streets are wide—wide as from here to the next village." The more he said, the more I wanted to know.

I thought and thought and one day I asked my father, "Don't we have any relatives in Chihuahua?" He answered that my godfather was there. I told him, "Father, I want to meet him. Maybe I can write." "Go ahead, write him," he agreed. I wrote the letter and asked my father, "Papa, isn't it true that the mail is sacred? You can't open a sealed envelope? Right?" "Yes," he answered. So I said, "Here's the letter for my godfather," and sealed it. He could do nothing but send it. In the letter I told my godfather that I wanted to come meet him and his wife. He wrote back saying that he's love to have me come and visit for a while. "My wife is expecting a baby and it would be fine." I wrote again asking him to ask my father for his permission, or to come if possible. He arrived. "How long it has been since we've seen each other, how great, couldn't she go with me for a while. My wife is having a baby, and it would be great if your daughter would accompany her." Since he was my godfather, my father accepted.

This woman came to the city, finished her studies and became a teacher. She married, had a family and decided once again to leave her home—this time for the United States. Hardship in Mexico pushed her, and promises of a better future for herself and her children drew her. Upon arriving in El Paso, she had to give up her teaching and enter Farah's factory. This was an immense shock to her hopes; the hardships continued. In making all of these decisions she made a radical departure from her upbringing and grew stronger as a woman. Part of this strength was her intense attachment to her origins.

Of course I still go back to Mexico frequently to see my parents in Cuateque. My father can no longer get papers to come here, but when he comes to Juarez, to visit my brother, I go to see him. My children go all the time. They love the ambiente there. I believe that this is a good country, but I don't want them to become Americanized so that they don't want to see their own people. Our roots are there. I became an American citizen by my own choice. This was my decision, but I don't want to negate my roots, or say that I don't want to be there [Mexico]. I love this country as much as I love my own [Mexico]. For that reason I live here. But my children should love both equally: the land is one and the same.

Many other women experienced profound physical and emotional changes; yet their ties to Mexico remained powerful.

A major change for those who came from Mexico involved no longer being a "native" but being stigmatized as an "alien." This identification was applied to all Mexican people regardless of citizenship, and included a population indigenous to the region and more "native" than the later white settlement.

The pride of many Farah workers in their Mexican heritage—a pride often fostered by their parents—protected them somewhat from this hostility and enabled them to stand up to it. "For not having much of an education my father was a pretty smart man," one striker remembered.

I wish I was like him. He kept up in his history . . . He used to say, "Americanos? We are the Americanos, we're the Indians, we were the first ones here." He was an Indian. He always argued about people calling an Anglo "Americano" and a Mexican "Mexicano." That really got him mad. He'd say, "*We* are Americanos; *they* are Anglos." That was one thing he always argued about.

Like their sisters in Mexico, Chicanas growing up in El Paso were expected to share responsibility for la familia at an early age. They were raised in poverty, received little formal education, began working when they were still children, married young, and spent their working lives in low status, low paying jobs.

Most of the Chicana workers at Farah had grown up in the barrio in south El Paso's Second Ward. Squeezed between the downtown area and the border, residents of "El Segundo" faced street violence, police indifference, or brutality, rip-offs from slumlords, and racism from uptown whites.

The violence in the streets was inescapable. "When I grew up," one woman recalled,

Life was a lot different at that time. Everything was harder . . . At that time there were no youth centers. There was nothing to do for the kids, no recreation or things like that. So they would hang around on the corners, they would have gangs and fight against each other. You know it became a *barrio* where policemen were there all the time. That kind of reputation. I guess that's one reason why the police didn't care what happened to them because they had that reputation. So they [the police] would beat them up and a lot of times they would just be sitting there with a quart of beer and the [police] would break it and kick them and take them to jail for nothing.

The unrelieved poverty operated as brutally on residents as attacks by the police. Many a childhood ended prematurely as young girls quit school to help support their families.

I grew up in the Second Ward. It was a poor neighborhood. We used to live in the projects. Some Mexican Americans try to help each other; others are selfish. My mother used to have three jobs: at Newark Hospital, at night, and at Levi's. After school I worked at Newberry's, babysitting, and as a maid when I was nine. With three young children and myself, I had to help my mother. It was a hard childhood. I didn't have a father. My mother had to work day and night. I told her to let me work for her at the Newark Hospital—so I cleaned the beds and floors.

While many quit school because of economic necessity, even more were driven out by systematic discrimination. They were penalized for being brown-skinned and Spanish speaking. Like the Anglo supervisors at Farah, Anglo teachers in El Paso schools instilled deep-seated feelings of inadequacy, humiliation, and disaffection in their Chicano students. Chicanos were discouraged from finishing high school, and the strict tracking system prohibited college and career aspirations. "To me it was hard in school," one woman recalled.

People making fun of you, especially the way you talked. Your English or your understanding [of English]. I believe my older brothers and sisters had the most difficulty getting adjusted here because they couldn't speak any English. Neither could I, but I was put in kindergarten so it didn't matter to me. People in that small village [outside of El Paso] didn't know how to speak English so we talked Spanish, but it was very difficult for them because they were put in the fourth or fifth grade and they were fourteen. People were making fun of them. I just went to eighth grade, then I quit and got married. I was sixteen and I'm still married to the same man. I was sixteen and I was still in eighth grade. I used to get very disappointed that most of my friends were fourteen or thirteen in the same grade. I was supposed to be in tenth grade at the age of sixteen. That used to bother me a lot. Because of the language problem I had when I came across the border[sic].

Whether at home, in the streets, at school, or on the job, there was no refuge from personal hostility or institutionalized discrimination. Mature women workers are still nursing their childhood wounds, looking back on childhood dreams which were crushed and scorned whichever way they turned.

Yet growing up Chicana in El Paso also provided these women with sources of strength, pride and courage. They drew strength from El Segundo's sense of community, which was formed in response to confrontations with the Anglo power structure of El Paso. Their families transmitted to them pride in Mexican culture, as well as countless individual examples of courage in difficult circumstances.

Whether they were raised in the U.S. or Mexico, these women by no means suffered passively. To survive they had to struggle. They responsed with anger to the racism, deprivation, and systematic oppression which they experienced as Raza women. While this anger was seldom expressed openly, it was always present and potentially explosive. The advent of a unionization campaign helped to give organized expression to this anger.

EARLY ORGANIZING

Despite the fact that most workers in the El Paso region were not organized into unions, some of the women had been exposed to labor organizing drives. Women from Mexico had parents who had fled to the United States after their attempts to organize workers in Mexico had failed. They had lost everything in the process. Some women, as children, had witnessed bloody strikes in the textile mills and mines of northern Mexico. Among those women, some had even worked as children in these industries. Others had undergone the dislocation and hardship of migrant life in the United States.

Among Chicanas at Farah, some had fathers, mothers, brothers, and husbands who belonged to unions in El Paso's smelting and packing plants. There was the example of the prolonged and successful strike of garment workers for union recognition at the Top Notch clothing plant in the 1960s. But experience with organized labor was by no means widespread among workers at Farah. The overwhelming majority of the women in the plant during the day-to-day activities of a union, and virtually no examples of working women's struggles in unions to guide them. Yet, Farah workers from both sides of the border had grown up in working class families, and many had had tragic personal experiences which dramatized for them the need for unionization. One woman recalled the early death of her father from lung cancer.

He died when he was young, only forty-four years old. Because where he was working, they didn't have no union and he was doing dirty work, smashing cans and bumpers. When you smash them, smoke comes up and he inhaled it and that's what killed him. He didn't have no protection; they didn't even give him a mask. He put only a handkerchief to cover his face. He died of cancer because of all the things he was inhaling. That's what the doctor told us . . . He died before I turned seventeen. They operated and said he had only half a lung and wasn't going to live long. He lasted three weeks. I'd do anything for him, I was very close to him. He told me it was too late to have another job. I couldn't stand it and would go into the next room to cry so that he wouldn't hear me. He was so husky until the sickness ate him away.

This woman never lost the conviction that her father's life could have been prolonged if he'd had a union's protection on the job. "When I started to know about the union," she concluded grimly, "I joined right away because of my father."

The earliest attempt by workers at Farah to present an organized response to management attacks was a brief petition campaign among markers at the Gateway plant in 1968. A more systematic effort to address workers' grievances began in 1969 when male workers from the cutting and shipping departments contacted organizers from the Amalgamated Clothing Workers of America (ACWA).[4] They acted in spite of Farah's repeated violent tirades against unions. Farah presented films about union corruption on company time and pronounced to his workers, "See what a union does? You don't want anything to do with that!" But Farah overestimated the impact of his blitz on organizing. He was sufficiently confident of union defeat in an upcoming election that he urged cutters to vote, insisting that not to vote was to vote for the union. The cutters turned out in force for the election, and on October 14, 1970, they voted overwhelmingly to affiliate themselves with the union. Not about to accept the unexpected turn of events, Farah immediately appealed the election result with the National Labor Relations Board (NLRB). The cutting room election was tied up in court until 1972, when the election victory was set aside on grounds that the cutting room was not an appropriate bargaining unit. But by that time, organizing had long since spread to the rest of the plant.

Soon after this first election, a handful of cutters began attempts to sign up workers in other departments. Reactions to the organizing drive varied. Most women had little idea of what the activists hoped to gain from union recognition. Others were fearful—with good cause—of supervisors' retaliation. Furthermore, many workers believed what Willie Farah said about labor unions taking their money and benefits.

Even so, some women were moved by their fellow workers' persistence in the face of personal harassment and threats to their jobs. Several workers signed cards and began to talk to their coworkers about the new organizing drive. Efforts to sign up workers took place clandestinely because of the virulence of management tactics against the organizers. Women hid union cards in their purses, met hurriedly in the bathrooms and whispered in the halls to persuade the indifferent. The cafeteria was the heart of the organizing efforts. During lunch time, workers circulated among the tables to sound out each other's sentiments about the union. The first union meetings in people's homes were a completely new experience. "Oh, I did like them," a striker reminisced. "There was a lot of—you know, talking about new things, about the union. And especially, I felt that somebody was talking for us."

Management responded to organizing activities with a series of repressive measures. Supervisors were stationed in the halls to monitor sympathizers and interrogate employees concerning their union loyalties. "They would say, 'What are they saying in there?' and I would respond, 'Who? I don't know what they're saying,'" a striker recalled.

> They'd say, "Don't believe about the union, the union's a bunch of bullshit. They only want to take your money away." That's what they'd say. And I just heard them, and I didn't say anything . . . But once they knew you were involved with the union, they'd start pressuring you . . . Some of us just quit, some were fired.

All personal conversations were restricted durign work time, and conditions worsened even for those not involved in organizing. "When we began organizing," one woman recalled," [the company] put even harsher supervisors who tried to humiliate people more. If there was a shortage of work on a line, they made me sweep. I refused, but other workers were afraid of being fired and obeyed. They did it to humiliate us and to assure that no organization would succeed."

Company intimidation frightened many people away. Workers treated union organizers as if they had some kind of disease. Union sympathizers were fired, among them four women. One woman described her firing, saying, "My supervisor, Hector Romero, sent me to Salvador Ibarra's line because my line had no work."

> After lunch, Hector Romero told me to go back to my machine because now there was work, and I worked at the machine the rest of the afternoon. About half an hour before quitting time, Ernest Boeldner, another foreman, asked me what I was doing at my machine since I had been told to work in Ibarra's line. I told him that I was only following Romero's orders. Without another word he sent me to the office where they asked me to turn in my badge and scissors.

I still did not know what was going on but the bell rang and I went home. The following day when I returned to work, Victor Chamali did not let me punch in and told me I was fired. Farah says I was fired for disobedience. Some people have spread the rumor that I was fired because I was lazy or that I quit to go to work for the union. But none of this is true. I was fired to stop me from organizing and to scare other people.

The firings intimidated workers, but also angered them. As one of the women who was fired observed, "It did give them some courage. They wanted to know why I was fired after all these years, with no earlier work problems." Few workers were willing to openly confront their supervisors, but as their anger grew they discussed the union among themselves more frequently.

Organizing continued at the Gateway plant, though there were no immediate plans to take action. The activists who were fired went down to the union office and vowed to continue the struggle. One woman organized a group of students from a nearby high school to distribute leaflets in front of the Gateway, Paisano, and Third Street plants. They were insulted, their leaflets were torn up and thrown in their faces, and some of them were assaulted. But the woman came every day at 6:00 a.m. and stood her ground until the day of the walkout.

THE WALKOUT

The campaign to unionize the Farah plants intensified in the spring of 1972. In March, twenty-six workers were fired when they attempted a walkout at the Northwest plant in El Paso. But it was a series of events in San Antonio that triggered the large-scale strike in El Paso.

One weekend, members of the union organizing committee in El Paso sponsored a march. Farah workers from San Antonio made the twelve-hour drive between the two cities to join the demonstration. Some of them did not return to San Antonio in time for work on Monday morning. On Tuesday, a supervisor confronted a worker with pictures of him marching under union banners in El Paso and then promptly fired him. Workers who objected to his dismissal were also fired. More than 500 San Antonio Farah workers walked out in protest.

Six days later, when El Paso Farah workers learned of the San Antonio strike, their frustration with working conditions and with Farah's continued suppression of union activity exploded into a spontaneous strike. On May 9, the machinists, shippers, cutters, and some of the seamstresses walked out. The walkout, which continued for almost a month, initially took the company by surprise. Women who had worked docilely at their machines for years, women who had been reduced to tears by a supervisor's reprimand, women who had never openly spoken a word in favor of the union, suddenly began to speak up.

That day that we walked out, the supervisor saw that I had a little flag on. He went over and he looked at me, sort of startled, and he said, "You?" And I said, "Yes!" And he said, "What have we done to you?" I said, "Oh, I wouldn't know where to begin." He said, "We haven't done anything to you." I said, "But you have done a lot to all of the people around me. I've seen it going on."

The startled management soon rallied with a skillful combination of promises and threats. On the first day of the walkout, as activists walked through the factory urging the workers to join them, supervisors followed them, telling the workers to let the dissidents go out on strike and suffer and lose their jobs. The loudspeaker system broadcasted "La Golondrina," a Mexican song of farewell, in a sardonic gesture to the strikers. The shop floor and the cafeteria were full of people shouting, arguing, or quietly trying to decide what to do. For many women, the decision was a difficult one which took several days to make, while the management did its best to frighten or cajole the women who were still undecided. For all of the strikers, the day on which they decided to walk out remains a vivid and memorable one.

I remember the first time of the walkout we were all in break, eating, having some coffee. And then suddenly there was a whole bunch in the cutting room—the girls and everything. They went over to my table and said, "Alma, you've got to come out with us!" And I just looked at them. I was so scared I didn't even know what to do. What if I go and lose my thirteen years? So long, having seniority and everything. I just looked at them and said, "Yeah,

yeah, I'll go. I'll go." That's all I said. And I had a whole bunch of people sitting there with me and I said, "Let's go!" And one of them said, "Well, if you go, we'll go."

So the next day I went and put pants on. I always wear dresses. I used to love to wear dresses. So I put some pants on and said, "I don't know what's going to happen. Maybe there's going to be fighting or something." You know, we were scared . . . We were scared maybe they would beat us and everything.

But I remember that day. When I was passing, the girls started yelling at me, "Alma, you'd better go out! We need you out here!" And I said, "Yeah, yeah, yeah. Wait, wait." "No, you're happy. That's what's the matter with you. You're just a happy one. The way they treat you in there, and you're still in there."

So around nine o'clock I started gathering everybody. "We're going out! Right now! When you see me get off my machine." So you should have seen all those supervisors around me. Somebody pinched a finger on me and told them I was going to go out. You should have seen them all around me. They said, "Alma, you're a good worker. We'll pay you what you want. Alma, the way you sew, the way you work, the way you help us." And I would just say, "Yeah, I know. I know." They thought I was going to stay there.

At nine o'clock I got off [the machine]. I went to the restroom and I started telling everybody, "Let's go!" So some of them just didn't go. I took a lot of people out with me.

Then I started walking through the middle of the— where all the people were working— they thought I was very happy [with work at Farah]. And they started, "Alma! Alma!" And everybody started getting off the machines. I couldn't believe it. It was something so beautiful. So exciting.

And then suddenly a supervisor got a hold of me on my shoulder, and he says, "Alma, we need you! Don't go!" So everybody started . . . I took a lot of people that were real good. I took them all out with me.

When I started walking outside, all the strikers that were out there, yelling, they saw me, and golly, I felt so proud, 'cause they all went and hugged me. And they said, "We never thought you were one of us" And I said, "What do you think? Just because I'm a quiet person?"

But it was beautiful! I really knew we were going to do something. That we were really going to fight for our rights.

As the walkout continued and spread beyond the shipping and cutting rooms, it began to include a wide variety of women. Some came from families with histories of union involvement, while others had no previous contact or experience with unions. Some who walked out had taken an active role in the union organizing campaign leading up to the strike, while others had never even signed a union card. For all of them, however, the act of walking out began a process of change in the way they looked at themselves and their work. "For me," one striker recalled,

> [The day of the walkout] was something out of this world. I was pleased with myself, but at the same time I was afraid. That night I couldn't sleep. I couldn't see myself out of Farah. So many years.

THE STRIKE

The Amalgamated Clothing Workers of America quickly moved to support the Farah workers; the strike was declared an unfair labor practice strike. One month later a national boycott of Farah products was begun, endorsed by the AFL-CIO. In El Paso the strikers began to picket the Farah plants and local stores which carried Farah products. But in a town where many regarded Willie Farah as a folk hero, the strikers found that public reaction to the walkout was often hostile. One woman remembers that:

> People were just very cruel. Everybody thought that Farah was a god or something. . . . I swear, they'd even turn around and spit on you if they could. There was one lady, I was handing out some papers downtown . . . and she got her purse and started striking me. . . . When she started hitting me, she said, "Ah, you people, a bunch of dumb this and that! Farah's a great man!"

Passers-by told the picketers that they were lazy bums who just wanted welfare and food stamps. The strikers were repeatedly reminded that Farah was a major employer in an area where unemployment was high, and that they should be grateful to him for giving them jobs.

Antiunion sentiment was not limited to random comments on the street. It was also expressed in a virtual blackout in the local media. A reporter for the *El Paso Times* who wanted to write a series of feature articles on the strikers was told that the strike was a "private affair" between Farah and his workers. The editor added, "Maybe if we let Willie Farah run his business he'll let us run our newspaper." It wasn't necessary for Farah himself to exercise direct censorship. His importance in the El Paso business community ensured that no newspaper would print material which was damaging to him. A striker describing the extent of his informal influence wryly observed, "Willie Farah conquered El Paso."

There was also considerable racism in the antiunion sentiment. Some members of the Anglo community felt that Mexican Americans were "aliens" and that Mexican American strikers were ungrateful troublemakers who should be dealt with severely. One woman angrily remembers:

> When we were on strike there was a program on TV and anybody could call up. You know, one man called the TV station and told them why didn't they send all the Mexicans back to Mexico? How ignorant! Here I was born in the United States and this stupid man has the nerve to say to send them all back to Mexico because we were on strike!

Racial tensions between Anglos and Chicanos, an ever-present feature of life in El Paso, were exacerbated by the strike and the political mobilization of Chicana workers which accompanied it.

However, opinions about the strike did not simply divide along racial or ethnic lines. The strike split the Chicano community. Many workers at Farah crossed picket lines and continued to keep the plant operating. They were known as the "happies" because they wore buttons which featured a smiling face and the slogan, "I'm happy at Farah." Especially at Farah's Third St. plant, where many of the people had worked for Farah since World War II, vehement opposition to the strike was expressed.

> There was this woman who was married to one of the supervisors. . . . She even yelled at us that we were going to starve. She said, "Don't worry! We'll give you the cockroaches!"
> They used to call us a lot of names. . . . "You should be ashamed after so many years that Willie has been supporting you with work." "Why don't you start working? All you want is to be loafing around. At your age!"

The strike divided families. Several women told of walking out while their sisters remained inside the plant. There was even one family where the husband was on strike and his wife was continuing to work at Farah. "He'd drive his wife up to the door," one striker recalled, "and get out of there as fast as he could. Now this was ridiculous!"

Striking workers were quickly replaced by strikebreakers from El Paso and the neighboring Mexican city of Juarez. There was no lack of applicants for the jobs: El Paso unemployment figures have soared as high as 14 percent in recent years, while Juarez, like much of Mexico, has a current unemployment rate of 40 percent.

Until shortly before the strike, Willie Farah, who liked to style himself as a superpatriot, had refused to hire Mexicans to work in his plant even if they had green cards. But when the strike began and he needed workers, he abruptly changed his policy, and became willing to hire Mexican nationals. Large numbers of green-carders appeared in the plant. Farah's hiring practices were partly successful in pitting workers against each other. Some Chicano strikers blamed Mexican workers for being hired by Farah, rather than blaming Farah and other employers along the border for using job competition to divide workers. However, many of the strikers recognized that the economic situation in Juarez forced people to find work wherever they could. And in spite of the economic squeeze, a small number of Juarez residents joined the strikers.

People on the picket lines faced continuing harassment from company personnel. Farah hired guards to patrol the picket line with unmuzzled police dogs. Several strikers were hit by Farah trucks, and one woman was struck by a car driven by Willie Farah's mother. Farah obtained an injunction limiting pickets to one every fifty feet; 1,008 workers were cited for violations, and many were ordered to report to the police station in the middle of the night and required to post four hundred dollar bonds. One woman was jailed six times. (The Texas law which permitted such injunctions was later declared unconstitutional, and all charges were dropped.)

Support

Although the strikers suffered physical and psychological harassment from opponents of the strike, they also discovered new sources of support. The Amalgamated Clothing Workers of America sent organizers to El Paso, gave weekly payments of thirty dollars to each striker, administered a Farah Relief Fund, and sponsored classes for the strikers on labor history and union procedures. For many workers, the films shown by the union were their first exposure to the history of labor struggles in the United States. One woman was deeply moved by a film about a strike in Chicago; another striker especially liked the movie "Salt of the Earth," because it showed the role of Chicanas in a strike in New Mexico.

Immediately after the strike began, the union organized a national boycott of Farah pants which became a crucial factor in the success of the strike. By January 1974, forty union representatives were working on boycott campaigns in more than sixty cities.[5] The Amalgamated issued leaflets, posters, and public relations kits, and worked closely with other unions, church and student groups to implement the boycott. Many Farah workers went on speaking tours to promote the boycott. All of these efforts transformed the Farah strike from an isolated local struggle to a national campaign with widespread support.

The Catholic Church was another source of help for the strikers. Father Jesse Muñoz, a priest at Our Lady of the Light Church, made church facilities available for union meetings and participated in several national speaking tours to promote the boycott of Farah products. He also came to the picket line at the Gateway plant to bless the strikers on Ash Wednesday. Bishop Sidney Metzger of El Paso publicly endorsed the boycott in a letter to his fellow bishops. Metzger said, "The fact that today over 3,000 workers are on strike is evidence that both grievances and resentment are real. And by listening to the people over the years one gradually became aware that things at Farah were not actually as they were made to appear."[6]

In El Paso, a town with a large and devout Catholic population, the approval of the church was a source of emotional as well as organizational support for the strikers and a setback for their opponents. Muñoz received threatening letters from unknown sources, and he contends that Farah hired someone to put LSD in his Coca-Cola at a union dinner.

When a group of happies announced that they planned to picket the church, the strikers quickly organized a counteraction. The happies arrived to find the church surrounded by strikers. One striker spotted the black ribbons worn by the protesters and called out, "What happened, did Willie die already?" The happies took stock of the situation and retreated.

Father Muñoz suggests that there were many reasons why the church chose to back the strikers in spite of the continuing controversy. He points out that the church has a commitment to social justice, which he personally had supported by joining the southern civil rights protests of the 1960s. "So when I came here and there was a roaring tiger in my backyard, I wasn't going to ignore it." Muñoz was also concerned that the strikers would be incited to violence by "communists from Red China, Cuba, and Berkeley," whom he charges came to town to disrupt the strike. By inviting the strikers to use church facilities, he hoped to isolate them from what he viewed as dangerous influences.

Workers at Asarco and the few other union plants in town also expressed their support for the strikers. Even more surprising to the strikers, given the prevailing mood of hostility, was the support given them by some local businesses.

> We got on that truck . . . and we went to ask everybody if they could give us some food. . . . That was when, I tell you, my life started changing. There you know who your good friends are and who cares about people. . . . We went to that fruit stand on Alameda. . . . He gave us, I guess, about twenty bags of potatoes. . . . Then we went to that Peyton [meat] packing company, and they gave us wienies. . . . Mostly we went to the stores to ask for baby food. Then we went to the *tortilleria* in Ysleta [east of El Paso] . . . and that man gave us about twenty dozens of tortillas . . . and tamales, and some juice. . . . Then we went back to report to the people, to tell them that we had support.

The strikers were also encouraged by messages of solidarity and financial support from other unions around the country. Particularly important to them was the visit to El Paso of Cesar Chavez. In addition, a variety of Chicano, student, and leftist organizations in El Paso and around the country supported the strike by publicizing the boycott and the conditions at Farah.

New Responsibilities

But the most profound changes among the Farah strikers began when they took on new responsibilities for organizing strike activities. Some women went to work for the union on a volunteer basis, writing strike relief checks, keeping records, and distributing the goods that arrived from outside El Paso. Almost immediately they began to realize that their capabilities were not as limited as they had been taught to believe. One striker asserted, "If I had not walked out, I would not have been able to realize all those things about myself."

You know, when we used to register the people from the strike, would you believe that we organized all those cards, all those people on strike? And you know, not realizing, here you can do this anywhere! You can go to any office and sit down and work! You know, you think to yourself, "How in the world did I ever think I couldn't do anything?" This is one of the things that's held us back. We didn't think we could do it. . . . Until you actually get there and sit down and do it, and you find out, "I'm not so dumb after all!"

Other strikers went on speaking tours organized by the union or by strike support groups to publicize the boycott and raise funds.

I had never travelled as much as I did when I was on strike. The only place I had gone was to L.A., one time, but that was about all. But I never thought that I could go to New York, or Seattle, or all these places. To me it was just like a dream, something that was just happening and I was going through, but I couldn't stop to think about it. I just had to go and talk to those people about the strike. . . . The first week it was hard [to get used to talking to groups of people]. Because over here I just used to talk to one or two persons when I was working— they hardly let you talk at all. . . . Sometimes I would try to talk just as though I was talking to the strikers right here. I just didn't think that they were other people that I didn't know.

One woman observed that antiunion harassment took similar forms all over the country; when she stopped to talk to workers at a non-

union plant, a supervisor appeared and shooed the workers back inside. When she spoke on the East Coast she noticed that racial and ethnic differences often kept workers isolated from one another. She returned to El Paso with a heightened perception of the difficulties involved in building a strong union.

Financial Troubles

As the months wore on, strikers faced increasing financial hardship. The union strike relief payments of thirty dollars a week were inadequate for many families. In one household both husband and wife were on strike, and there were eight children to feed and clothe. Unable to handle their house payments, the family moved in with the husband's mother. The uncertainties of the strike, the financial troubles, and the change in living arrangements were a strain on the marriage:

My husband was worried too, because of the financial [situation], and he would start to drinking to take it off his mind. I . . . even told him to go to the hospital, because he was getting awful. And I had an operation too at that time. And he did, he went to the hospital and he got cured. . . .
[Drinking was a big problem among the strikers] because there was nothing for them to do. . . . He had to be there [on the picket line] from 7:30 until 4:30 in the afternoon, because he was the [picket] captain. Mostly the kids wouldn't see him at all, and neither did I, until two in the morning when he got home.

For single women workers living with their parents, the situation was somewhat easier. Their parents supported them, and working brothers and sisters often helped with car payments and other bills. But many single women were themselves working to support widowed parents and younger siblings. For them the strike meant financial desperation.

Women who could find work in other clothing factories did so, continuing to picket at Farah before and after work and on Saturdays. Only the small number of unionized plants in El Paso were willing to hire Farah strikers. At nonunion plants, however, the jobs only lasted as long as the striker's identity was unknown.

On my application I lied. I said I had worked at Farah . . . and then I had gotten married and I had left. . . . I had an interview with this man. He was real nice about it. He said, "How come you didn't go back to Farah?" I said, "Oh, my husband says they're having a lot of trouble in there." [laughs] . . . So he said, "I might as well put you as an inspector on the lines."

It was a very good job, better than being an operator. . . . He called me in when I had about two months there, and he says, "I like your work. . . . You're going to get a raise, but don't tell anybody about it." . . . About four months later . . . he called me in again. . . . "Listen," he says, "I'm thinking of giving you a bigger raise." . . . Well, finally what I earned there in six months I didn't earn in those seven or eight years that I had in Farah! . . .

But there were some of the girls in the plant that had brothers and sisters that were happies. . . . and they would say, "She's the striker from Farah, and doesn't anybody know about it?" "No, but she's an inspector and she got a better job than I did!"

The third time . . . they called me into the office and he also had a tape recorder there. And then they got my application out . . . and he said, "You know what's going to happen, don't you?" And I said, "Yeah, I guess you're going to fire me. . . . Tell me, why am I getting fired? It couldn't be about my work—you just gave me two raises!" And he [pointed at the tape recorder and snapped at the other man in the office], "Turn it off!"

For strikers who could not find other work and for those who had to meet unexpected expenses, the struggle to get food stamps and other forms of aid was crucial. After a lengthy delay some strikers were declared eligible for food stamps. Unemployment benefits, of course, were unavailable to strikers. When one woman began work at another factory and was laid off after a year, she found that she could not collect unemployment benefits because she was a Farah striker.

Because of these problems, it was imperative that strikers obtain contributions and money from other unions across the country. They staffed an emergency committee which dispensed funds to strikers who could not meet medical and other payments. They formed a Farah Distress Fund to supplement the fund-raising efforts of the union-sponsored Farah Relief Fund. They helped to arrange their own speaking tours in addition to speaking on the

union tours. Strikers who did not need the groceries distributed by the union passed them on to those who did. But in spite of all these measures, their financial situation continued to decline. One ex-striker comments tersely, "A lot of people lost their homes, cars—you name it, they lost it."

Social Relations

If the strike created new pressures and anxieties, it also cemented new relationships. "The good thing about the strike," recalls one woman, "is that we started knowing a lot of people—what they felt, who they were, what their problems were." Women who had been too busy or too shy even to speak to their fellow workers found themselves involved in discussions and arguments.

I never used to come and talk to people about their beliefs. I never used to go and tell someone "do this" or "do that" or "this is good for you" or "bad for you." But everyone was so enthusiastic that I started [saying to the non-strikers], "Come on, girls! It's for your own good!"

Picket duty and strike support activities brought new groups of people together.

People made a lot of friends. Some of us know each other by nicknames, that's all. Believe it or not, I have a whole bunch of friends at Farah, and they call me up, and they have to tell me their nicknames, because I won't know them by their first name or their last name.

The difficulties of being a striker in an antiunion town also inspired camaraderie. When groups of women were arrested for mass picketing and ordered to report to the police station, they took advantage of the inexperience of the police in dealing with female detainees, and created havoc.

We got on the scale and they weighed us, and then they got our fingerprints, and they asked us how old we were, and then we used to say, "You really want to know?" And then they said, "What's your phone number?" "Ai, you *really* want to know!" We were just playing around. The jailman was going all kinds of colors, because he was an old man.

In working-class areas, particularly in the sprawling eastern end of town, many workers felt a sense of solidarity with their neighbors.

Here the whole neighborhood, you know, the majority of us were on strike! . . . The guy on the corner was on strike, the girl across the street, the one on the corner over there, then there was Virgie and all her sisters, and then we had one lady down the other corner that was working. . . . my neighbors in front—her father's always been fighting for unions. A lot of these things, I think, kind of made you feel good.

The Home

As women became more and more involved in running strike support activities, and as they developed new friendships among the strikers, they began to spend more time outside the home. This was a source of tension in many households.

I was so involved that I was forgetting everything. My husband started getting very angry at me, and I was giving him a hard time. You know, at the time I didn't realize that I was hurting my kids and my husband. At the time I just felt that this was something I had to do, and if my husband liked it or didn't like it he was going to have to accept it. . . . Lucky that he was able to accept [it], because this went on and on during the strike. . . . Now I stop to think, and I tell myself, good grief, he really did put up with a lot! How would I like it if he was gone every day of the week! . . . So I'm just glad that he was able to stand behind me, and it didn't destroy our marriage, but it did destroy a lot of marriages. . . .

In some cases, differences of opinion about the merits of the walkout were fueled by financial insecurity. In other homes the husbands did not think that attending public meetings was an appropriate way for their wives to spend their time.

Well, at the beginning they didn't like it. They thought [the women] should be at home, because here they were kind of old-fashioned, the women were always supposed to be home. The only time she'd be working was if she had to work to keep up with the bills, and both wife and husband had to work. Otherwise there was no way that the man himself could support the house. But that's about all they thought about,

just for them to work—they didn't think they could go to meetings.

But the women felt strongly enough about their involvement in the strike to put up a spirited defense of their activities.

My ex-husband told me, "You're not gonna make it, and I'm not gonna help you!" And I said, "If God made it, and his followers made it, like Peter, he left his boat behind, his wife . . . everything, he left everything behind, all his belongings to follow God, yet he didn't die! Right now he's in better shape than we are. He's in heaven, holding that door—isn't that true!"

For many women the changes in their marriages were more profound than a few disagreements over meetings or money. The strike made them more confident of their ability to make decisions, and they began to question their own attitudes toward their husbands.

Maybe it's just the Mexican woman, maybe it's just that the Mexican woman has been brought up always to do what somebody tells you, you know, your father, your mother. And as you grow up, you're used to always being told what to do. . . .
For years I wouldn't do anything without asking my husband's permission. . . . I've been married nineteen years, and I was always, "Hey, can I" or "Should I . . . ." I see myself now and I think, good grief, having to ask to buy a pair of underwear! Of course, I don't do this anymore. . . . [The time of the strike was] when it started changing. All of it. I was able to begin to stand up for myself, and I began to feel that I should be accepted for the person that I am.

Most marriages survived the ordeals of the strike, and many women feel that their growth as individuals has strengthened their relationships with their husbands. But it was also not uncommon for husbands threatened by the new eloquence, assertiveness, and political awareness of their wives simply to walk out.

The strike also transformed the relationship of women workers to their children. Many brought their children to meetings and to the picket line. "My little boy was only three months, and you should have seen me, I had him always in my arms, going everywhere," remembers one striker. Children who were slightly older took an active part in strike support work, and formed their own opinions about unionization.

> See my little boy? . . . I used to take him with me to go picket. We [adults] used to go give people . . . papers, and they would hold their papers, or throw them at us right in the face, or say "Shove it down your you-know-what." He would get them—you know, he's a small boy. People would not pay attention to him. So he would say, "Here, sir!" "OK!" He would put it in his pocket, or read it. . . . He was always out with me, always out picketing. He was about seven or eight. . . . Anybody talks about unions, he'll tell you, "Go out there and join the union." Tell him, "Unions are no good." "They're good. They educate. They educated my mother."

One teenager commented, "Mom used to be a slave. But since the strike she thinks for herself. It's a lot better."

Women also consciously reevaluated their ideas about child-rearing and their hopes for their children.

> I used to be a very nervous person when my kids were little. I almost had a nervous breakdown. . . . My husband used to drive me batty, you know. The kid couldn't be bawling over there in the other room—I had to get up and run and see what's the matter with the kid! Because my husband was an overly protective person with his children. . . . So here's the idiot wife, running like crazy to look after these kids, and it was driving me batty! . . .
>
> These are the things that I was able to begin to stand up for. It was crazy, you couldn't watch the kid constantly . . . And I've come to where now I don't feel this . . . pressure. I don't feel this anymore. I'll look out for my kids the best I can. . . .
>
> My ideas are a whole lot different than they used to be. I want my kids to be free. I never want them to feel oppressed. I want them to treat everybody as an equal. . . . I don't think they should slight someone because he's black or he's any different than they are. And this is what I want—I want them to be free people. And to be good people. . . .
>
> I want my daughter to be able to do what she's gotta do . . . and not always comply to whatever her boyfriend or her husband [wants] . . . that she should be the person that she is. And I want my boys to be the person that they are.
>
> You know, it's very funny, when my daughter and my son were little, you know my husband wouldn't let my boy wash dishes? . . . So he grows up never washing a dish! And I tell my husband, "I think it's your fault that he doesn't know how to wash dishes . . ."
>
> You know, I think it [the strike] has made my kids more outspoken. . . . Maybe some people would call it disrespect. I don't. I think that being outspoken is not harmful if you do it in the right way. Like my son—if somebody, if an adult, gives him a hard time, I expect him to stand up and speak for his rights.

Unidad Para Siempre

Women strikers turned a critical eye on their personal lives and their home; as they became more experienced they developed criticisms of the union campaign as well. Some women felt that the Amalgamated Clothing Workers of America was not promoting the strike and boycott actively enough, particularly in El Paso.

The union, hard-pressed to pay each striker thirty dollars a week, stopped encouraging more workers to come out on strike. (The union organizers felt that the strike could not be won unless there was a successful national boycott, and that funds should be channeled into boycott organizing rather than support of additional strikers.) There were squabbles about eligibility for emergency funds and relief payments. More important, many strikers felt that they were not being encouraged to take independent action to raise funds or publicize the strike. They wanted the process of education which had begun with the walkout to continue. One woman remembers that she and her fellow activists "were trying to get those people to reorganize—not only the union, but actually to really try to stand on their own two feet . . . trying to talk things out for yourself without having somebody else talk them out."

Some strikers began to meet independently of the union, in a group which was known simply as the rank-and-file committee. (This group took the name Unidad Para Siempre—Unity Forever—when it was reactivated after the strike.) The members of the group—about forty—shared a strong sense of themselves as workers and a desire to build a strong and democratic union. They put out their own leaflets, participated in marches and rallies, helped to found the Farah Distress Fund, and talked to other strikers about the need for a strong union. "We wanted a union with action, not just words.

That's why we were having meetings and going out, really doing more, making our own papers...."

Politicization of Women

For the women on strike at Farah there was no artificial separation between personal and political change. Their experiences during the strike altered the way they looked at themselves as women and as workers.

> Of course, we never did anything wrong, really. What we were fighting for was our rights, because we were very oppressed. For one thing, I was a very insecure person way back then. I felt that I was inferior to my supervisors, who were at the time only Anglo. None of this affects me anymore. I have learned that I am an equal. I have all the rights they have. I may not have the education they have, and I may not earn the money they earn.... But I am their equal regardless. And it's done a lot for me, it's changed a lot for me. It made me into a better person....
>
> It used to be if a supervisor got after me for anything I'd sit there and cry. Well, they don't do this to me anymore. They don't frighten me anymore. Two of them can take me into the office—it does not affect me at all. I have my say, and if they like it or not, I'm going to say so.... Before I wouldn't say anything. I would just hold it in and cry it out, and stay and stay....
>
> And I believe very much in fighting for your rights, and for women's rights.... I don't believe in burning your bra, but I do believe in our having our rights, that even if you're married you can make your marriage work. I know that sometimes we have to put up with a little bit more, but it has changed a lot of things for me....
>
> Maybe the company doesn't feel this way, but it's done a lot for us....

The strike made women more conscious of political and social movements which they had regarded as "outside" and irrelevant to their own lives. These ranged from the support of local union struggles to the struggles of the UFW and Texas Farmworkers to the women's movement.

"During the strike," says one woman, "every place I turned around there'd be a strike. They [other strikers] used to go to the stores where they were selling Farah pants, and they used to picket at the stores, and in return we used to go and help them picket." Farah workers have supported recent strikes at a local cannery and the municipal bus lines. Some of them joined the picket lines when Asarco, a nearby smelting plant, went on strike in the summer of 1977.

Recently, ex-strikers have also been involved in other unionizing drives. One woman who now works in a hospital is contemplating an organizign campaign among health care workers. Another has helped her father and uncles to begin signing up people at a bread factory. Several other women have joined a Texas Farmworkers support committee, which publicizes the working conditions of the farm workers and tries to raise funds for their unionizing campaigns.

People have also begun to discuss the women's movement in their homes. Although it is still perceived as a movement that is taking place somewhere outside of El Paso, it evokes both sympathy and support.

> Well, all of us women, we like it. And we sure would like to join them. Some of the husbands they don't like it at all. They're not happy about it.... [My husband] doesn't like it.... Sometimes [we argue] and my daughters help me, my daughters back me up. [My sons] like it too.

For all of the women, the strike made them more conscious of themselves as working people with interests distinct from other classes. One woman began to argue with her dentist, who complained to her that her strike was causing him to lose money he had invested in Farah Manufacturing Company. She commented that he could afford to lose money, and added,

> It's like I tell him, "Just because you happen to be one Mexican out of many that made it to the top—and I bet you worked your butt off to get up there. I'll respect you for your ideas as long as you respect me for mine. I happen to be of the working class, and I happen to be one of the minority (i.e. Chicana), that I feel work at the lowest type of job there is, and I feel that we have a right to fight.

For others the strike altered the way they looked at their jobs, and for the first time made them feel that their workplace was the site of an important struggle.

For myself, I would like to continue working where I am. I think about going to school and getting a secretarial job, and I think it would be a boring thing. I like to be where the action is. For my kids, if they want a college education, I expect to give it to them. . . . I'd rather have them have a better job than me.

But I like being there. I like the challenge. You don't know what the next day's going to bring you. You might get fired! . . . I don't think I could see myself sitting there in back of a desk, answering phones. When you could be fighting somewhere else, in a grievance, fighting with your supervisors, giving them hell. . . .

[Before the strike] it was just a job to go to. Now it is kind of challenging, you know, you can never tell what's going to happen.

Inside the Plant: The Pressure Builds

By the beginning of 1974, the nationwide boycott organized by the ACWA was having a noticeable effect on Farah's business. Sales, which were $156 million in 1972, dropped to $126 million in 1974.[7] By the end of 1973 four Farah plants outside of El Paso had been closed, and the El Paso plants had been put on a four-day week.

The five El Paso plants, which had been operating with scab labor throughout the strike, began to resemble ghost towns. One striker who maintained a close friendship with a strike-breaker recalls:

She told me all the things that happened in there. That sometimes there wasn't even work and they would send them home. She said sometimes they would just play tic tac toe for hours. . . . She said she used to get tired of staying waiting hours in there for material. And they would just sit down and talk, or go into a bathroom and spend thirty minutes in there. . . . I think that their orders weren't coming in [because of] the boycott.

Even among the business community in El Paso, there was concern that the city was acquiring a reputation as a bad place to invest, and there was embarrassment at the outrageous and frequently racist statements that Farah periodically made to the press. When Farah publicly blamed the Catholic Church for his problems with the union, national press coverage was not sympathetic.

The final blow came at the end of January

1974, when an Administrative Judge of the National Labor Relations Board issued a decision which accused Farah of "flouting the (National Labor Relations) Act and trampling on the rights of its employees as if there were no Act, no Board, and no Ten Commandments." Farah was ordered to offer reinstatement to the strikers (whom the company asserted had voluntarily quit), to reinstate with back pay several workers who had been fired for union activity, and to allow the union access to company bulletin boards and employee lists.

Farah initially indicated that he would appeal the decision, but several weeks later he abruptly changed course. On February 23, apparently after preliminary discussion with union officials, he recognized the Amalgamated Clothing Workers of America as the bargaining agent for Farah employees. The union simultaneously announced that it would terminate the boycott.

The strikers, exultant and relieved, celebrated the fact that they had outlasted El Paso's major business figure.

It's like Rome. Remember, at that time, Caesar and all of them, he had a big throne. He said, "I am a god. I make these people do that and and I make these people do this." Yet his throne, his empire, crumbled down. That's what happened to Farah. It was an empire. . . . And yet, his empire came down. Farah's empire came down. . . .

However, for many strikers the feeling of triumph was marred by a confusion about who had decided to end the strike. They resented the fact that they were not involved in the discussions which preceded Farah's capitulation. Many people first heard the news on the picket line.

All of a sudden the strike was over. [We heard about it] the day before, because they said, "Nobody's gonna picket tomorrow." After I got out of the check committee I went out picketing. . . . [The picket captain] knew, I'm pretty sure he did, because he's working now as a business agent. . . .

We really didn't know what was going on. "We don't picket tomorrow." "Why don't we picket?" "I don't know. The strike is over, I guess." "Oh, really?" And then the newspaper, the headlines. . . . I didn't like it, because I thought it was something they had already made up their minds to it, you know. We were not involved. . . . I wasn't really pleased about it, but I said, "Well, at least we got the union in."

Most strikers believed that the decision to end the strike had been made in New York.

When the negotiating committee for the first contract was elected, strikers discovered to their dismay that happies were to be represented on the committee. In the few weeks before Farah recognized the union, his supervisors had been ordering people to sign union cards, telling them that if they didn't comply the factory would close. As nominal union members, these people had the right to participate in contract negotiations. The committee was thus badly split.

You know, we were strikers, and they told us we were going to have a committee for the negotiations as strikers. And I believe that as long as you're on strike, that you have the right to decide what contract you want. . . . They [the union officials] decided that it was only fair that the people that were inside [should] have another committee.

So there was the table, this side were happies, and this side was strikers. We wanted something, they voted against us. We wanted thirty cents, they wanted five cents. That's where I believe we got screwed. If we had the chance, not having that committee there, I believe we would have gotten a better . . . contract.

Other strikers on the negotiating committee felt that they were powerless, that the union officials had decided what they wanted before they held meetings with the workers. "The negotiating committee never really had much to say. . . . [The officials] say they know what is right and what isn't." If a member of the negotiating committee raised a question about a specific contract provision in negotiations, recalls one committee member, the senior union official would say: "Well, let's have a little break now." And he would talk to the people and say, "You shouldn't do that, you know. They know how much they can give you."

The final contract included pay increases of fifty-five cents an hour over three years, a medical insurance plan financed by the company, job security and seniority rights, and a grievance procedure. It also gave union repre-

sentatives the right to challenge production quotas for individual operations. It was ratified at a meeting of employees on March 7.

Many workers were angry that there was little time taken to explain the contract or hear people's questions and objections.

They put us all in the cafeteria of one of the factories. And we were in there along with all the people. There was a lot of people, a lot of noise. Some of the clauses that were in there, we didn't even get to understand them very well. He [a union official] would explain it in English, and Sanchez [the ACWA Joint Board Manager] would just translate it. . . . But he was going so fast with it that we didn't have a chance to really understand it. But then they said that we had to take that contract regardless because Mr. Farah had said that if that contract was not signed he wasn't about to change his mind and go for another contract. That contract had to be taken or else he would just close down the factory and that was that. . . .

So he read the contract real fast and then he asked, "Does anybody disapprove?" and then a few of the people raised their hands and they were ignored. . . . He said, "OK, this means we go back to work." . . . We didn't vote on it.

Strikers felt that two years of suffering entitled them to a stronger contract. But Farah was in financial trouble as a result of the boycott and a series of management mistakes, and his threat to close the factory was a real one. The strikers, inexperienced at contract negotiations, felt outmaneuvered by a process in which the company set the terms and the union lawyers made most of the decisions.

AFTER THE STRIKE

In spite of their misgivings about the contract, and a pervasive feeling that the situation was no longer under their control, most strikers concluded that the contract was "all right for a first try," and that it was "a beginning." They realized that their fight for better working conditions was by no means over, but at least they now had the protection of a union and a grievance procedure. They were determined that they would no longer be intimidated by supervisors; if they were mistreated they were going to climb off their machines and protest. "I'm going to say something if I have to say it," one striker insisted. "And I'll be nice if they're nice. If they're not very nice I can also be very unnice."

When they returned to work in the spring of 1974, the strikers faced tremendous obstacles. Texas was (and still is) a right-to-work state, so workers were not required to join the union. If enough workers took the benefits without joining the union, the company could move to have the union decertified. This made the task of organizing the unorganized at Farah both very necessary and immensely difficult. It was complicated by the fact that the conclusion of the strike did not dilute Willie Farah's notorious antiunion sentiment. He had recognized the union with great reluctance, and was determined to break it. Finally, there were serious divisions among the workers in the plant. Strikers determined to build a strong union would have to overcome tensions between themselves and the "happies," as well as divisions between Chicanas and Mexicanas which had been created during the strike.

When the strikers returned to the factory, they found that the organization of production had changed dramatically during the two years of the strike. In an attempt to keep up with the changing men's clothing market, Farah was diversifying production to include men's leisure suits and jackets. Workers were placed in new production lines without adequate retraining. Women who had been sewing straight seams for ten years were suddenly expected to set sleeves. One woman said, "They just sat me on the machine and said, 'Try to do this.' That was my training."

Workers who previously had been working with a six-piece pattern for pants were now working with a thirty-piece pattern for jackets. Seamstresses accustomed to sewing cotton fabric suddenly had to adjust to sewing brushed denim, plaids and double-knits—fabrics which were much more difficult to handle. In addition, sewing collars and cuffs of jackets were much more delicate and time-consuming work than most operations involved in the production of pants.

These changes in materials, patterns and techniques were not taken into account when new production quotas were established. Women whose wages had been based on their ability to produce a certain number of pieces at one operation were expected to produce just as many at a new operation. As a result, quotas were often impossibly high. Unable to meet their new quotas within the prescribed time limit, many women suffered wage reductions and eventually were fired for low production. Some ex-strikers believe that by selectively assigning them to the most difficult new operations and establishing outrageous quotas, the company hoped gradually to weed them out of the plant.

At the same time that Farah was changing production, the company plunged into a serious financial disaster. The recession of 1974–1975 hurt the company, and in addition, Willie Farah made major miscalculations in production and marketing.[8] He had always been able to stockpile his most dependable styles and sell them on a stable market year after year. Lightning changes in styles meant that Farah could no longer predict the market. For example, one year he would corner the market in leisure suits, stockpile thousands of leisure suits, and then find that the next year no one was wearing leisure suits. In 1974 Farah decided he wanted to produce his own fabrics, and opened a textile mill in El Paso. The venture was a six million dollar flop.

Farah's financial predicament was exacerbated by marketing problems. In the past, Farah had been known for the high quality of its merchandise. But under severe pressure to meet quotas on new operations, workers were simply unable to concern themselves with perfection. "When you're pushing people they can't get their work out right," one ex-striker commented.

> So they were getting it out as fast as they could, without caring how it was coming out . . . They made all these jackets lopsided and crooked. Who are you going to sell them to once the stores see how they are? They are definitely going to return them. And that is what started happening. They were sending back truckloads of jackets, sportcoats, and pants.

In addition, retailers who disliked Farah's high-handed business practices had gladly removed Farah pants from their shelves during the boycott, and were reluctant to resume dealing with the company again after the strike.

All of these management problems resulted in a 40 percent decline in sales and a $3.5 million loss in the last quarter of 1976. Five thousand of the original 9,000 employees were laid off. Several of the Farah plants were closed, including plants in San Antonio, Victoria, and Las Cruces, New Mexico.

Union Troubles

These financial setbacks hindered the efforts of union activists to continue organizing. First, there was a visible cutback in services provided for the workers by the company. Bus service to and from the plant was curtailed, coffee and donuts no longer were served during breaks, the already inadequate medical care available to workers was cut back, and Thanksgiving turkeys and Christmas parties were no longer provided. Many workers complained that the plants were dirtier and more dust-covered than they had ever been in the past. Since these cutbacks coincided with the end of the strike, many nonunion members blamed the union, not Farah, for the decline in their working conditions.

A more serious consequence of Farah's financial setback was that it required a drastic reduction in the size of the workforce. This need to layoff workers provided Farah with an opportunity to harass and eliminate his most vocal opponents among the union activists. Some were given extremely erratic work schedules. Some days they would be required to work until noon, other days until three o'clock, and frequently they were called to work on Saturdays. They were rarely given much advance notice of their hours. Some ex-strikers were switched to production lines which were scheduled to be phased out. Others were placed on extended layoff and after one year were let go by the company.

Farah's management devised several further strategies which undercut the ability of union activists to organize. One was to isolate union members. At the end of the strike almost all of the strikers were assigned to the large Gateway plant. (By keeping them all in one place the company apparently hoped to prevent strikers from "infecting" other workers in the various plants.) After the strike, one woman recalled,

> We were closer. We didn't let our chain break. They tried to break it. At first they put us all together. And then suddenly they knew that we were so strong, they started separating us. They went to Northeast, and the other ones went to Paisano. So then suddenly you were all separated . . . Then they put "happies" with you. It was hard to make them understand.

While, in the past, an effort had been made to assign women to the plant nearest their homes, after the transfers many workers found themselves working at plants across the city from their residence.

Grievances

It is against this background of changes in production, financial setbacks, the establishment of high quotas, and transfers of workers that many grievances were filed. (During negotiations for the second contract in March 1977, union officials stated that more grievances were filed at Farah than at all other ACWA plants in the United States combined.) When workers had grievances it was up to the shop stewards to investigate the complaint, collect all the necessary information, discuss it with the immediate supervisor, fill out the forms and deliver them to the union office. If a grievance could not be resolved on the shop floor it would be turned over to a business agent.

Most of the shop stewards were inundated with grievances. Some were responsible for lines of a hundred workers, stretched out over a quarter mile. Unlike the supervisors, they did not have roller skates and bicycles at their disposal to traverse the distances within the plant. They had to do all union-related work during lunch hours and breaks. One ex-striker said:

> I'm a very active person and I *love* to help people. They wouldn't let you talk during work, they wouldn't let you talk about the union or anything. At breaktimes I would go real fast, I would go in the plant and start talking to the people, start going line by line.

Work for the union did not end with the end of the working day at Farah, and most shop stewards spent several hours each day driving to and from the union office. "Some people don't understand the time you put into it," one shop steward complained,

... the time you have to leave your kids to go fight their cases ... We don't get paid for being shop stewards, we don't get gas money, we still pay our union dues, everything. We get nothing out of it, other than our self-satisfaction that we are helping our people.

In addition to being overworked, shop stewards were systematically harassed. One union activist noticed that every time she went to the bathroom a supervisor followed her, and if she took time to smoke a cigarette, the supervisor would hurry her back to work. Another found that whenever she had problems with her sewing machine and signalled the supervisor, he would consistently ignore her, and it would be hours before the machine was repaired.

The ability of shop stewards to effectively solicit and process grievances was further hindered by their isolation from other union activists and from workers in general. "They have a great big cutting room," one shop steward commented

> And on the corner where all the machines start, that's where I'm at, on the very corner. They kind of keep me isolated from the other people ... I had one woman tell me—she saw me in the bathroom. She said, "Are you the shop steward here?" I said, "Yeah." And she said, "You know, I'd never seen you before here." I said, "Yes, I've been here, but I've never been on the other side." She said, "Well, they keep telling me there was one [shop steward], but I never saw you."

There is at least one case of a steward being fired for carrying out her duties. In this instance, an ex-striker who had filed a grievance was being harassed by the supervisor. The entire production line had stopped work to watch the argument. The shop steward stepped off her machine and walked down the line to investigate. The supervisor started yelling at her to return to her machine. Outraged that she had climbed down from her machine in the first place, and then refused to go back, he phoned the plant manager who fired her for disobedience. She had witnesses and was rehired after her case went to arbitration.

A final factor which made the shop stewards less effective than they might have been was the continuing apathy of nonunionized workers.

The ex-strikers clearly understood that they had to organize to defend their interests, and were continually frustrated by the complacence and lack of support from workers who refused to act on their own behalf.

There were never enough women willing to serve as shop stewards. When shop stewards were laid off, or transferred from one plant to another, there was rarely another worker willing to take their place.

The effectiveness of the grievance procedure depended largely on the resources of the union staff. The business agents, hired by the union, were chosen from among the ex-strikers. Inexperienced and inadequately trained, they were overwhelmed by the volume of grievances. In addition, some ex-strikers charge that the union carefully selected the most passive and malleable strikers to work full-time for the union.

Another union staff member who played a decisive role in implementng the grievance procedure was the union engineer. Because of the changes in production from pants to leisure suits and the introduction of new operations, many of the grievances dealt with allegedly unfair quotas assigned to those operations. Quotas for new operations were initially set by company engineers. If they were to be challenged, a grievance had to be filed within thirty days; then a union engineer would be sent to the plant to determine whether or not the quota set by the company for that operation had been reasonable.

There was only one union engineer for the five Farah plants, and he was responsible for all the other ACWA plants in El Paso as well. Not only was the union engineer overworked and unable to investigate every dispute, but all too often, ex-strikers complained, the union engineer would back up the quotas set by the company.

One union activist, switched to a new production line and given an impossibly high quota, received a pink slip for low production. She called in the union engineer to observe the operation. She could not even produce half of the quota, and another person he observed was also not able to make the quota. Nonetheless, he agreed with the company that the quota was a reasonable one. The repeated occurrence of similar cases led many strikers to conclude that the union engineer could not be counted on as an advocate for the workers.

Many ex-strikers felt victimized by a combination of the company's determination to manipulate and undermine the union and the union's reluctance to actively challenge the company. The union seemed willing to take to arbitration only those cases in which a favorable decision was certain. Only a small percentage of all the grievances filed were taken to arbitration.

Decline of Unidad Para Siempre

Militant union members were left in a particularly vulnerable position. The rank-and-file group, Unidad Para Siempre, pushed for reforms which had not been included in the contract. These reforms included elimination of the quota system, compensation and training for shop stewards, and greater rank-and-file participation in settling grievances between workers and the company. In this way, they hoped to build a stronger and more responsive union. The continued growth of Unidad was hampered by the fact that a large number of its members —the most vocal and militant union activists— were among the first to be laid off by Farah during his cutbacks in production. Unidad members feel that the union did not actively prosecute their cases because, like the company, it felt threatened by their presence. By 1977, few members of Unidad still worked in Farah plants.

Unidad's ability to form a strong organization was further inhibited by fundamental divisions among the workers. There were differences among the ex-strikers and nonstrikers about how much and when to criticize the union. Among the workers at Farah, there were some who still actively opposed the union. They blamed the union for Farah's financial predicament; they blamed the union for the termination of services they had previously enjoyed. They did their best to aggravate union activists in the plant. "Oh, I had so many things done to me," one shop steward remarked.

They [workers hostile to the union] used to get into my car, put gum on my chair. . . . One time I was setting the cuff. People would come by and knock them all down. They would take all my union papers and leaflets. They'd take them off or throw them on the floor. . . . One time somebody cut all the threads off my machine. Can you imagine?

Other workers were simply indifferent to the union. As far as they were concerned they could take advantage of union benefits without paying dues or suffering the harassment inflicted upon union activists. Some Mexicans feared that they might lose their green cards if they became union activists.

Union members viewed the union in a variety of ways. Some uncritically supported it. In their view the major obstacle to the growth of a strong union was the apathy of the workers who refused to share the responsibility of working to improve conditions. There was another group of union activists who expressed frustration with passive, nonunion workers in the plant, but who attached equal importance to the weaknesses of the union machinery. There was still another group, many of whom belonged to Unidad, who emphasized the extent to which the union had collaborated with the company, and who saw democratizing the union as the major requirement. Finally, there was a small group of ex-strikers who became disillusioned with the union, and simply signed out.

The Second Contract

The continuing layoffs, loss of rank-and-file activists, tensions among workers in the plant, and inadequate support from the international union all combined to weaken the position of the workers during contract negotiations in early 1977.

Negotiations took place with both sides assuming that Farah was in serious financial difficulties. Workers on the negotiating committee spent several days listening to detailed descriptions of Farah's woes, and finally were told, "You can ask for the moon, but if we give it to you we'll fold tomorrow and you'll all be out on the street."

This bleak picture was accepted by union lawyers, who urged the negotiating committee to accept Farah's terms. The union officials clearly were worried about Farah's financial status, and felt that no further challenges to the company's authority should be mounted. Instead of giving an organized voice to workers' grievances, they tried to devise a strategy which would help the company back to financial health. As one union official put it, "Once Farah was a union plant, it was in the union's interest to sell pants." If selling pants more cheaply meant accepting a serious setback in working conditions, the union officials were willing to pay that price to keep Farah from going under.

The 1977 contract granted the workers a scanty thirty-cent pay raise over a three-year period. It eliminated dental benefits and retained the hated quota system. Most damaging of all, it permitted Farah to lay off experienced workers and call them back to work on a different production line—at the minimum wage. Some members of the negotiating committee reluctantly voted to accept the contract, certain that once it was taken to the workers for ratification it would be rejected.

Many workers now believe that the company exaggerated its problems so that the union would settle for a weak contract. Although it is still uncertain whether Farah Manufacturing Company will recover from its economic crisis, it is already clear that under the terms of the 1977 contract, the workers are paying for Farah's problems.

The contract was hastily presented in a short meeting held in the cafeteria at the Gateway plant. The meeting was called at the end of the working day, and most workers did not know until the last minute that the meeting was to take place. The contract was read in legalistic Spanish which few workers could understand, and questions from the floor were discouraged. When a vote was called, Tony Sanchez (the ACWA Joint Board Manager) requested that those in favor of the contract stand up. Since the room was packed, most people were already standing up. There is a great deal of controversy about what happened at this point. Many who attended the meeting say that a clear majority of workers raised their hands in opposition to the contract. No formal count was made, however, and Tony Sanchez declared that the contract had passed.

Before workers could raise their objections to the terms of the contract and the way in which the vote was conducted, the bell signalling the end of work rang. Workers swarmed out of the Gateway cafeteria, many angrily pulling their union buttons off their shirts and throwing them onto the ground. Lacking experience as well as the presence of a strong rank-and-file organization, the remaining union activists were unable to challenge the proceedings. This created even greater divisions among the work-

ers, as many felt that they had been sold out by union militants.

Since March 1977, Farah has closed another of its El Paso plants. The number of workers at Farah, particularly union members, continues to decline.

CONCLUSION

Events at Farah since the strike show the continuing difficulty of union organizing in the Southwest. The right-to-work law, the consolidated opposition of powerful employers, the timidity of union officials, and the many incipient tensions in the border area which employers can use to divide the workforce—all of these are formidable obstacles in the way of a strong workers' organization.

The story of the ACWA at Farah also illustrates some of the problems specific to organizing workers in the garment industry. In contrast to relatively monopolized, capital-intensive industries such as auto and steel, the garment industry is highly competitive, volatile, and labor-intensive. In this context of constant business fluctuations, it is possible for a large and established company like Farah to suffer a dramatic decline within a period of several years.

The development of runaway shops during the last decade has made this instability even more pronounced. Increasing workers' organization and the relatively high cost of American labor have prompted labor-intensive industries such as garments and electronics to move south across the border, or to southeastern Asian countries, where labor is cheaper and less organized than in the United States. In border cities such as El Paso, industries have been able to take advantage of the proximity of an abundant supply of documented and undocumented workers from Mexico.

In an attempt to prevent industries from leaving the country, many unions such as the ACWA have adopted the strategy of bailing out the company in times of financial hardships. As recent events at Farah suggest, this may often be done at the expense of the workers. Although this is not a problem whose ultimate solution lies solely within the borders of the United States, current union strategy has not even provided a partial answer. Instead, it has failed to prevent runaway shops and simultaneously has helped to undermine the development of a strong union movement.

It is clear from the Farah experience that a successful unionization effort does not end when the union wins a contract. Organizing and training of workers in everything from a grievance procedure to labor history must continue on a long-term basis. In addition, workers must develop a strong rank-and-file movement—one which can overcome divisions among the workers, build a democratic local union, and encourage women workers to develop leadership skills and an analysis of their working situation.

While the Farah strike did not produce a strong, mature rank-and-file movement, it did help to create the conditions in which one can develop. The workers who made the strike were irreversibly changed by it. All of them say that they would organize and strike again; most of them recognize the need for strong support from an international union like the ACWA, as long as it does not undermine the independent organization of rank-and-file workers. "We're sticking in there and we're not going to get out and we're not giving up!" one ex-striker insisted.

In the words of one striker:

I believe in fighting for our rights, and for women's rights . . . When I walked out of that company way back then, it was like I had taken a weight off my back. And I began to realize, "Why did I put up with it all these years? Why didn't I try for something else?" Now I want to stay here and help people to help themselves.

The Chicanas who comprise the majority of strikers learned that they could speak and act on their own behalf as women and workers, lessons they will not forget.

NOTES

1. El Paso, Texas is located on the western tip of the Texas panhandle, near the point where the boundaries of Texas, New Mexico, and Mexico intersect. In July 1975, the population was estimated by the U.S. Bureau of Census at 414,700 people, of whom 57 percent were "Spanish American." El Paso is directly across the U.S.-Mexico border from Ciudad Juarez, which has an estimated population of 600,000.
2. General Executive Board Report "Farah Boycott: Union Label," to the 1974 Convention, Amalgamated Clothing Workers of America, p. 1.
3. Allen Pusey, "Clothes Made the Man," *Texas Monthly* (June 1977), p. 135.
4. In June 1976, ACWA merged with the Textile Workers Union of America, and became the Amalgamated Clothing and Textile Workers Union. Since the events in this article occurred before the merger, the union will be referred to as ACWA.
5. "Farah Boycott: Union Label," General Executive Board Report, op. cit.
6. Bishop Sidney Metzger to Bishop of Rochester, October 31, 1972, reprinted in *Viva La Huelga: Farah Strike Bulletin No. 15* (Amalgamated Clothing Workers of America, AFL-CIO).
7. *Moody's Industrial Manual*, 1975, p. 1099.
8. Critics of the union have blamed the strike and boycott for the company's business troubles. However, the boycott never actually destroyed Farah's profit margin. In fact, some analysts argue that the short-term effect of the strike was beneficial because it forced the company to stop overproduction. They note that "during the only full year of the boycott (1973), the company jumped from $8 million in losses to a modest $42,000 profit." Pusey, loc. cit. The losses predate the union and can be traced to management errors on Farah's part.

THE ELECTION DAY IMMIGRATION RAID AT LILLI DIAMOND ORIGINALS AND THE RESPONSE OF THE ILGWU

Mario F. Vázquez

Lilli Diamond Originals is a division of Campus Casuals, one of the fastest growing women's sportswear and dress manufacturers in southern California. Between 1973 and 1976 their gross sales rose from $19,576,000 to $29,986,747—an increase of over ten million dollars. Net profits rose from $782,000 in 1973 to $2,083,000 in 1976. While gross sales increased by approximately 33 percent, net profits increased by more than 62 percent.

Lilli Diamond Originals occupies a large, new building located slightly south of downtown Los Angeles. The ethnic composition of the work force is approximately 10 to 15 percent black and white workers, 25 to 30 percent Asian (mostly Japanese and Korean, but also Chinese, Philippinos, and Vietnamese). The larger work force, about 60 percent, is composed of Mexican and Central American workers. Over half of the Latinos working there are undocumented, as are many of the Asians.

The company manufactures evening gowns, robes, and other expensive apparel. For this reason, many of the workers are highly skilled and their pay is considerably higher than that of the average garment worker in Los Angeles.

This report was made to the General Executive Board of the International Ladies Garment Workers Union (ILGWU), by Mario F. Vázquez, Western States Region Organizing Department, February 1977.

ORIGINS OF THE ORGANIZING CAMPAIGN

On October 26, 1976, the Western States Region Organizing Department of the International Ladies Garment Workers Union (ILGWU) was informed by a cutter from Lilli Diamond Originals that the workers at the plant were highly dissatisfied with the company and wanted to unionize. The cutter, Jesse Haro, was an undocumented worker and he was also a member of the ILGWU. He and his brother Tomas, also a cutter, had been working at Lilli Diamond for over a year building support for the union and waiting for the right moment to launch the organizing drive. That moment came when the company refused to raise the minimum wage of $2.30 per hour to the new state minimum wage of $2.50 per hour.

In addition, workers were equally dissatisfied with the abusiveness of the plant manager, Jerry Salk, and of the sewing department's supervisor, Alma de Payne. During the unionization campaign, de Payne made numerous individual threats that she would call the Immigration and Naturalization Service (INS) if the union won the election. She stated several times that she had a friend who was an agent and that he would "help her."

The initiation of the organizing drive resulted

in immediate firings. Carlota Gonzalez, a receptionist for the company, overheard Salk's plans for the firing of two women in a move intended to intimidate workers and discourage them from participating in unionization efforts. Carlota was fired when she protested the firing of the women.

Subsequently, union organizers filed charges of unfair labor practices against the company on behalf of the three women. The National Labor Relations Board (NLRB) Region 21, however, dismissed the charges.

Meanwhile, at meetings held on company time, Jerry Salk and a hired labor consultant intimidated workers by reminding them of their illegal status in the country. Those who were suspected of being leaders among the workers were often called into Salk's office, singly or in small groups, for interrogation and intimidation sessions. During one of these sessions, Salk slandered one of the shop committee members, Maria Victoria Pena, in an attempt to blackmail her into betraying the union. He accused her of marital infidelity with a fellow employee. Mrs. Pena became hysterical. She called her doctor to prove that on the day that Jerry Salk claimed to have witnessed the affair she had in fact been bedridden in a hospital. She also called her husband and he demanded an explanation from Salk. Union organizers again filed charges against the company for these actions and put Maria Victoria Pena in contact with an attorney to initiate a lawsuit against the company charging slander and intentional infliction of emotion distress. Mrs. Pena has since settled this case out of court and has been awarded a cash settlement.

As the organizing campaign progressed, union organizers found their strongest support among Spanish speaking workers. In fact, half of the shop committee and over half of all those who signed authorization cards were undocumented workers. Close to half of all the workers in the shop signed authorization cards within a relatively short period of time. However, union organizers were only able to obtain the support of three or four black and white workers. Not a single Asian worker signed an authorization card, and many of them literally ran from organizers when they tried to hand them leaflets. Organizers found them extremely suspicious and unfriendly. In fact, the company found the loyalty of Asian workers so reassuring that plant managers didn't bother to hold intimidation sessions for them. In the end, the inability of organizers to gain the support of Asian workers forced them to file for an NLRB election while still short of a majority vote.

IMMIGRATION RAIDS

The election date was set for Friday, January 14, 1977. On the early morning of January 13, as organizer Miguel Machuca handed out leaflets at the plant gate, he observed two men in civilian clothes detain two female workers (both had signed authorization cards) and identify themselves as immigration officers. Miguel immediately informed them that an election was scheduled the next day, and that he knew there was an agreement with INS District Director Joseph Sureck that the INS would not interfere during a labor dispute or organizing campaign. The INS agent, Officer Brechtel, ignored Miguel.

The next day, a picket line consisting of members from several labor unions and the Los Angeles County American Federation of Labor-Congress of Industrial Organization (AFL-CIO) was set up to give support and solidarity to the workers on their election. Shortly after 9:00 a.m. the picketers broke for breakfast at a nearby cafe. Immediately after they left, three immigration vans and six agents descended upon the company and were allowed into the premises. Once inside they arrested ten workers. Of these, all but one were union supporters or members of the shop organizing committee. Collusion between the company and the INS against unionization efforts was clearly evident.

The INS had come prepared with a list containing the names of the ten workers arrested and those of five or six others who were not at the shop at the time of the arrests. In addition, Jerry Salk showed unusual concern in learning Tomas Haro's whereabouts the morning of the election. When the INS arrived at the shop, Salk took Tomas's time card and gave his address to the INS. That evening, Officer Brechtel and his partner visited Tomas at his home, identified themselves as INS officers and warned him not to go back to work at Lilli Diamond.

Equally suspicious was the INS' selective arrests of Latino workers back at the plant. During the raid ten women (most of them Asian) hid in the restroom, but Alma de Payne sent a message to Isabel Quintero (prounion), who was hiding there too. She was told that she was wanted at the main office. Once out of the restroom she was arrested by INS agents waiting outside for her. Although agents knew of the other women hiding inside, they did not arrest them. Alma de Payne also assisted in the identification of undocumented prounion workers by falsely warning them to run and hide but in their attempts to do so INS agents, standing nearby, easily identified them and arrested them. By mistake an Asian worker was arrested and was already in the INS van when Jerry Salk came out, spoke to the agents, and right there obtained her release.

The raid over, several workers saw and heard Jerry Salk approach the supervising INS agent and say to him: "You guys did a great job!" Union organizers also noticed that many of the antiunion workers arrived very late to work the morning of the raid. They said they heard Alma the day before order many of them to not come to work earlier than noon on the day of the election. During the election, the cutting room supervisor and another antiunion worker made at least two trips each to pick up other antiunion workers at their home so they could vote and then drive them back home.

Union Organizers Respond

The company tried desperately to blame the ILGWU for the raid and sought to take credit for bailing out those arrested. When the first two workers were arrested February 13, organizers were led to believe that the vice president of the company had authorized the posting of bail on their behalf. The union's attorney had called the INS in an effort to post bail but was informed that the company's attorney was already there and that he was taking care of the matter. Unfortunately, this was not true. The attorney present was representing only one worker through a private arrangement, who was released on her own recognizance. But when she returned to the plant, Salk immediately gathered the workers and told them that he had posted $5,000 bail for her and that "his" attorney had handled the matter.

The raid on the factory, however, had a positive effect on the trade union consciousness of most of the workers and the villainy of management had caused great anger among the work-

ers. It is believed that both Lilli Diamond Originals and Campus Casuals incurred financial loses due to a loss of production; workers at Lilli Diamond were afraid to go to work for several days after the INS raid. At Campus Casuals undocumented workers pressured the company into opening a second shift for them in hopes of avoiding INS raids.

The day of the election, organizers Miguel Machuca and Mario Vázquez were at the INS office shortly after 9:00 a.m. trying to obtain the release of Victoria Villanueva, the other woman arrested the day before the election. But Victoria, they were told, had been deported the night before. Her relatives told them that she had been pressured into signing a "voluntary deportation" form, even though she and her husband were due to get their permanent residence visas in less than two months. The normal procedure involving these cases is releasing these individuals on their own recognizance, yet Victoria was not even allowed to be released on the bail that organizers were ready to post for her. (It has since been learned that Victoria became increasingly despondant over being separated from her husband and their three small children. She suffered a nervous breakdown in Tijuana, Mexico, and was hospitalized.)

Of the other ten arrested, seven were released on their own recognizance. Organizers posted bail of $1,000 and $500 each to release two others (including Jesse Haro, a principal organizer); another worker was forced to sign a "voluntary deportation" release, but she has since reentered the country and is back at work.

Salk, who boasted of having posted bail for one of his workers, refused to help any of the others. He publicly stated to the rest of the workers that it was illegal for an employer to bail out illegal aliens. At a meeting, Salk told workers: "The union people are not stupid, they spent a lot of money trying to organize Lilli Diamond because they know that we are the key to organizing Los Angeles—they know that if Lilli Diamond goes union many others would follow."

The Western States Region Organizing Department of the ILGWU soon launched a campaign in the Spanish language media in an effort to present the truth and expose practices at Lilli Diamond. Organizers and workers, via television newscasts, radio presentations, and press releases, charged the INS and management of conspiracy. Organizers took the position that now as before, the only way in which workers could protect themselves against the attacks of the employers or corrupt and repressive forces such as INS is through the organization of workers—the trade unions. This publicity directly generated a quick and militant organizing campaign at Condor Sportswear, a major local manufacturer.

POSTSCRIPT

The Western States Region Organizing Department saw the Lilli Diamond election day raid as an extremely serious threat to the ability of the union to grow stronger and healthier in the West Coast and wherever unorganized workers without documents are to be found. In our public positions and in our propaganda we have followed ILGWU unionization policies to the effect that we organize *workers,* not "citizens," "legal residents" or "illegal aliens."

However, because of the extremely low trade union consciousness of many of the workers in the industry (many thousands of them are now receiving their first experience as industrial workers). There is a grave danger that in their minds they may equate union organizing campaigns and National Labor Relations Board elections with immigration raids and deportation. For this reason, we feel that something has to be done to deny unscrupulous employers the use of a government agency as their private, union-busting police force.

PART FOUR
PAST STRUGGLES

WORKING-CLASS
WOMEN IN NINETEENTH
CENTURY MEXICO

John M. Hart

The Islamic-Moorish heritage of Spain played an important role in the attitudes toward women that developed during the formative period of Spanish America. It was believed that a lady of the "gente decente" should be protected from inconvenience, secluded, and not bothered with the harsh, competitive atmosphere of the outside world. During the baroque period of the Mexican colony, Spanish and Creole ladies were patronized, sheltered, and protected. They played little or no role in affairs outside of the family circle and the family was usually dominated by a male patriarch. Women of the castas or, even worse, Indians, were not treated with such benign tenderness. During the colonial period in New Spain the most unfortunate Indian women worked the mines with their husbands and sons, while the lucky ones served as domestic help or sold goods in the market place. These socioeconomic patterns played an important part in the roles assumed by lower-class women in industry and within the labor movement after the beginning of the late nineteenth century Mexican Industrial Revolution.

John M. Hart is Associate Professor of History at the University of Houston, Texas. An earlier version of this paper was read at the Eighteenth Annual Meeting of the Pacific Coast Council on Latin American Studies, October 27, 1972, Monterey, California.

Mexican industrialization, which began during the second half of the nineteenth century, was paralleled by the appearance of women in the new factories and as a factor in the urban labor movement. Industrialization resulted in a sudden concentration of new workers from the countryside in a few urban areas—especially Mexico City. Living conditions for the new city dwellers were generally intolerable and were compounded by chronic economic and political instability. Crowning the laborer's difficulty were the almost impossible working conditions for men, women, and children in the new factories. Lower-class women, usually wives and mothers, were subject to virtually the same working conditions as the men, to comparable hours, and were paid much lower wages. The working class, virtually in self-defense, began to organize and from the beginning the exploitation of women was one of its principal concerns.

An open letter of protest written by the participants in one of Mexico's first large strikes vividly portrayed the situation in the valley of Anahuac:

... there are female workers who receive a weekly salary of sixteen cents and this cannot be denied. The working day extends from 5:15 a.m. to 6:45 p.m. in the summertime, ... in the wintertime from 6:00 a.m. to 6:00 p.m., . . . the foremen only concede five minutes daily to the workers in order for them to eat.

The conditions within the factories in Puebla are not much better, working men receive a salary of two and a half to three and a half reales daily while working women receive from one half to one and a half reales. The work day spans eighteen hours with two fifteen-minute lunch breaks.

Nevertheless, in the twenty years between 1853 and 1873, while the workers and peones have lived in unbelievable misery, the nation has had sixteen presidents, four imperial regents, and the emperor; a total of twenty-one governments which have tried to achieve happiness for the Mexican people.[1]

Intolerable living and working conditions profoundly affected the nature of the emerging labor movement. They encouraged a strong radical-revolutionary bent, while corrupt local and unstable national government increased worker belligerency and distrust of formalized political institutions. The indiscriminatory wages and the hardships suffered by women in the textile factories inevitably resulted in special demands on their behalf by striking workers and their participation in the unrest.

In March 1865 the workers in the textile factories of San Ildefonso, in the neighboring town of Tlalnepantla, and La Colmena began "to organize in order to protect their interests." Conferences held between the workers and some organizers from Mexico City's already existing mutualist societies produced the Sociedad Mútua del Ramo de Hilados y Tejidos del Valle de México.[2] On March 15, 1865, a delegation from the Mexico City mutualist organizations joined the newly organized laborers and other employees of the two textile factories in an inauguration dance celebrating the formation of the new mutualist societies.

The circumstances behind the workers' decision to organize were indeed harsh. In an apparent economy move in January 1865, the workers in the San Ildefonso plant had suffered a reduction in their already pitiful pay. Despite this, the tienda de raya maintained its previous price level and, as usually occurred under these conditions, commanded the greater part of each worker's salary at the end of the weekly pay period.[3] Working hours for women were reset to extend from five in the morning to six

forty-five in the evening. For the men the work day was now from five in the morning until seven forty-five in the evening. About fifty workers were then laid off. The factory owners explained that the earlier release time for women was made necessary by their domestic obligations.

On June 10, 1865, the workers of the San Ildefonso plant walked off their jobs. The following day the workers at La Colmena followed their example.[4] Thus began the first strike in Mexican labor history. The strike leaders, all men, hoping to gain government protection, sent a short and pathetic appeal describing their plight to the imperial government of Maximiliano. As a direct response a Gendarmería Imperial was created to maintain order in Mexico City and its environs, and a directive was sent to the imperial representative in the Tlalnepantla district ordering him to offer assistance to the proprietor of the San Ildefonso Factory.[5]

On June 19, 1865, the government representative, Eulalio Núñez, arrived at the factory with a contingent of about twenty-five armed men. When confronted by an angry crowd of workers comprised of men, women, and children, he ordered his men to fire. Several workers were wounded, and about twenty-five were arrested. The prisoners, who were taken to the jail at Tepejí del Río, were advised that if they ever returned to San Ildefonso they would be shot. There was no record of women casualties as a result of the confrontation, but given their militancy and the potential shock effect that such a report would have had on public opinion it is likely that there were and that the news was suppressed. The first strike in the long struggle of the Mexican labor movement had ended.[6]

Throughout this episode organizing efforts among the workers were unimpeded by an imperial government obviously preoccupied with its continuing struggles with the Liberals under Juárez. Thus, the political instability of Mexico that bred contempt in the long run for government had permitted in the short run the organizing success of a handful of artisan labor activists who circulated among the industrial workers of the central region creating the first unions in the nation's history. Women joined the movement from the beginning, but initially were not expected to participate in the leadership. Belated government repression only alienated the workers further and made them even more receptive to radical ideology.

In early 1866, Santiago Villaneuva, the first leader of the Mexican labor movement and a member of an anarchist organizing group known as La Social, reinstituted a mutualist organization that had expired several years earlier, as a new workers' central council. This association, La Sociedad Artistica Industrial, was critically important to the labor movement and thus, to the advancement of women's rights during the next few years. It was dominated by artisans who declared themselves dedicated to the study and discussion of the works of Proudhon and Fourier and one of the themes that they stressed was the belief that women should be granted full rights and responsibilities both in Mexican society and within the labor movement.[7] Villanueva and the Sociedad membership began to proselytize the industrial workers of the Mexico City area and recruit them into mutualist societies. Mexico was now entering its first stage of intensive labor organizing.

In January 1868 Villanueva succeeded in organizing the textile factory La Fama Montañesa in Tlalpan. This advance was followed up with the formation of the Unión Mútua de Tejedores del Distrito del Tlalpan, which was comprised of newly organized workers, both men and women, at the factories of La Fama Montañesa, Contreras, La Abeja, and Tizapan. The factories would remain hotbeds of worker militancy well into the 1930s. Women were recruited, but were still not active in the leadership.[8] On July 8, 1868, the workers at La Fama Montañesa launched the first successful strike in Mexican history. Their moderate demands consisted mainly of a call for better working conditions, but article four of their list of priorities demanded "that women work only twelve hours per day in order that they may attend to household duties."[9] The shortened hours for female employees was one of several demands grudgingly granted by the employers who probably saw no contradiction between the protected and pampered lives of their wealthy wives and the utter desperation of poverty-stricken working-class women who endured an unbelievably high neo-natal death rate of over fifty percent caused by inadequate nutrition and virtually nonexistent sanitation and health facilities.

Following the successful strike several new workers' associations espousing Proudhonism appeared during the months of July and August 1868. In addition, the previously defeated and disbanded mutualist societies in the factories of San Ildefonso and La Colmena were reorganized. Villaneuva was now surrounded by new helpers in the labor movement leadership, still all men and all Mexico City artisans, who were to be very important in the advancement of cooperativist doctrines. They were Benito Castro, Pedro Ordóñez, Agapito Silva, and Ricardo Velatti.[10] All except Silva were later active members of the central anarchist group, La Social, and would support the rise of women labor leaders a few years later.[11] Villanueva planned for a general labor congress to meet in 1868, but the idea failed because of a lack of funds. He then proposed convening a permanent assembly composed of three delegates from each mutualist society, but the idea again failed for the same reason and apparently no women were included. Finally, in 1869, he formed a group of labor militants which was named the Círculo Proletario and was comprised of the above named cooperativists joined by the newcomers José María González, Juan de Mata Rivera, Evarista Meza, and Rafael Pérez de León who attempted to coordinate urban labor organizing activities and disseminate their ideology. Some of the anarchists, on the basis of their equalitarian ideology, were already demanding that women be represented in the workers' councils.[12] At this time they were defeated by a majority of the men. Late in 1869 Villaneuva's enthusiasm for a central council was rekindled by a newsletter from the International Workingmen's Association circulated by the Geneva Congress in 1866. The three-year delay before it reached Mexico indicates the isolation of that country's socialist movement. On January 10, 1870, Villanueva and his associates sent out a call asking for the formation of a "Centro General de los Trabajadores Organizados in order to more effectively defend the interests of labor."

On September 16, 1870, delegates from all over central Mexico convened the Centro for the first time and called it the Gran Círculo de Obreros de México. Once again there were no women delegates. The pro-Villanueva faction immediately established its dominance in the organization. Villanueva served as president until he died in 1872. Throughout the two-year period he conducted an intense campaign to win new industrial workers adherents. On July 9, 1871, El Socialista, the first Mexican newspaper that can be described as socialist, began publication in Mexico City. Several of its writers expressed their "socialist" ideology in clearly anarchist terms. The paper joined the Círculo, became its "official organ," and was duly granted the customary three delegates. La Social also joined and sent Velatti, Ordóñez, and Castro as representatives. Most of the other recently formed mutualist organizations in Mexico City and its environs belonged to the Círculo and as a result there was an increased intermingling of anarchists and working men and women, the latter attended as observers.[13] Individuals who wished to could join, provided they were workers and did not belong to any political party. Employers who were "on good terms with their employees,"— usually artisans who had expanded their trade —were admitted to associate membership. The organization was made accessible to almost any sympathizer who cared to join in its activities.[14] However, at this early date there is no indication that women were permitted to take part in the decision-making process of what constituted a workers council for greater central Mexico.

Elsewhere in the country, workers were influenced by ideas emanating from Mexico City and began forming mutualist societies and cooperatives. In San Luis Potosí the Asociación Potosina de Obreros was comprised of three new mutualist groups and was in contact with the Círculo in Mexico City. In Toluca a mutualist society was formed and, on November 8, 1871, affiliated with the Círculo.[15] In both towns industrial workers including women were recruited. Textile factories in the Orizaba area were also organizing and they included a sizeable number of women workers. By 1874 the Círculo's membership was estimated at 8,000.[16] At this time moderates sympathetic to president Lerdo de Tejada took over the organization. It continued to grow, but its moderate leadership left it vulnerable to criticism. By 1876 the more radical members of the group began to break openly with the moderates. They objected to the acceptance of money

from the government; to the formation of several "company unions" sponsored by factory owners in conjunction with the Círculo leadership; and to the group's refusal, through decisions of the leadership clique, to support a serious strike at La Fama Montañesa factory. They also strongly attacked El Socialista for its relatively conservative editorial stance. In the polemics the hardships endured by women were cited, but the question of their participation in union leadership was once again avoided.[17]

During the early 1870s, it was the growing conviction of virtually every prominent member of the urban labor movement that a nationwide organization was needed, and by the end of 1875 steps were being taken to convene a national workers' congress.[18] The anarchists had long supported this idea, and Villaneuva had worked toward it as early as 1869. Mata Rivera, the editor of El Socialista, was the man who presented the formal proposal for a national workers' congress to the special junta designated by the Círculo to consider the project.[19] The junta apparently completed its work successfully, because the Congreso General Obrero de la República Mexicana, with Círculo support, met for the first time on March 5, 1876, in the salon of the Sociedad Artística Industrial with thirty-five of the approximately seventy-three appointed delegates present.[20]

The first Congreso spent most of its time with the tedious details of organizing special committees and electing officers. The main event of the Congreso revolved around the role to be played by women. Two of the anarchist representatives sent by La Social to the Congreso were the women Jesús Valadés and Soledad Sousa.[21] The moderate Mata Rivera, from the Círculo, opposed their being seated. Although he professed the utmost regard for La Social, he charged that admitting female delegates would violate precedent. José Muñuzuri of La Social, the editor of the more radical El Hijo del Trabajo, which was not the official organ of the Círculo, led the debate in support of the women. Thus, the editor of El Socialista, who had close ties with the moderate faction, debated the editor of El Hijo, who was the voice of the more militant elements, regarding the seating of women delegates in an asamblea which repeatedly claimed working-class women's rights as a high priority. After a prolonged and heated debate the assembly supported Muñuzuri and to standing applause the female delegates were seated in a regional or national conclave for the first time in the history of the Mexican labor movement.[22] No doubt passions generated during the moderate-radical rivalries of several years affected the decision of the Congreso as much as did any ethical consideration of women's rights. This event, in its own right, however, did have lasting consequences. Women soon became important in the affairs of the Congreso, and Carmen Huerta was elected its president in 1879, again in 1880, and several times thereafter.[23]

The anarchists, whose radical libertarian ideology prospered for a time, had a significant impact on emergent women workers' militancy. The membership of the Congreso supported the anarchists between 1879 and 1882. It did this in part because of the chaos and despair that had been brought about by the civil war of 1876 and because some of them believed that the oppressive and disappointing policies of the Díaz regime had fulfilled anarchist prophesies regarding the ultimately evil nature of the national government. One of the anarchist leaders, Carmen Huerta, was from the Rio Blanco textile factory zone and she had a lasting effect upon female workers in that region. Years later Margarita Martinez and the women workers at Rio Blanco played a leading role in the 1907 rebellion there.

The labor movement accepted not only the anarchists' ideas on women's rights but their domination of the movement itself because of the anarchists' increased strength in the period 1876–1882. During 1877 and 1878, La Social had continued to organize; and it reached the peak of its strength in 1879–1882. In 1878 the organization claimed to have sixty-two regional sections located in, and propagandizing in, urban centers throughout the country.[24] The anarchists had become, by far, the strongest force in Mexican labor and they continued to advocate feminine equality. In the early 1880s they dominated the Congreso which, in 1882, after its reorganization and official entry into the European based anarchist International Workingmen's Association, claimed one hundred affiliated societies and a total enrolled membership of 50,236.[25]

But urban industry during the 1880s was still too weak to give rise to a sufficiently powerful labor movement capable of resisting a Díaz regime that was consolidating its power and preparing to move against dissidents. The Rurales, decimated during the civil war of 1876, were rebuilt by Díaz in the late 1870s. During the same period the army was reconstructed. Díaz at the same time created a wide following within the national community at large and even enjoyed limited support within some elements of the working class. With this base the dictator was in a solid position to confront industrial working-class dissent.

In the next few years several agrarian leaders affiliated with La Social and the Congreso were arrested and exiled to the northern frontier. A series of anarchist inspired agrarian uprisings and labor strikes were violently suppressed between 1878 and 1884, when they were finally snuffed out. Finally, General Trinidad García de la Cadena, the most consistent military supporter of the urban labor movement, was killed in 1886 by his army captors in Zacatecas under the conditions of the Ley de Fuga.[26] The working-class press was shackled.[27] In 1881 the Congreso invited trouble with Díaz by affiliating with the anarchist international. The Mexicans were represented at the 1881 London convention of the international by an American delegate from Boston named Nathan Ganz.[28]

By 1883 the organizational network built up by La Social had vanished. The Gran Círculo of Zacatecas suffered the same fate after García de la Cadena was killed. That they were dispersed by the government is clear. Unfortunately, the position of working-class women also deteriorated. Textile strikes, while frequent, were rarely tolerated, and after 1884 attempted strikes in the textile mills of central Mexico were routinely broken up by troops or police. Large numbers of women were employed in those mills. In 1882 the women of Rio Blanco joined their male counterparts in a secret "sociedad de resistencia" which continued in existence until the 1907 uprising.

The Congreso, with the bulk of its original revolutionaries removed, and at the sufferance of the government, continued to proselytize on behalf of cooperativism and to organize workers until the mid-1890s. The official newspaper of the Congreso during this period, La *Convención Radical,* betrayed its ideological commitment with observations such as "Paris proclaimed the Commune, this is . . . the municipio libre, la autonomía municipal."[29] But most leaders, including Pedro Ordóñez, at times president of the Congreso and vice president of *La Convención,* found accommodation with the regime a more personally rewarding approach. He ran successfully for election as a regidor of Mexico City.[30] In the late 1880s the city and national governments cooperated with the Congreso, now led by Ordóñez and Carmen Huerta, who also turned more moderate with advancing age, in a few experimental cooperatives.[31] Since these projects stressed housing and a well-integrated community as well as economic self-sufficiency, women and children would have especially benefited. The government soon lost interest however, and the projects died for lack of funds.[32]

During the 1880s and 1890s Huerta remained one of the principal leaders of the Mexican labor movement. In the mid-1880s she presided over a group known as the Junta Patriotica Privada de las Sociedades Mutualistas de México. The purpose of the organization is unclear, but among its members were José María González and Ordóñez.[33] In 1885 she was president of the recreated Congreso Nacional de Obreros, and then in 1888 she served as first pro secretary of *La Convención Radical,* the latter day Congreso's newspaper.[34] During the 1880s and 1890s Díaz permitted the organization of many unions, as long as they did not cause trouble. Huerta was organizing actively in the Orizaba region. It is not known if she was a part of the workers' underground society at Rio Blanco, but in 1895 an aging Huerta was a delegate to the Congreso from the neighboring Agricultora de Nogales, Orizaba.[35]

Several women rose to prominence in the Mexican labor movement during the late 1870s and early 1880s. But, it is interesting to note that within the next two decades, in the midst of declining real wages and outright repression, traditional attitudes once again prevailed and the women's role in the leadership of the labor movement vanished. During the Revolution of 1910, despite the ideological heritage from the nineteenth century claimed by leaders of the Casa del Obrero Mundial, no women occupied primary positions of leadership al-

though they were members of the Casa strike committees of 1916 and thus far more important than in the years of decline since the Casa's defeat.

NOTES

1. *El Socialista* (México D.F.), 23 January 1873.
2. Manuel Díaz Ramírez, *Apuntes Historicos del Movimiento Obrero y Campesino de México 1844–1880* (Fondo de Cultura Popular, México D.F., 1938), p. 77.
3. José Valadés, "Precursores del Socialismo Antiautoritario en México," *La Protesta,* (Buenes Aires), 22 May 1928, p. 411.
4. Díaz Ramírez, *Apuntes,* pp. 31–32.
5. Diario del Imperio, (México D.F.), 19 June 1865.
6. "Pequeña Biografía de Plotino Rhodakanaty," *La Paz,* (Chilpancingo, México), 17 March 1873.
7. For example see José María González, "Nuestras Ideas," *El Hijo del Trabajo,* (México D.F.), 3 September 1876. Some went so far as to advocate a divorce law. See Plotino Rhodakanaty, article in *El Socialista,* 8 June 1883.
8. Alfonso López Aparicio, *El Movimiento Obrero en México* (Editorial Jus, México D.F., 1958), p. 107; and *El Socialista,* no. 10, 1872.
9. Díaz Ramírez, *Apuntes,* pp. 33–34; and Lino Medina Salazar, "Albores del Movimiento Obrero en México," *Historia y Sociedad,* (México D.F.), Invierno 1965, p. 60.
10. Díaz Ramírez, *Apuntes,* pp. 33–34; and Medina Salazar, "Albores del Movimiento Obrero en México," *Historia y Sociedad,* Invierno 1965, p. 60.
11. *El Hijo,* 9 May 1876; and 9 July 1876.
12. For example see Rhodakanaty, *El Craneoscopio,* (México D.F.), 5 May 1874.
13. *El Socialista,* 9 July 1871 and 1 March 1874.
14. *El Socialista,* 29 September 1872.
15. *El Socialista,* 15 October 1871; and 12 November 1871.
16. *El Obrero Internacional,* (México D.F.), 27 October 1874.
17. *El Hijo,* 1 May 1876; 22 May 1876; 2 July 1876; and 27 August 1876.
18. The first recorded newspaper reference to a national workers' congress can be found in "Los Obreros de San Luis Potosí," *El Socialista,* 15 October 1871. This need was discussed repeatedly in the pages of *El Hijo* in 1876, *El Obrero Internacional* in 1874, and in *El Socialista* during the period extending from late 1875 throughout 1876.
19. *El Socialista,* 27 February 1876.
20. *El Socialista,* 5 March 1876.
21. *El Socialista,* 7 May 1876; and *El Hijo,* 9 May 1876.
22. *El Hijo,* 22 May 1876. Also see the article by Juana la Progresista.
23. *El Hijo,* 20 December 1879; and 16 May 1880.
24. *La Internacional,* 25 August 1878; and 6 October 1878.
25. *El Socialista,* 26 September 1882.
26. General Carlos Lueso, a ministerio de Guerra y Marina, Zacatecas, Octubre 25, 1886, Expediente 15–395, Documento 220, Archivo Historico de la Defensa Nacional; Noviembre 11, 1886, Expediente 15–395, Documento 218, ibid.; Documentos 204, Octubre 19,

1886; 214, Octubre 20, 1886; and 219, Noviembre 16, 1886, ibid. For a newspaper account see *El Siglo XIX,* (México D.F.), 3 November 1886. The practice of killing prisoners became common during the Porfiriato and was referred to as the Ley de Fuga—"killed while trying to escape."

27. The working class press did not submit without some protest. For example, see Luigi, "La Revolución es Necessaria," *El Hijo,* 28 December 1879; and *El Hijo,* 6 March 1881.

28. Nathan Ganz, "What We Will and What We Will Not," and "War Against the Authorities by Various Methods and Means," *El Socialista,* 10 January 1881. See also, Valadés, Mexico City, to Nettlau, April 26, 1924, Nettlau Archive, Instituut Internationaal voor Sociale Geschiendenis, Amsterdam. For a description of Ganz' antics at the convention see George Woodcock, *Anarchism: A History of Libertarian Ideas and Movements,* (The World Publishing Company, Cleveland, 1962), p. 258.

29. Andrés Díaz Millán, editorial in *La Convención Radical,* (México D.F.), 9 January 1887.

30. For a brief biography of Ordóñez see *El Socialista,* 30 June 1881.

31. *La Convención Radical,* 9 January 1887; and 16 January 1887.

32. Mexico, Memoria de Fomento, *Colonización É Industria de la República Mexicana, 1883-1885,* (México D.F., Tip. de la Secretaría de Fomento, 1887), pp. 195-203; and Mexico, Memoria de Fomento, *Colonización É Industria de la República Mexicana,* 1892-1896 (México D.F., Tip. de la Secretaria de Fomento, 1897), pp. 13-16.

33. Carmen Huerta, et. al., Letter to the Editor of *El Socialista,* 28 June 1885.

34. *La Convención Radical,* 15 January 1888.

35. *La Convención Radical,* 9 March 1895.

A LA MUJER
(TO WOMEN)

Ricardo Flores Magón

PREFACE

In recent years, we Chicanos have begun to study our history with renewed determination. We have done so because it is in knowing our past that we come to understand the sources of our present situation and are better equipped to determine our own future.

To understand our current reality, we have gone all the way back to our indigenous origins; we have gone to the birth of Mexico and the birth of the mestizo. To the Aztecas, Mayas, Toltecas and beyond. Some of us, however, have refused to leave the mystical skies of Huitzilopochtli.

It is time we study and utilize another aspect of our history, for we find ourselves at that stage of revolutionary struggle again. The struggle of Zapata and Villa, so much romanticized over the last few years, was not a spontaneous event but represented the long revolutionary development of a movement against the exploitation and corruption of the ruling

From *Regeneración,* September 24, 1910. *Regeneración* was a newspaper established by Ricardo Flores Magón in 1900 as a "periódico jurídico independiente." The preface in this article and the English translation of Magón's editorial was done by Prensa Sembradora, March 8, 1974, Oakland, California.

class of Mexico. Much of the ideological influence was generated by men like Ricardo Flores Magón and organizations like the Partido Liberal Mexicano.

Mexico at the turn of the century was an underdeveloped peasant society which, while it embodied a capitalist mode of production, remained under the burden of feudal social institutions. Porfirio Díaz and the class he represented had been in power for nearly thirty years. There was a stirring of liberals and other sectors of the bourgeoisie around economic stagnation and political corruption. The issue of the liberals was the manipulation of democratic elections.

Magón and the Partido Liberal Mexicano, while using the language of liberalism, already understood then that inequities in capitalist society were not incidental to the system but an integral part of it and therefore could not be corrected by piecemeal reforms. Their agitation and calls for revolution forced Magón and other members of the Partido into exile in the United States where they intensified their organizational efforts.

Newspapers, armed groups, political organizations, and communications networks which, although well organized, were also so well infiltrated by Díaz and the United States agents that their effectiveness was continually undermined.

Ideologically, one would have to call Magón and his compañeros anarchists. Although they saw the need for total revolution, they did not seek to establish a socialist state which would reorganize the means of production and methods of distribution. Their slogan, "Tierra y Libertad," called for the repartition of lands and their return to those who worked them, but it took little into account the coming industrialization of Mexico and the role she would have to play in a modern society. Their manifestos and political pamphlets and revolutionary newspapers are filled with the most poetic and often romantic calls to revolutionary action, but rarely do we see the hardheaded analysis of objective political conditions so necessary for the development of successful revolutionary strategy. Thus we learn for our struggle that in revolution one must combine the spirit and heart of the anarchist with the analysis of scientific socialism; that we must create correct theory as well as an insurrectionary spirit.

Prensa Sembradora chose to translate Flores Magón's essay "A La Mujer," not at random, but to demonstrate that within our revolutionary tradition there have been serious and progressive statements on women's rights. If we are to examine seriously and critically our historic revolutionary tradition, it is obligatory that we deal with Magón's essay. It demonstrates to our "revolutionary" machos that women's emancipation is an integral aspect in our struggle for liberation. We must not regress to cultural stereotypes, placing the Chicana's role exclusively within the kitchen and with the children, for that would be self-defeating. There is a rekindled revolutionary attitude among Chicanas today which will not be appeased by tokenism and patronage. A revolutionary movement can succeed only when its forces are free from the restraints of sexual chauvinism.

Ricardo Flores Magón's position is that for women there is no other solution but rebellion. This essay is a call to action. However, the role today is more demanding than what he proposed in 1910—to be supportive or agitative. As for any revolutionary, the duty of Chicanas is to make revolution!

March 8, 1974
International Women's Day

TO WOMEN

Compañeras:

Revolution approaches! With angered eyes, and flaming hair, her trembling hands knock anxiously on the doors of our nation. Let us welcome her with serenity, for although she carries death in her breast, she is the announcement of life, the herald of hope. She will destroy and create at the same time; she will raze and build. Her fists are the invincible fists of a people in rebellion. she does not offer roses or caresses; she offers an axe and a torch.

Interrupting the millennial feast of the content, sedition raises her head, and the prophecy of Balthasar* has with time become a clenched fist hanging over the heads of the so-called ruling class. Revolution approaches! Her mission will ignite the flames in which privilege and injustice will burn. Compañeras, do not fear the revolution. You constitute one-half of the human species and what affects humanity affects you as an integral part of it. If men are slaves, you are too. Bondage does not recognize sex; the infamy that degrades men equally degrades you. You cannot escape the shame of oppression. The same forces which conquer men strangle you.

We must stand in solidarity in the grand conquest for freedom and happiness. Are you mothers? Are you wives? Are you sisters? Are you daughters? Your duty is to help man; to be there to encourage him when he vacillates; stand by his side when he suffers; to lighten his sorrow; to laugh and to sing with him when victory smiles. You don't understand politics? This is not a question of politics; this is a matter of life or death. Man's bondage is yours and perhaps yours is more sorrowful, more sinister, and more infamous.

Are you a worker? Because you are a woman you are paid less than men, and made to work harder. You must suffer the impertinence of the foreman or proprietor; and if you are attractive, the bosses will make advances. Should you weaken, they would rob you of your virtue in the same cowardly manner as you are robbed of the product of your labor.

---

*In 538 B.C., Balthasar, the last king of Babylon, held a feast. Words appeared on the wall which Daniel translated as meaning that Balthasar was an unfit ruler and would be overthrown. (Daniel V:1)

Under this regime of social injustice which corrupts humanity, the existence of women wavers in the wretchedness of a destiny which fades away either in the blackness of fatigue and hunger or in the obscurity of marriage and prostitution.

In order to fully appreciate women's part in universal suffering, it is necessary to study page by page this somber book called Life, which like so many thorns strips away the flesh of humanity.

So ancient is women's misfortune that its origins are lost in the obscurity of legend. In the infancy of mankind, the birth of a female child was considered a disgrace to the tribe. Women toiled the land, carried firewood from the forest and water from the stream, tended the livestock, constructed shelters, wove cloth, cooked food, and cared for the sick and the young. The filthiest work was done by women. Should an ox die of fatigue, the women took its place pulling the plow, and when war broke out between rivaling tribes, the women merely changed masters, and continued under the lash of the new owners, carrying out their tasks as beasts of burden.

Later, under the influence of Greek civilization, women were elevated one step in the esteem of men. No longer were they beasts of burden as in the primitive clan, nor did they lead secluded lives as in oriental societies. If they belonged to a free class, their role was one of procreators of citizens for the state; if they were slaves, they provided workers for the fields.

Christianity aggravated the situation of women with its contempt for the flesh. The founding fathers of the Church vented their outbursts of rage against feminine qualities. St. Augustine, St. Thomas, and other saints, before whose statues women now kneel, referred to women as daughters of the devil, vessels of impurity, and condemned them to the tortures of hell.

Women's position in this century varies according to their social stature; but in spite of the refinements of customs and the progress of philosophy, women continue subordinated to men by tradition and laws. Women are perpetually treated as minors when the law places the wife under the custody of the husband. She cannot vote or be elected, and to enter into civil contracts she must own a sizeable fortune.

Throughout history women have been considered inferior to men, not only by law but also by custom. From this erroneous and unjust concept derives the misfortune which she has suffered since humanity differentiated itself from lower animal forms by the use of fire and tools.

Humiliated, degraded, bound by chains of tradition to an irrational inferiority, indoctrinated in the affairs of heaven by clerics, but totally ignorant of world problems, she is suddenly caught in the whirlwind of industrial production which above all requires cheap labor to sustain the competition created by the voracious "princes of capital" who exploit her circumstances. She is not as prepared as men for the industrial struggle, nor is she organized with the women of her class to fight alongside her brother workers against the rapacity of capitalism.

For this reason, though women work more than men, they are paid less, and misery, mistreatment, and insult are today as yesterday the bitter harvest for a whole existence of sacrifice. So meager are women's salaries that frequently they must prostitute themselves to meet their families' basic needs, especially when in the marketplace of marriage they do not find a husband. When it is motivated by economic security instead of love, marriage is but another form of prostitution, sanctioned by the law and authorized by public officials. That is, a wife sells her body for food exactly as does a prostitute; this occurs in the majority of marriages. And what could be said of the vast army of women who do not succeed in finding a husband? The increasing cost of life's basic necessities; the displacement of human labor by the perfection of machinery; the ever-decreasing price of human labor—all contribute to the burden of supporting a family. The compulsory draft tears strong and healthy young men from the bosom of a society and lessens the number eligible for marriage. Migration of workers, caused by economic and political phenomena, also reduces the number of men capable of marriage. Alcoholism, gambling and other ills of society further reduce the number of available men. Consequently, the number of single women grows alarmingly. Since their situation is so precarious, they swell the ranks of prostitution, accelerating the degeneration of the human race by this debasement of body and spirit.

Compañeras: This is the frightful picture offered by modern society. In it you see men and women alike suffering the tyranny of a political and social environment in complete discord with the progress of civilization and the advances of philosophy. In times of anguish, however, do not look up to the heavens for solutions and explanations because in that lies the greatest contribution to your eternal bondage. The solution is here on earth! That solution is rebellion.

Demand that your husbands, brothers, fathers, sons and friends pick up the gun. Spit in the face of those who refuse to pick up a weapon against oppression.

Revolution approaches! Jimenez and Acayucan, Palomas, Viesca. Las Vacas and Valladolid are the first gust of the inevitable wind.** A tragic paradox: freedom, which is life, is gained by imparting death!

Ricardo Flores Magón
[From *Regeneración,* September 24, 1910]

**A reference to the insurrections led by the Partido Liberal Mexicano in 1908 and 1910. Too premature, they failed in their intent. Still, they gave the signal for the later general insurrection, the Revolution of 1910.

SARA ESTELA RAMÍREZ: UNA ROSA ROJA EN EL MOVIMIENTO

Emilio Zamora

This paper has a two-fold purpose. First, it introduces the reader to Sara Estela Ramírez, a heretofore unknown political and literary figure of the early 1900s in South Texas. Second, it examines three pieces that are thematically and stylistically representative of her total collected works. More generally, this paper is an attempt to contribute modestly to the development of the history of a significant segment of our population, Mexicanas. Since a general history of Mexicanas remains distant, our efforts in that direction are necessarily our first steps. Thus, this paper is chiefly biographical.

Ramírez was born in the Mexican state of Coahuila. She came to Laredo, Texas in 1898 to assume a teaching position with a local educational institution. During the twelve years that she lived in Laredo, Ramírez was notable for her literary activity in local Spanish language newspapers and for her political association with the Partido Liberal Mexicano (PLM). Many of her political writings are philosophical contributions to PLM activities and, by extension, to the Mexicano socio-political movement of South Texas.

Emilio Zamora is director of the Ethnic Studies Center, Texas A & I University, Kingsville, Texas. An earlier version of this paper was read at the Floricanto Festival held at San Antonio, Texas, 1976.

Ramírez arrived in Laredo approximately fifty years after the signing of the Treaty of Guadalupe Hidalgo. During that fifty-year period the Southwest had undergone a significant economic transformation. It had developed from a semifeudal to a capitalist society. The attendant racially defined social relations constituted a class structure with Mexicanos at the bottom. By the turn of the century, the economic dye had been set. Increased immigration from Mexico, the concentration of Mexicano workers in the urban areas, and occupational immobility further assured the economic subordination of Mexicanos.[1]

More specifically, in South Texas, Mexicanos were affected by the particular phase of capitalist development that their home region was undergoing. The United States economy integrated three distinct economic areas at different rates. This entry variation produced different sets of economic activity and labor relations. The three regions were: the large and middle scale ranching corridor approximately fifty miles wide extending southward from the Nueces River to the Rio Grande River; the large pockets of commercialized agricultural production in Dimmit County, Nueces County, and the Rio Grande valley; and the urban centers of Laredo and Brownsville.[2]

Some Mexicanos in the first region retained land ownership. Thus, they remained influential in political and social circles. Mexicano workers, on the other hand, were relatively stationary and governed by a patron-peon relationship in the political and economic activity of the area. The second region had been rapidly transformed from a ranching to a highly commercialized agricultural economy. Mexicano workers were seasonal, mobile, and exploited wage laborers. Mexicano sharecroppers, on the other hand, were stationary and governed by a system of debt-peonage. Of the three regions, the last one represented the more advanced stage in economic activity, labor relations, unionization, and civic organizing activity. Since this paper focuses on Ramírez, I shall examine Laredo, her place of residence, with particular attention to the organizing climate there.

The iron horse of the industrial revolution had replaced the familiar ox cart that passed through Laredo. By the late 1800s, railroads effectively linked the city with the developing capitalist economies of the United States and Mexico. The pace of economic activity quickened and the work force increasingly became free wage labor. Industrial activity in Laredo during the early 1900s included construction; garment work; cigar making; railroad work in the Mexican Railway Company shops of Laredo proper and on the lines in the Laredo area; coal mining in the outlying communities of Minera, Cannel, and San Jose; smelting work; and binational commercial related activity.

Although some Mexicano wage laborers worked in the ranches and farms of the areas, the greatest number of workers were probably employed by local industry. For instance, in 1906, when the population of Laredo was 16,000, the Mexican Railway Company alone employed approximately 1,000 workers in the shops. In Minera, Cannel, and San Jose, the great majority of the male labor force worked in the mines. During the period 1905–1907, organized labor activity led by Federal Labor Union Local No. 11,953 among these railroad and mine workers indicates that the industrial nature of labor relations was in an advanced state.[3]

Nonmaterialist forces also induced organizing activity among Mexicanos in Laredo. Its location on the international border was strategic for binational politics. In 1904, it became the headquarters for the exiled PLM. In 1918, it was selected as the site for the Pan American Federation of Labor Conference. Also, the city was removed from the central Texas area where racial conflict was most severe. Mexicanos still maintained political and economic control. As a consequence, some Mexicanos saw Laredo as a secure homefront in the sociopolitical movement. This may have been the reason why El Congreso Mexicanista was held at Laredo in 1911. This meeting was an important development in the Mexicano sociopolitical movement of Texas.[4]

The spontaneous and organized responses by individuals and groups to a situation of domination and to subjective acts of oppression constitute the nascent Mexicano sociopolitical struggle of the early 1900s. Laredo was central in its development. This movement reached a developmental peak with the convening of El Congreso Mexicanista. At this meeting, delegates from various organizations in Texas and Nuevo Laredo, Tamaulipas, convened in Laredo to form a statewide structure that was to function as an umbrella organization. El Congreso signals the advent of a formal, mass-based movement of Mexicanos in Texas.[5]

This organizational development partly originated in political activities emanating from Mexico. According to Professor Gómez-Quiñones, the PLM and its ideology of the early 1900s was one of the chief political factors that influenced the development of the Mexicano sociopolitical movement in Texas. The PLM's opposition to the Porfirio Díaz regime provided a focal point for organizing. Its early form of Mexican liberalism was undoubtedly applicable to socioeconomic conditions in Texas.[6]

Ricardo Flores Magón and his PLM associates chose Texas as their first exiled base of operations. They arrived in Laredo in 1904 and re-established in San Antonio during the same year. Harassment by United States and Mexican authorities prompted them to move to St. Louis, Missouri, in 1906.[7] While in Laredo, they established their headquarters in the home of Sara Estela Ramírez, a PLM supporter since 1901. In a letter to PLM members, Magón described Ramírez as

Una digna correligionaria que siempre ha colaborado y colabora activamente en nuestros trabajos, y que firma con nosotros la presente.[8]

Magón further stated in the letter that correspondence be addressed to Ramírez because PLM mail was being intercepted by Mexican postal officials.[9] This observation partly reveals Ramírez's role in the PLM organization.

Ramírez was a member of the local core of female leaders that assumed the public roles that other more popular PLM leaders were unable to undertake. Harassment by local police, Pinkerton men, and Furlong detectives often forced the men to be less conspicuous and prompted the women to fulfill the more public roles of propagandizing and transmitting PLM policy.[10] Ramírez was such a central figure in the PLM.

During the period between 1901 and 1906 Ramírez was one of Magón's principal contacts in Texas. They corresponded frequently.[11] Her friendly communications denote a close working relationship. On one occasion, for instance, Ramírez wrote in personal terms about the conflict between two PLM leaders, Magón and Camilo Arriaga:

> I've become sad and weary Ricardo, of so many personal antagonisms. I tell you frankly, I am disillusioned with everything, absolutely everything . . . I don't want to analyze the causes of your quarrels with Camilito. I believe you both are right and both to blame.[12]

Ramírez's involvement was direct, as evidenced by her public and personal support of PLM activities. However, she made her most lasting contribution through her literary works.

SARA ESTELA RAMÍREZ AND SELECTED WORKS

Sara Estela was born in 1881 in Villa de Progreso, Coahuila, and died in Laredo, Texas, at the young age of twenty-nine.[13] Although she lost her mother at an early age, she managed to finish her public education in Monterrey and to graduate from a teachers' college in Saltillo called Ateneo Fuentes. She accepted an offer to teach at the Seminario de Laredo. When she arrived there in 1898, she was accompanied by her only sister, María. During the following twelve years that she spent in Laredo, Ramírez became a popular literary and political figure of the South Texas and northern Mexico region.

Ramírez accumulated a sufficient number of accomplishments to warrant the following praise during her funeral: "Ha fallecido la mujer mexicana mas ilustrada de Texas." She was also called "La mas noble, mas sentimental y primera de las poetisas de la region" in an obituary entitled, "La Musa Texana Esta de Duelo; Sara Estela Ramírez, La Mimado de Las Musas, Ha Muerto." A young woman named Jovita Idar added:

> . . . siempre estaba pronto para impartirnos del caudal de los vastos conocimientos que atesoraba; soberana de la moral, sus enseñanzas iban impregnadas de inteligencia, ternura y talento.[14]

Such praise denotes a prodigious career.

Her literary career spans the period 1898–1910. She published her poems, essays, and literary articles in the local Spanish language newspapers, *La Crónica* and *El Demócrata Fronterizo*. In addition to these works, the local papers often reproduced her public speeches. She also demonstrated her artistic capabilities on the stage. Once, *El Demócrata Fronterizo* announced Ramírez had donned the double laurels of the famous French dramatist Moliere by writing a play titled "Noema" and by participating in its acting cast before enthusiastic audiences at several local theaters.

The continuous printing of Ramírez's works by the local papers, favorable newspaper reviews of her writings, and well attended stage productions suggest that Ramírez was a popular literary figure in the Laredo area. This locally based popularity must have extended beyond Laredo, since *La Crónica, El Demócrata Fronterizo*, and Ramírez's own newspapers were regional publications.

She published two literary periodicals, *La Corregidora* and *Aurora,* between the years 1904 and 1910. The former was a daily, printed and distributed out of Mexico City, Laredo, and San Antonio. It was published while Ramírez traveled throughout Mexico and Texas as a member of the PLM. The latter paper was a daily published in Laredo during the last years of her life. Copies of these papers have been lost to time. Luckily, some issues of *La Crónica* and *El Demócrata Fronterizo* have survived. They include a sufficient number of her writings to eventually produce a complete study of Ramírez and her works.

The nineteen works that this writer has collected span a fifteen-month period, between December 28, 1907, and April 10, 1909. We know that she began to publish her writings as soon as she arrived in Laredo around 1898. Therefore, the pieces we are to examine reflect the last stage of an approximately eleven-year writing period, between 1898 and 1909. Since they are three of her most recent, they probably represent refined products in her literary career. "Alocución," is a public talk delivered before the Sociedad de Obreros; "Igualdad y Progreso" during the organization's twenty-fourth anniversary; "Surge," is a literary composition directed at women; and "La Página Blanca," is a love poem.[15]

In "Alocución," Ramírez does more than just pay tribute to a mutual aid organization that has consistently protected the material and spiritual interests of its members. She makes a moral statement. The original state of humans is by nature good, yet fragile. Although we are capable of exercising inherent qualities in the interest of humanity, our free will often betrays nature. Avarice, selfishness, jealousies, apathy, and other "gérmenes morbosos" disrupt and destroy a natural tendency to practice "mutualismo."

For Ramírez, mutualismo is the logical concept that should govern social relations. It is "un sentimiento de altruísmo ennato en el corazón." Sadly, many workers have fallen from the grace of nature. Alienated and divided, they often actively participate in negating basic principles of solidarity, cooperation, and goodwill. Ramírez calls for a reaffirmation of a humanizing spirit. We need to draw

> . . . de entre nuestros egoísmos, algo inmenso,
> algo divino, que nos haga noblemente humanos.

Ramírez viewed moral behavior in terms of a dialectical process between two prominent forces in the universe—determinism and free will. This theme runs through most of her other political works. She believed that humans are inherently equipped by nature to actively care for the general welfare of others. However, we often exercise our free will and reject the determinants of nature. Those that reject the dictates of such a universal law disrupt the natural order of things. Logically, Ramírez's views on morality provide the justification for social movements that propose to create a new society free of class, racial and sexual discrimination. As such, they are philosophical contributions to PLM activity and the Mexicano sociopolitical movement of South Texas.

The work titled "Surge" speaks to women who are exclusively fulfilling prescribed roles of a pedestal nature. Ramírez calls on women to reject these roles to work for loftier goals: "Surge, pues, a las bellezas de la vida; pero surge asi, bella de cualidades, esplendente de virtudes, fuerte de energías."

Ramírez warns that women who act as queens and goddesses are glorified objects whose existence is dependent on forces external to the woman. A woman is fundamentally and irreversibly a woman. "Los dioses son arrojados de los templos; los reyes son echados de sus tronos, la mujer es siempre la mujer."

It may appear that Ramírez fails to adequately describe the roles that she wishes women to fulfill. We are told that women should be authentic in thought and behavior. However, she does not describe this desired thought and behavior in direct and clear terms. It may have been socially unacceptable for Ramírez to openly appeal for the organization of women as women. Possible social mores notwithstanding, Ramírez tells women:

> la mujer vive siempre y este es el secreto de su dicha, vivir.
> Solo la acción es vida; sentir que se vive, es la mas hermosa sensación.

The key word in this statement is *acción*. When she speaks of action in her other political works she is usually exhorting Mexicanos and workers to organize as Mexicanos and as workers. Thus, when Ramírez remarks that "solo la acción es vida," she may be suggesting that women can achieve authenticity by participating in struggles for democratic rights.

In "La Página Blanca," Ramírez confronts rejection by the man/men she loves. This theme gives most of Ramírez's love poems a tone of sadness and loneliness, but never remorse. She tells us her favorite poem is an unwritten one symbolized by an empty, or white page, in her album of poems. It is the dearest and saddest of all because it affirms her undying love and his/their rejection.

The empty page symbolically represents:

"tu desden y cariño de mi alma"; true creativity, as it renders a continuous and unfolding process unburdened by the time-thought-space inherently associated with a written poem; an effort to submerge the reader in her world of rejection by describing a poem yet refusing to share it; and a metaphorical relationship between man/poet and Ramírez the women, on one level, and Ramírez the empty page, on the other.

CONCLUSION

This paper is an initial study of Sara Estela Ramírez and three of her representative works. Her participation in PLM activity is direct and noteworthy. Her intellectual contribution to the PLM logically extends to the Mexicano sociopolitical movement, principally through her writings. Her works legitimize these and other such movements by justifying the application of given moral and ethical considerations. As such, her works can be said to be contributions to contemporary efforts to create a more humane society.

Appendix

Alocución
(Leida por su autora en la velada
con que la Sociedad de Obreros Celebro
el 24 Aniversario de su Fundacion.)

Suplico al Sr. Presidente, a la respetable Sociedad de Obreros y a tan distinguido auditorio, se sirvan dispensar mi ineptitud. Invitada para tomar parte en esta fiesta, simpatica por mas de un motivo, y deseosa de cooperar al esfuerzo social con lo que mi pequeñez permite, vengo, ferviente admiradora del mutualismo, a llamar a los obreros, mis hermanos, y a decirles: luchadores, ¡adelante!

Para tan sencilla expresion no necesito elegancia de lenguaje, retorica, ni sabiduria alguna. Para llamar hermano al obrero, me basta tener corazon, y para decirle ¡adelante! me basta tener, como el, el alma henchida de anhelos de lucha.

Celebramos el vigesimo cuarto aniversario de la tan bien conocida cuanto respetable Sociedad de Obreros.

¡Vigesimo cuarto aniversario! ¡Cuanto dice esa fecha!

Veinticuatro años de noble lucha contra tantos y tantos germenes morbozos que aniquilan el esfuerzo de la agrupacion, que se disponen terribles y rastreros a devorar el mutualismo; veinticuatro años de ir matando egoísmo y ambiciones, de ir sugetando rebeldias y enlazando las manos sobre esas rebeldias caidas; veinticuatro años de ir enlazando las almas por un principio de humanidad, por un sentimiento de altruismo innato en el corazon, altruismo que nos permite partir de nuestro haber con el querido compañero, visitarlo en sus enfermedades, consolarlo en sus tristezas y darle la mano en toda amargura y en toda prueba, hasta despidirlo cuando llegue su turno de llamar a la eternidad.

Ese es el mutualismo. Noble mision en verdad, mision sublime y santa, mision de caridad que desconocen o han descuidado los pueblos; los pueblos, cuyo elemento obrero disperso, segregado, extraño entre si y . . . cuantas veces, triste es decirlo, mas que extraño sugeto a enemistades ruines, ese elemento obrero se esquiva en lugar de buscarse, se ofende en lugar de ayudarse, y no rechaza odiandose, en vez de abrazarse amandose; se rechaza sin mirar que su sangre y sus congojas van amasando juntas el pan amargo que los dos devoran; sin mirar que sus brazos son los que mantienen viva la industria de los pueblos, su riqueza y su engrandecimiento.

Cuantas veces tambien por apatia permanecen aislados los gremios obreros, por falta de ese espiritu vigorizador que da energias y paciencia para afrontar reveces y salvar escollos.

El mutualismo necesita vigor de lucha y firmeza de conviccion para avanzar en su obra unionista, necesita sacudir la apatia de las masas, encadenar con eslabones de abnegacion las pasiones que desgarran sus fueros; necesita corazones que digan: soy para ti, como quiero que seas para mi, el mutualismo necesita de nosotros los obreros, los humildes, los pequeños gladiadores de la idea, necesita que saquemos de entre nuestros egoísmos, algo inmenso, algo divino, que nos haga sociables, que nos haga noblemente humanos. Y no piense el obrero en su humildad, no piense en su insignificancia, no razone nulificandose y apartandose con desaliento del concierto social. ¿Que importa que sea un atomo, que importa?

Los atomos invisibles por su pequeñez son los unicos factores del universo.

Asi es el. El obrero es el brazo, el corazon del mundo.

Y es a el, luchador incansable y tenaz, a quien esta encomendado el porvenir de la humanidad.

Que vosotros, obreros queridos, parte integrante del progreso humano, celebreis aun, incontables aniversarios, y que con vuestro ejemplo enseñeis a las sociedades a quererse para ser mutualistas, y a unirse para ser fuertes.

From *El Democrata Fronterizo,* April 17, 1909, p. 1.

¡Surge!

(A la mujer)

¡Surge! Surge a la vida, a la actividad, a la belleza de vivir realmente; pero surge radiante y poderosa, bella de cualidades, esplendente de virtudes, fuerte de energias.

Tu, la reina del mundo, Diosa de la adoracion universal; tu, la soberana a quien se rinde vasallaje, no te encierres asi en tu templo de Diosa, ni en tu camarin de cortesana triunfadora.

Eso es indigno de ti, antes que Diosa y Reina, se madre, se mujer.

Una mujer que lo es verdaderamente, es mas que diosa y que reina. No te embriague el incienso en el altar, ni el aplauso en el escenario, hay algo mas noble y mas grande que todo eso.

Los dioses son arrojados de los templos; los reyes son echados de sus tronos, la mujer es siempre la mujer.

Los Dioses viven lo que sus creyentes quieren. Los reyes viven mientras no son destronados; la mujer vive siempre y este es el secreto de su dicha, vivir.

Solo la accion es vida; sentir que se vive, es las mas hermosa sensacion.

Surge, pues, a las bellezas de la vida; per surge asi, bella de cualidades, esplendente de virtudes, fuerte de energias.

From *La Cronica,* April 9, 1910, p. 3.

La Pagina Blanca

Tengo un album, sus paginas llenas
    Recorro seguido.
Porque gusto de ver las violetas
Que dejaron alli mis cariños.

Hay en el una pagina en blanco,
    Una sola . . . parace un olvido,
Una sola, en que leo y no acabo,
¡Leo mas que en las otras del libro!

Siempre, siempre que el libro recorro
    Miro todas las paginas llenas,
Y al mirarlas, ninguna a mis ojos
Es tan dulce y tan triste como ella.

¿Y tu sabes porque? Si, lo sabes.
    ¡Tu comprendes excelsos amores!
Ella fue para ti or para nadie;
¿No escribiste? . . . que nadie la toque.

Blanca esta; en su veste de armiño
    No pondra su violeta otro amigo,
No pondra su cancion otro bardo.

    ¡Blanca esta! Que poema mas bello
Su blancura intocable me guarda.
¡Con razon a mirar me detengo
Mas que a todas, la pagina blanca,
Mas que a todas, la estrofa querida,
    La nota callada . . .
Con razon cual ninguna la quiere,
Con razon cual ninguna me habla,
Esa pagina blanca en que leo
Tu desden y el cariño de mi alma!

From *El Democrata Fronterizo,* April 10, 1909, p. 2.

NOTES

1. For a view on the historical development of racial and class oppression of the Mexicano people, see: Tomas Almaguer, "Historical Notes on Chicano Oppression: The Dialectics of Racial and Class Domination in North America," *Aztlán: Chicano Journal of the Social Sciences and the Arts,* (Spring and Fall, 1974), pp. 27–54. Also consult: Juan Gómez-Quiñones, *Sembradores, Ricardo Flores Magón y El Partido Liberal Mexicano: A Eulogy and Critique* (Los Angeles: Chicano Studies Publications UCLA, 1977) pp. 31–32; and Américo Paredes, *With His Pistol In His Hands: A Border Ballad and Its Hero.* (Austin: University of Texas Press, 1973), pp. 7–32.

2. For readings in various aspects of South Texas history during the early 1900s, consult appropriate sections in the following books: Theodore R. Fehrenback and Joe B. Frantz, *Texas: A Bicentennial History* (New York: W.W. Norton and Co., Inc., 1976); Donald W. Meinig, *Imperial Texas: An Interpretative Essay in Cultural Sociology* (Austin: University of Texas Press, 1965); and Rupert Noval Richardson, *The Lone Star State* (New York: Prentice-Hall, Inc., 1947). Readings that are more pertinent to this section of the paper include: David Montejano, *Race, Labor Repression and Capitalist Agriculture: Notes From South Texas 1920-1930;* Working Paper Series No. 102 (Berkeley: Institute for the Study of Social Change, 1977); Paul S. Taylor, *An American Mexican Frontier: Nueces County Texas* (New York: Russell and Russell, 1971); Paul S. Taylor, *Mexican Labor in the United States: Dimmit County, Winter Garden District, South Texas,* University of California Publications in Economics, Vol. 6, No. 5 (New York: Arno Press, 1970); José Limon, "El Primer Congreso Mexicanista de 1911: A Precursor to Contemporary Chicanismo," *Aztlán: Chicano Journal of the Social Sciences and the Arts,* (Spring and Fall, 1974), pp. 85-117; and Emilio Zamora, "Chicano Socialist Labor Activity in Texas, 1900-1920," *Aztlán: Chicano Journal of the Social Sciences and the Arts* (Summer 1975), pp. 221-236.

3. Federal Labor Union Local No. 11,953 was organized for the expressed purpose of improving wages and working conditions for Mexican industrial workers of Laredo. Its socialist leadership and newspaper made urgent appeals for all workers to help form a citywide labor federation. Besides railroad and mine workers, it organized barbers, electricians, bricklayers, seamstresses, cigar workers, butchers, store clerks, water carriers, cooks, common laborers, laundresses, and female dancers. Although the union disbanded in 1907, its successful organizing activity denotes a high class-consciousness among workers in Laredo. Zamora, "Chicano Socialist Labor Activity in Texas 1900-1920," op. cit., pp. 221-236.

4. For PLM related activity in the Mexicano Community of South Texas: Juan Gómez-Quiñones, *Sembradores.* Also, consult the following for added information on the Mexicano movement of the early 1900s in Texas: Gómez-Quiñones, "The First Steps: Chicano Labor Conflict and Organizing, 1900-1920," *Aztlán,* (Spring, 1972), pp. 13-49; Limon, "El Primer Congreso Mexicanista," op. cit., pp. 85-117; Zamora, "Chicano Socialist Labor Activity," op. cit., pp. 221-236.

5. The statewide organization was called La Liga Mexicanista. Although La Liga was short-lived, its establishment remains a significant development in the Mexican movement. It is the earliest recorded organizing effort of its kind for South Texas during the twentieth century.

6. Gómez-Quiñones, *Sembradores,* pp. 6-7. According to Professor Gómez-Quiñones, the PLM appealed to Mexican migrants and Chicano natives in three ways. "It rejected the present order and offered a different and better world as a hope and possibility. Secondly, it supplied a coherent set of secular beliefs and values for denying the legitimacy of the existing order and morally justifying its overthrow. Thirdly, PLM clarified, relatively, the means for achieving the overthrow: propaganda plus organization culminating in overt violence against the state; and though somewhat vaguely, PLM put forth a proposition for administering the new order: fraternal communal cooperation."

7. Ibid., pp. 27-29

8. Ibid., p. 97

9. Ibid.

10. Gómez-Quiñones, *Sembradores.* When Ramírez moved to San Antonio to publish *La Corregidora,* PLM supporters were told to address their mail to another woman by the name of Antonia Mendes. Draft of a letter dated March 2, 1904, Laredo Texas, in Asunto Magón, Archivo, Secretario de Relaciones Exteriores, México D.F.

11. Correspondence between Magón and PLM sympathizers, deposited in an archival collection in Mexico City, shows that Ramírez was the single most prolific letter writer. Asunto Flores Magón, Archivo, Secretaria de Relaciones Exteriores, Mexico, D.F.

12. Sara Estela Ramírez (San Antonio Texas) to Ricardo Flores Magón (Laredo Texas), March 9, 1904. Quoted from excerpts that appear in James D. Cockroft, *Intellectual Precursors of the Mexican Revolution* (Austin: Von Boeckmann-Jones, 1968), p. 118-119.

13. Unless otherwise noted, all biographical data has been taken from the following sources: "Sara Estela Ramírez," *El Demócrata Fronterizo,* August 27, 1910, p. 1; "La Musa Texana Esta De Duelo; Sara Estela Ramírez, La Mimada de Las Musas, Ha Muerto," "A La Memoria De Mi Inolvidable Amiga, Sara Estela Ramírez," *La Crónica,* September 3, 1910, p. 5; and Clemente Idar, "Oracion Funebre: Pronunciado Por Su Autor Ante El Cadaver de La Señorita Sara Estela Ramírez Al Ser Depositado En La Tumba," *La Crónica,* September 3, 1910, p. 5.

14. Jovita Idar, *La Crónica,* September 3, 1910.

15. "Alocución," Leida por su Autora en la Velada con que la Sociedad de Obreros Celebro el 24 Aniversario de Su Fundacion, *El Demócrata Fronterizo,* April 17, 1909, p. 1; "¡Surge!", *La Crónica,* April 9, 1910, p. 3; "La Pagina Blanca," *El Demócrata Fronterizo,* April 10, 1909, p. 2.

LA COSTURA EN LOS ANGELES, 1933-1939: THE ILGWU AND THE POLITICS OF DOMINATION

Douglas Monroy

In the lives of many Mexicanas, employment in la costura, the garment trade, figures prominantly, as does the International Ladies' Garment Workers' Union. The valiant and successful effort to organize Farah in Texas was one of many episodes in the saga of Mexicana organization in the garment industry. Therefore the problems associated with the ILGWU and the AFL—bureaucratic control, self-interested leadership, ethnocentrism—are not new to Mexicanas. In fact, the problematic relationship between the ILGWU and Mexicanas had emerged as early as the 1930s. The following essay describes the situation which Mexicanas in Los Angeles confronted in la costura during the Depression, the enthusiastic union organization drives, and the ideology and political philosophy of the ILGWU as related to the Mexicana rank and file. From this analysis we see some negative side effects of successful union organizing. Often another layer of authority, the union leadership, rarely Mexicano or female, burdened Mexicanas. In this case, while making crucial gains in wages and hours, the union did not significantly increase the power and control which the rank and file in la costura exercised over their work lives.

LA COSTURA Y LOS ANGELES

Competitive and service industries have overabounded in Los Angeles economic history. Low profit rates relative to the monopoly sector, and the rugged competition and high degree of turnover that the low profit rates produce, make work in these industries undesirable. Low pay, underemployment, seasonal work, and bad working conditions characterize such competitive sector industries as clothing and accessories, restaurants, service stations, and the laundry trade. Since these labor intensive enterprises require little capital investment, they proliferate rapidly. Markets tend to be local, unstable, and seasonal, yielding little opportunity or incentive to stabilize production and employment. Inability to find full-time, well paid work in the monopolistic or state sectors of the economy forces people to accept employment in the competitive sector on virtually any terms.[1]

In such industries as garment, restaurant, service, and smaller agricultural enterprises,

Douglas Monroy is an instructor in the History Department at the Colorado College, Colorado Springs, Colorado.

Professor Juan Gómez-Quiñones and Professor John Laslett nurtured and criticized this work in a previous form. The Colorado College extended funds for the completion of this manuscript, and Mary Friedrichs provided editorial assistance. Their help is acknowledged and appreciated.

the capitalist is unable to determine prices. An increase in the costs of production must be absorbed by the capitalist unless the market allows him or her a price increase. If the capitalist in the competitive sector can drive his or her costs below the competitive market price, the profits and power within the industry increase. This process provides the primary incentive for employers in the competitive sector to pay the lowest possible wages, spend as little as possible on maintaining decent work conditions, and neutralize any collective efforts by workers to alter these work conditions. Furthermore, as the entire economy becomes increasingly concentrated, monopoly pricing is able to appropriate an increasingly larger share of the spending power of consumers. Having to spend more money for the same amount of goods from the monopolized sector, such as for petroleum products, consumers have less to spend in the competitive sector, such as for clothing, thereby intensifying the already ruthless competition.[2] In addition to the employers' desire to escape the unions, this relationship between the monopoly and competitive sectors of the economy has produced the modern-day scourge of garment industry workers, the runaway shop.

These aspects of the competitive sector of the economy produced the working conditions for the many Mexicanos employed in the women's clothing, restaurants, laundries, and food related industries. Only about 2,000 worked in Los Angeles' 150 dress factories at the nadir of the Depression. However, by 1939 Los Angeles had 634 dress factories employing about 15,890 workers of which 75 percent were Mexican women and girls. "Garment factory owners," an International Ladies' Garment Workers' Union organizer claimed, "regarded their employees as casual workers, in the same class as migrants who harvested fruit and vegetable products." Maria Flores, a garment worker of the 1930s, described one way that garment factory owners extorted the maximum from their workers for the minimum pay:

> I come in the morning, punch my card, work for an hour, punch the card again. I wait for two hours, get another bundle, punch card, finish bundle, punch card again. Then I wait some more the whole day that way.[3]

Employers had other ways to achieve the most from their workers. They exploited the language barrier, operated the vicious kick-back system whereby workers gave back some of their wages, and kept a high turnover of workers. Frequently they paid below the minimum wage.[4]

Even after the establishment of the union by the strikes of the 1930s, the $20.00 per week pay of women's clothing workers was the lowest earned in the state except for hotel and restaurant workers. Before that, wages averaged between $13.00 and $17.00 per week when the state minimum wage was $18.90 per week in 1935. In the early years of the Depression when the minimum wage was $16.00 per week, the unregulated employers could chisel weekly wages to less than $5.00 per week by the methods described above.[5]

THE AFL AND THE ORGANIZATION OF MEXICANOS

Actual indifference, despite lip-service support for strikes, summarized AFL attitude toward Mexicano workers in Los Angeles during the Depression. The Los Angeles AFL verbally supported the Mexicano agricultural strikes in all of California. In April 1934, the local AFL's newspaper, *The Citizen,* published a letter by the Secretary General of the Confederación de Uniones de Campesinos y Obreros Mexicanos, Guillermo Velarde, requesting support for a local strike. Similarly, the local AFL verbally supported strikes in the Imperial Valley, Salinas, Orange County, and elsewhere, and even urged financial aid. There is no evidence, however, of actual material support. Local AFL Chief Buzzell, was said to have worked out plans "to boycott 'hot' Salinas lettuce, but it never appears that he did." In 1927 Los Angeles street paver Luis Tenorio summed up the actual practice of the local AFL craft unions:

> I don't belong to any union because they don't want to admit the Mexicans. Once the workers in asphalt, all Mexicans, organized a union, but they wouldn't admit us into the Asphalter's Union of the American Federation of Labor because they said that these same Mexicans were going to take their jobs away from them by accepting lower wages. So our union was broken up.[6]

With good reason, Mexicanos did not hold the AFL in very high esteem.

The local AFL operated under a pluralist ideology. They acted in their own homogeneous and particular interests as skilled workers trying to secure power and benefits. They did this by acting in league with other groups rather than by promoting a broader, ongoing policy that might tie or restrict the organization to a program such as welfarism or the government. The AFL feared the effect which any such compulsion might have on the federation's allegedly unending effort to improve its members' standard of living. As Samuel Gompers said:

> ... the workers, as human beings, will never stop in any effort, nor stop at any point in the effort to secure greater improvements in their condition, a better life in all its phases. And wherever that may lead, whatever that may be, so far in my time and my age I decline to permit my mind or my activities to be labeled by any particularism.[7]

The AFL, nationally and locally, operated on a day to day and practical course opposed to compulsion or paternalism by the state.

This policy meant that the AFL did what they perceived correct for the moment. The campaign for the union label, not the strike, placed first on the local AFL's list of strategies for establishing unionism in the city. They supported the efforts to free Mooney and Billings; they supported Upton Sinclair for governor in 1934. The AFL in Los Angeles also supported conservative Sheriff Daniel C. Murphy against liberal Culbert Olson for governor in 1938 (because the CIO supported Olson) and thrilled over the "drubbing" given Communists William Francis Dunne and Louis Weinstock before the Senate Judiciary for their support of the Black Bill which would have given labor the thirty hour week.[8] They also paid no substantive attention to Mexicano workers.

Yet the AFL's ILGWU organized Mexicanos in la costura. They could do so because they organized industrially and because the organizational drive emanated from New York, not Los Angeles. David Dubinsky, president of the ILGWU, assigned the Jewish labor leader Rose Pesotta to organize Los Angeles and Israel Feinberg to lead and coordinate the efforts on the West Coast.[9]

THE ILGWU

In its stronghold of New York, the ILGWU functioned beyond merely the economic aspect of its members' lives. The leadership consistently asserted how "the union must provide information and guidance in matters of health, social security, family, housing, and political matters." In New York the union became a Jewish cultural institution as well as an economic organization. This fact, while far from hindering efforts on the wages and hours front, actually served to reinforce the solidarity of the largely Jewish work force in the garment industry prior to World War II.[10]

Nationally, the ILGWU had achieved a degree of success in stabilizing employment and working conditions in the volatile and competitive women's wear industry. Los Angeles was the exception, however. The ILGWU had achieved this stability by accepting joint responsibility with management for production and for the welfare of the industry. The ILGWU, a nominally socialist organization, epitomized the corporate ideology of North American labor, in which labor leaders have attempted not to change, but to integrate labor into American society. This conception follows from the view of society by both labor and business leaders "as composed of various functional economic groups caused by the division of labor (in which) workers are defined as producers rather than as a social class." The goal of such a society was to create a community of interest between capital and labor within one unified corporate body.[11] The political implications of such a strategy on the part of labor leaders are, of course, myriad. The AFL aped general North American society by excluding minority groups and women.

The policies and actions of the AFL nationally and in Los Angeles resulted in frequently working hand in glove with employers against the interests of the rank and file.[12] "There can be no security in an insecure industry," said the general manager of the ILGWU's joint board of the dressmakers' union. "It is therefore our duty, in the interests of the workers we represent, to concern ourselves with every phase of our industry and to do everything in our power to put it on a sound and solid basis." The leaders of the 1933 general strike of Los Angeles garment workers reflected this philosophy:

We want union recognition so that the union can police the industry and see that evaders are made to come to terms and to see that everyone abides by the (NRA) code. . . . That's the all-important reason for this strike.

The ILGWU sought more control over their workers to make work more efficient, and therefore more profitable, to workers and capitalists both. "In very few factories," this general manager continued, "is there any sort of supervisory assistance. No effort is made to guide the workers in the one best method of making any particular style."[13] To remedy these defects the ILGWU consciously sought cooperation with management. Los Angeles garment factory owners would be forced to accept this joint responsibility which would produce stability, higher wages, and descipline, for Los Angeles garment workers.

HUELGA EN LA COSTURA

To confront the miserable and unscrupulous conditions under which Mexicanos labored in the garment industry, the somewhat revitalized ILGWU went to work. Before the arrival of Pesotta in September 1933, virtually no organization existed in the dress shops. The withdrawal of the Communists from the old Local No. 65 and formation of their Trade Union Unity League dual union, the Needle Trades Industrial Union in 1929; the quick discharge of anyone suspected of union activity; and the difficulty of communication between the Mexicana (the majority), Italian, Russian, and Anglo women, conspired to produce an inneffectual union local. The ILGWU initiated a propaganda drive which included meetings, radio talks, and twice weekly bulletins in Spanish and English. The drive attracted hundreds of workers to the union and the international chartered a new Local No. 96 which enrolled over a thousand workers in a short time.[14]

On August 27, 1933, Los Angeles dressmakers, fifteen hundred strong, met in Walker's Orange Grove Theatre and voted unanimously for a general strike if employers refused the demands drawn up by the local. The leadership received full power to act on the dressmakers' behalf. The demands included union recognition, the thirty-five hour work week, a guaranteed minimum wage, a shop chairman and price committee elected by each shop, elimination of homework, and a grievance procedure.[15]

Employers strengthened their organization as well. The Associated Apparel Manufacturers of Los Angeles, affiliated with the parent open shop organization, the Merchants and Manufacturers, not only urged its members to stand firm or else "be forced to strictly adhere to the minimum wage laws of California" and even lose their open shop, but they also bound their members (in at least the garment and cabinet and fixture industries) not to deal with unions or provide raises. The Merchants and Manufacturers provided valuable anti-strike and informational services, made the signing of such a contract a condition of membership, and promised fines for weak-kneed member employers.[16]

The local National Recovery Administration office stepped into the matter and proposed a settlement in line with the rest of the United States. This action contented the ILGWU leadership which was "satisfied with the NRA provisions" and "agreed that there will be no strike in the garment trade." Union recognition remained the only bone of contention between the ILGWU and the employers.[17] As the ILGWU soon discovered, the NRA functioned only to cooperate with employers to buy more time.

Employers then began discharging workers for union activity. Such activity steadily mounted with Mexicanas leading the swelling ranks of Local No. 96. Factory owners locked out several shops entirely and by October 8, the union had a strike on its hands. Sanctioned by the AFL Central Labor Council, Local No. 96 now called for a general dressmakers' strike on October 12.[18]

The strike call brought an immediate response from the largely Mexicana work force. The two to three thousand strikers' ranks held firm despite many arrests. The militant strikers sang and chanted on the picket lines in front of the dressmaking shops. Parades of unionists and supporters, huge quantities of food, and union label propaganda all assisted in the stirring effort. The massive numbers which the union marshalled on its picket lines made an employer injunction against picketing ineffectual.

Within two weeks, the local NRA office proposed an arbitration of the strike issues. The ILGWU, in accord with its corporate ideology of cooperation, quickly accepted. The employers, however, did not. The "impartial" board granted little: at best there was technical recognition of the union, NRA minimum wages, and an equal distribution of work in slack periods. Somehow the membership ratified the agreement by a five to one majority.[19]

The Communists, who through the dual Needle Trades Workers' Industrial Union became active in the strike, vociferously denounced what they called a sell-out on the part of the ILGWU, first for submitting to arbitration, and then for accepting the settlement. The strident nature of their hyperbole makes difficult the task of sorting out the situation. Realistically one doubts if "the Communist element," as the ILGWU officially charged, "continued giving the employers all the aid and comfort they were capable of," or if the strike was lost through "the treacherous class collaboration politics of the AFL and the 'Socialist' misleaders," as the Communists asserted.[20]

The Reds promised, mostly to themselves, that the growing militance of the strikers would turn rank and file support away from "the officials of the international, the reactionary Feinberg and . . . Rose Pesotta, Anarchist" and to their own NTWIU. The Communists, probably correctly, told the garment workers, "your officials have handed you over to the mercy of an arbitration board, to the mercy of so-called impartial citizens! . . . Arbitration never gave anything to the workers. Struggle on the picket lines did!"[21] However correct they may have been, Communists got nowhere in the needle trades either nationally or locally.

While most of the ILGWU leadership found the decision of the arbitration board less than satisfactory, they did realize that the strike efforts of October 1933, laid the foundation for a dressmakers' union in Los Angeles. In 1934 Local No. 96 continued to gain strength in individual shops. The following year several quick strikes or mere work stoppages strengthened the union and technically established the closed shop.[22]

By 1936 the ILGWU established itself firmly as the representative of the dressmaking industry's largely Mexicana workers. On August 5 3,000 workers engaged in another general strike with accompanying picketing and arrests. Luckily the ILGWU, led by Feinberg, signed agreements for 2,650 workers in fifty-six firms achieving a weekly minimum wage of twenty-eight dollars for women and thirty-five dollars for men on a three-year contract. Though the ILGWU

was still threatened by migrant workers from the South and Midwest, the general volatility of the garment industry, and the continuing resistance of the intensely competitive factory owners, it had nearly managed to establish a closed shop. The union had a membership of about 3,000 in 1937 after becoming a CIO union in the same year.[23] (It rejoined the AFL in 1940.)

Why did the ILGWU succeed in organizing dress factories? During the 1933 strike the ILGWU organizer, Rose Pesotta, noted that "the Mexican girls and women . . . acted almost like seasoned unionists," something that should not surprise one with any knowledge of Mexicana history. Many have noted how labor militancy infused the Mexicanos of Los Angeles. Such militancy has been an integral part of the culture. Frank López, organizer for the United Furniture Workers (CIO), United Cannery, Agricultural, Packinghouse and Allied Workers of America (CIO), who also briefly organized for the ILGWU, noted a similar militance from the Mexicana women. López found the women "essentially much more vocal, militant and aggressive" than the men, as well as "highly indignant of any abuses or demeaning attitudes toward them" within the union. Women in factories dealt speedily and definitely with a stool pigeon or "toady" to the boss. One of their favorite weapons was the "silent treatment."[24]

Garment workers dealt less liberally with police and scabs. The 1933 strike saw many scuffles between the striking dressmakers and the odious "Red Squad" of police captain Red Hynes. In the strike of August 1936, ILGWU members beat up two women scabs and a "Black Jack" wielding police lieutenant who attacked their picket line.[25] While family obligations may have kept women from asserting a more dominant role in their unions, the gender of these particular unionists did not decrease their militance and solidarity. Actually, once moved to action, the Mexican women appeared more militant than their men. Their strength and solidarity won the strikes. This greater militance, and their additional labor and responsibility in the home, makes the role of Mexicana workers a more intricate study.

Pesotta and the ILGWU leadership in Los Angeles exhibited a more enlightened attitude toward Mexicanos and their culture than the rest of the AFL and the ILGWU. In Texas, for example, as late as 1956 the ILGWU attempted to organize Mexicanos without the benefit of Spanish speaking leadership or staff. "We get them," explained Pesotta, "because we are the only 'Americanos' who take them in as equals."[26]

Pesotta did much to reach the Mexicano community. During the 1933 strike the ILGWU did short broadcasts at 7:00 p.m. on a Mexican cultural society's radio program until it was shut down after a few days. Then the Mexicana women in the union facilitated the purchase of time on a Tijuana station, "El Eco de México," so that at 7:00 a.m. each morning "Spanish speaking workers all over Los Angeles learned of the progress of our strike before starting to work each morning." The leadership also produced a four-page, semi-weekly newspaper, *The Organizer,* in Spanish and English. The "Spanish Branch" of the ILGWU had Halloween parties for niños, adult parties featuring professional Mexican singers, and two-for-twenty-five-cents admission parties "to have members of all unions, regardless of their classification, come and make friends with the Spanish speaking members." Photographs of Labor Day parades show those on the ILGWU's Spanish Branch float regaled in Mexican costumes.[27]

However, in other aspects, the Jewish leadership of the ILGWU did less well. Among those officers elected to the board of Local No. 96, Mexicanos only numbered six out of nineteen, and held none of the important positions.[28] Even with the efforts of this union leadership, Mexicanas, who amounted to about three-fourths of the membership, apparently did not fully integrate into the workings of the union.

¿CUÁNTO VALE?

Consistent with its corporate ideology, the ILGWU leadership was not so much interested in assisting Mexicana workers in establishing their own strength in the dress factories, as it was interested in establishing its own strength in the garment industry. This does not mean that the ILGWU did not care to organize garment workers into its ranks or to gain benefits for its members. The ILGWU, and any other union interested in stabilizing so competitive and fragmented an industry as the various garment trades, needed a high level of organization to give it weight in dealing with employers and to impose consistent wage and price agreements. By 1941, the ILGWU could claim: "There

is really nothing new in our concern for the welfare of the industry. What is new is that we are in a position to do something about it." The union leadership sought to establish this ideology in the 1933 strike: "We will police the industry and force NRA members to live up to the code." It appears that the ILGWU ultimately desired sufficient power to have a hand in the running of the garment industry. While this may sound like a good thing for the dressmakers, it really amounted to little control and power in the work place. Power and control went only to the ILGWU leadership who wanted more order and discipline from both employers and employees in the garment industry.[29]

Like most unions, even industrial ones, the ILGWU remained a union run from the top down. The union remained in the hands of the cutters, such as its president, David Dubinsky, and other highly paid garment workers from the "craft" categories of the industry.[30] The leadership in Los Angeles, most of which was from New York, managed and directed the organizational campaign and the strikes. The ILGWU and the Amalgamated Clothing Workers under Sidney Hillman, sought power within the garment industry for themselves and their corporate ideology, which they wished to establish through industry government cohesion.[31]

This left the ILGWU's rank and file in a morass. Except for the Communists, there appears to have been no opposition to this ideology. One important sector of Mexicano political leadership, the consul Ricardo Hill, consistent with the rigorous anti-communism which he demonstrated in the famous El Monte strike of 1933, sanctioned the ILGWU leadership, recommended which Spanish speaking organizer be hired, and exhorted the Mexicano workers of the ILGWU to accept their leadership.[32]

The union delivered to those working in la costura in Los Angeles better wages and greater stability of work in the economically turbulent 1930s. The union also delivered greater control and discipline over them as well. Paternalistically, the ILGWU maintained that "the Mexican dressmakers were normal humans, who simply needed honest and intelligent guidance."[33] They allegedly needed, and got, "honest and intelligent guidance" from the top, from the personally successful and elite-minded ILGWU leadership, who sought, above all else, to integrate themselves into the North American political and economic power structure. No one can question the economic gains which ILGWU organization brought to unskilled Mexicana dressmakers; one can, however, question the long-term benefit of such organization.

NOTES

1. James O'Connor, *The Fiscal Crisis of the State* (New York: St. Martin's Press, 1973), pp. 13–15.
2. This discussion extends the concepts contained in Paul M. Sweezy, *The Theory of Capitalist Development: Principles of Marxian Political Economy* (New York: Monthly Review Press, 1968), pp. 274–277; James O'Connor, *The Fiscal Crisis of the State*, pp. 13–16.
3. International Ladies' Garment Workers' Union, *Report and Proceedings of the Twenty-Fifth Convention of the Ladies' Garment Workers' Union, 1944* (New York: 1944), p. 122; Rose Pesotta, *Bread Upon the Waters* (New York: Dodd, Mead & Co., 1945), p. 20, 23.
4. Pesotta, *Bread Upon the Waters*, pp. 20–23; *Western Worker*, 28 February 1935.
5. State of California, Unemployment Reserves Commission, James L. Mathews, Chairman, *A Study of Seasonal Employment in California* (Sacramento: 1939), p. 69; *Western Worker*, 28 February 1935; Pesotta, *Bread Upon the Waters*, p. 40.
6. Manuel Gamio, *The Mexican Immigrant, His Life Story* (Chicago: University of Chicago Press, 1931), p. 127; *Los Angeles Citizen*, 1 September 1933.
7. Testimony of Samuel Gompers, President of the American Federation of Labor, cross-examined by Morris Hillquit, Socialist Party Leader, May 22, 1914. U.S. Congress, Senate, *Final Report and Testimony Submitted to Congress by the Commission on Industrial Relations*, 64th Congress, 1st Session, Senate Doc. 415 (Washington: 1916), pp. 1526–1529, reprinted in Leon Litwack, *The American Labor Movement* (Englewood Cliffs, New Jersey: Prentice Hall, 1962), p. 39.
8. *Los Angeles Citizen*, 27 May 1935, 21 May 1937, 2 November 1934, 20 January 1933; Louis B. Perry and Richard S. Perry, *A History of the Los Angeles Labor Movement, 1911–1941* (Los Angeles: University of California Press, 1963), p. 241.
9. ILGWU, *Report and Proceedings of the Twenty-Second Convention of the International Ladies' Garment Workers' Union* (New York: 1934), p. 107; *Report and Proceedings of the Twenty-Third Convention of the International Ladies' Garment Workers' Union* (New York: 1937), p. 100.
10. Mark Starr (Educational Director of the ILGWU), "Role of Union Organization," in William Foote Whyte, ed., *Industry and Society* (New York: Viking Press, 1946), p. 152. See Lewis Lorwin, *The Women's Garment Workers: A History of the International Ladies' Garment Workers' Union* (New York: Huebsch, 1924).
11. Ronald Radosh, "The Corporate Ideology of American Labor Leaders from Gompers to Hillman," in James Weinstein and David M. Eakins, eds., *For a New America, Essays in History and Politics from Studies on the Left, 1959–1967* (New York: Vintage, 1970), p. 126, 127.
12. Philip S. Foner, *History of the Labor Movement in the United States, The Policies and Practices of the American Federation of Labor 1900–1909* (New York: International Publishers, 1964), *Volume 3*, pp. 78–110 provides some of the most striking examples of the corporate ideology at work against the workers.
13. Julius Hochman, *Industry Planning Through Collective Bargaining, A Program for Modernizing the New York Dress Industry as Presented in Conference with Employers on Behalf of the Joint Board of the Dressmakers' Union* (New York: 1941), p. 8, 19; *Los Angeles Illustrated Daily News*, 14 October 1933.
14. Pesotta, *Bread Upon the Waters*, pp. 19–33; Perry and Perry, *A History of the Los Angeles Labor Movement*, p. 251; *Report and Proceedings of the Twenty-Second Convention of the International Ladies' Garment Workers' Union*, p. 107.
15. Pesotta, *Bread Upon the Waters*, pp. 29–31.
16. Quote is from a bulletin from the Associated Apparel Manufacturers of Los Angeles reprinted in Pesotta, *Bread Upon the Waters*, pp. 30–31; Congress of Industrial Organizations, Industrial Union Council, Los Angeles, *Unions Mean Higher Wages: The Story of the LaFollette Committee Hearings in Los Angeles* (Los Angeles: 1940), p. 20.
17. *Los Angeles Illustrated Daily News*, 9 October 1933.
18. *Report and Proceedings of the Twenty-Second Convention of the International Ladies' Garment Workers' Union*, pp. 107–108; Pesotta, *Bread Upon the Waters*, p. 34.
19. *Report and Proceedings of the Twenty-Second Convention of the International Ladies' Garment Workers' Union*, p. 108; Pesotta, *Bread Upon the Waters*, pp. 34–58; *Los Angeles Illustrated Daily News*, 6 November 1933.
20. *Report and Proceedings of the Twenty-Second Convention of the International Ladies' Garment Workers' Union*, p. 108; *Western Worker*, 11 December 1933.
21. *Western Worker*, 30 October 1933 and 11 December 1933; a Communist leaflet reprinted in Pesotta, *Bread Upon the Waters*, pp. 58–59.
22. U.S. Department of Labor, Bureau of Labor Statistics, "Collective Agreements in the Ladies' Garment Industry," *Monthly Labor Review*, Vol. 41, No. 5 (November, 1935), p. 1301; *Los Angeles Citizen*, 29 July 1935; *Report and Proceedings of the Twenty-Third Convention of the International Ladies' Garment Workers' Union*, p. 100.
23. *Los Angeles Citizen*, 14 August 1936; Los Angeles Police Department, Office of Intelligence Bureau memo of September 30, 1937 in U.S. Congress, Senate Subcommittee of the Committee on Education and Labor, *Violations of Free Speech and the Rights of Labor*, 76th Congress, 1940, pt. 64, p. 23614.
24. Pesotta, *Bread Upon the Waters*, p. 40. For Mexicano labor militancy see Rodolfo Acuña, *Occupied America: The Chicano's Struggle Toward Liberation* (San Francisco: The Canfield Press, 1972), Luis Leobardo Arroyo, "Chicano Participation in Organized Labor: The CIO in Los Angeles, 1938–1950. An Extended Research Note," in *Aztlán*, Vol. 6, No. 2 (Summer, 1975), pp. 277–304, Juan Gómez-Quiñones, "The First Steps: Chicano Labor Conflict and Organizing 1900–1920," in *Aztlán*, Vol. 3, No. 1 (Spring, 1972), pp. 13–49, and Carey McWilliams, *North from Mexico: The Spanish Speaking*

People of the United States (New York: Greenwood Press, 1969). Interview with Frank López.

25. *Los Angeles Illustrated Daily News,* 21 October and 26 October 1933; *Western Worker,* 13 August 1936.

26. George N. Green, "ILGWU in Texas, 1930–1970," *Journal of Mexican-American History,* Vol. 1, No. 2 (Spring, 1971), p. 146; Pesotta, *Bread Upon the Waters,* p. 32.

27. Pesotta, *Bread Upon the Waters,* pp. 24–25, 43; *Los Angeles Citizen,* 25 October 1935 and 22 May 1936; also photographs in my possession.

28. Pesotta, *Bread Upon the Waters,* pp. 60–61.

29. Hochman, *Industry Planning,* p. 8, 19; *Los Angeles Illustrated Daily News,* 24 October 1933.

30. Stanley Aronowitz, *False Promises: The Shaping of American Working Class Consciousness* (New York: McGraw Hill, 1973), p. 173.

31. See Len DeCaux's comments on Sidney Hillman in *Labor Radical: From the Wobblies to the CIO, A Personal History* (Boston: Beacon Press, 1971), pp. 328–344.

32. *Los Angeles Citizen,* 30 March 1936.

33. Pesotta, *Bread Upon the Waters,* pp. 21–22.

PART FIVE

PROFILES

I'M TALKING FOR JUSTICE

Maria Moreno

I am Maria Moreno, forty years old, mother of twelve children. Born in Karnes City, Texas. Raised in Corpus Christi. Since 1928 I start working in agricultural work. I been a worker all my life. I know how to handle a man's job like a man and I'm not ashamed to say it. I'm American citizen, and I'm talking for justice. I'm asking for justice. Not only for me or for my family, but all the migrant workers. We been suffering for so long. Waiting and hoping, but it seems like that our hope been lost. I guess we got the right to do it. I guess we got the right because we are human beings as everybody.

For so many long years ago our children been suffering. I'm going to tell a little of my life with my own children. My first child was born, had no doctor. Was born alone, me and my husband.

Maria Moreno was an organizer for the Agricultural Workers' Organizing Committee, (AFL-CIO) between 1960 and 1962, in the Fresno area. She was one of four delegates elected at a farm workers' conference to drive 3,000 miles to the AFL-CIO convention in Miami Beach, Florida. Although Mrs. Moreno has had only six months formal schooling, she is a forceful speaker in both English and Spanish, and has testified at a number of public hearings.

The following talk was delivered by her at a meeting in Berkeley to raise funds for the lettuce workers of Imperial County who, in January 1961, were striking for $1.25 an hour. Her talk is provided here unedited as it appeared in *Regeneración*. Last year the family left California and Maria went back to work in the fields.

And I didn't know that a woman supposed to go to the doctor. Second child born, me and my husband alone. The third one born. Same thing.

We were working in Texas. Picking cotton, chopping cotton. 1932 we're picking cotton, twenty-five cents a hundred. We're chopping cotton, ten cents a row. And have to support the children who in those days did never know what shoes were on their feet. Our children didn't know that they have to drink milk every day. Our children drink milk once a week. Our children eat meat once a week. Why? We can't afford it. That is the reason we are working, trying to get the agricultural workers organized.

I guess we got rights. I guess we been suffering so much. It is time to ask for justice. We're demanding $1.25, which is, I think, not very much for a grower to give us. We're asking, we're waiting and we're hoping for get this $1.25.

1940, we came to California. Waiting and hoping to find a better living, a better living condition for ourselves and for our family. The braceros came in. We had to move on from the Imperial Valley. We hit Salinas. Here come the braceros. Well, we're tickled anyway when we work a little. We can earn a little money. We can feed our children. Half eat. Don't you think that our children [should have] their stomachs full of food like the rest of you people, the rest of you people that have a union or a better decent wage than we got. The road is our home. The ground is our table.

I've got a twenty-three-year-old son. When he was nineteen years old he was blind because he was without eat. 1958 it start raining so hard we can't earn very much money. The little money that we earn. It start raining and raining. And kept on raining a month. We couldn't go to work. All our food was gone. All our money was gone. No hope held.

One day I decided to go to the welfare and ask for something to eat. They refused to help out. Some people think that the welfare help everybody, but they help them when they want to and when they like. If they help them the food they give we have to work for. They don't give it to us. We have to work and pay for it.

I went to the welfare and they refused to help me. We already had when I went to the welfare no hope and no place to get money or food or anything, so I went to the welfare. We had three weeks without eating more than once a day. Three weeks. I had my baby, three month. I was feeding him water and sugar. The days sped on.

The investigator came home and I told her that she might as well come in the home and search and see what she can find. Anyhow, she did it, and she was satisfied. There was not a thing to eat in that place. Said, "Mrs. Moreno, if you don't get the food for Thursday, you're not going to get anything."

Three days passed by three weeks which we were eating once a day. Three days, my son got blind. He got so weak, he lost all his strength. He was blind for three days. The day that he was blind, my heart was broken in pieces. When I see a strong American. I see how richest America will live. And the real miserable life that we're living. I'm not ashamed to say this in front of nobody because it's truth.

I've got nothing to do. Nowhere to go. All my hopes were lost. Went, called the police and brought them home. Said, "I want you to look at my son. He is real blind." He got surprised. Said, "What happened?" Said, "He lost his strength. He went blind."

We were leading him by his hand. Nineteen year old boy. Just imagine what a mother has to pass by. How you think I feel, my son blind only because we got nothing to eat while some other tables are full and wasting food? The days pass on, then the door was opened.

Said, "Mrs. Moreno, we didn't know that you really need the food." They did know because I went and knock the doors but got no answer because the agricultural workers been ignored, been forgotten for so many long years.

People been forgotten. They don't care about us. Our home is under the tree. That's the way that we have been treated. We never screamed. We never had a word until now. Like I said, I'm mother of twelve children and I'm working for discovering the things that been hiding for so long—that people must know what we been suffering, what we been through.

People think that because somebody else have something to eat, they think that the whole world have some. But, people, I want you to understand that my family been suffering greatest mockery in the world that I ever seen. When every flame goes out, when you hear no fry pan noise at the stove. Potatoes and beans are gone. The only hope we have is God. We call for Him because we been calling to the people. They don't hear. They don't care. We have an old piano that we bought for $25 with a lot of sacrifice. We get together at that piano and we rejoice and we feel happy.

But the thing that really hurts me is this: that we are living in a rich America, that the people been sending food, the clothing overseas. And then forgotten us. That we are citizens, and we're living in America. That's what really hurts me, but like I said, I hope that you people help us do something for this situation. You won't have to go very far. You travel a little up here to Mendota. Woodlake. Visalia. Firebaugh. Huron. All places around here. You can find out. People sleeping on the floor for so long.

This is the way the agricultural worker lives. This is the way that we have been treated. This is the way that we have been keeping on going.

We're asking for a little different wages. And I hope we'll get it. Growers said that we don't need the $1.25, that we got enough. I'm not trying to say that we're taking away the bread of the ranchers or the farmers. The ranchers say they don't make any money, but one thing I know for sure; they're lying. I never heard about a rancher go and knock at the welfare doors and ask for something to eat like the agricultural workers do.

What I say it's truth, and I'm not afraid to say it. For too long the agricultural workers been afraid. When somebody hollers, we jump. We never answer back. Well, I'm not afraid no more. These are the things I have to say and I'm hope that you understand the things that I say.

LUCY DURAN—
WIFE, MOTHER,
AND ORGANIZER

"If you're a farmworker, you probably begin working at dawn and finish when the sun sets. But if you are a woman farmworker, your work doesn't end at sundown. You have to prepare dinner, do the laundry, get the children ready for bed, fix lunches for the next day, do the dishes, and all of the other things that need to be done."

Those are the words of Lucy Duran, wife, mother, organizer, and central committee member of FLOC. She recently returned from an organizing trip to Florida and Texas, where she and other FLOC organizers met with several hundred interested farmworkers. She talked with us about her organizing experiences and the special difficulties of organizing women farmworkers.

"We met with workers in San Antonio, Crystal City, Weslaco, and McAllen in Texas. In Florida, we talked with workers in Homestead, Immokalee, Zolfo Springs, Bowling Green, Wauchula, and several other small towns whose names I can't remember. But whether in Texas, Florida, or my experiences in the camps here in Ohio, the problems of organizing women farmworkers

are the same. The men would sit outside and talk with the men organizers, but the women couldn't because they had housework to do. This is a real organizing problem and it makes me very sad. Women make up nearly half the farm labor work force. Their voice needs to be heard. In the camps last summer, I remember thinking of the women being invisible. Many times I would never get a chance to see them. When I did get a chance to talk with them, we talked about the farmer, wages, working conditions, jobs, and all of the things the men were talking about . . . But it was hard for them to talk because they were so busy. Women have special concerns too. A lot of personal things. Because I am married and have children and am a little older than some of the organizers, they tended to trust me and be willing to talk with me. It was very valuable to me. But our time together was so short. This isn't right. FLOC is a democratic organization. If it is to continue to be democratic, women must be encouraged to participate in the decision-making right along with the men.

"Often times the women might say, 'ask my husband' or 'ask my brother.' These ideas must be overcome. I know that men have certain fixed ideas about women. My father never did the dishes in his entire life. It was an accepted kind of thing. We were poor, and so just to survive meant that each family member had certain

From *Nuestra Lucha*, an independent Chicano newspaper published by the Farm Labor Organizing Committee (FLOC), Guadalupe Community Center and Latinas Unidas Para Acción, Toledo, Ohio. (Vol. 1, No. 6, April 1977). Reprinted with permission from *Nuestra Lucha*.

jobs and responsibilities. My father had his and my mother had hers. It was kind of an economic thing. It still is.

"For example, when we were in Crystal City, we stayed with two people. She worked in a cannery during the day and he had a night job. When we arrived, she was preparing dinner and couldn't be a part of our conversation. If maybe the man had helped her to finish, she too could have talked with us about FLOC. These things can't change over night, I know. But if FLOC is to grow, it is essential that these problems be overcome."

FLOC encourages greater participation by women. Several women are members of the Central Committee, while others are organizers in the field. Among other things, FLOC allocates money for the payment of child care, so that women may be free to participate to a greater extent.

PERSONAL CHRONICLE OF CRYSTAL CITY

Irene Castañeda

Well, daughter, as I remember there was lots of Mexican families and they'd go to pick cotton—Ganado, Texas, Corpus Cristy, Agua Dulce, Kerney, and lots of other little towns. When the cotton picking was done they'd come back to their shacks—they'd start to cut spinach, tomatoe, onion, watermelon, melon, radishes, then—in time—they started traveling to Minnesota, North Dakota and Ohio, Wisconsin—to top beets—the people who had transportation would carry people in the trucks and charged ten dollars per person or five dollars—depending on the price they got paid for beets. Some of the people had houses—only two rooms—a room to sleep and a little kitchen. The toilets were outside or in the chaparros. The people who couldn't get out to work the crops because they had too many little kids, well they had adobe houses or houses made from old tin cans that they hammered open and nailed—they'd fix a little shack. They would sleep on the floor or make wooden benches to sleep on. Mattresses weren't very common then—there wasn't enough money to buy them.

My parents—I think they got to Crystal City in 1910—there wasn't too much there then—they didn't sell lots. Everything was like a ranch, cows and horses roamed loose in 1910. [In] 1911 they brought people from Mexico, they started to clear the land. My father was the foreman because he was the only one who could understand English—so that's how they started to make up lots and sell them and many people stayed.

Mother had a small house and a little tent. Once when they came to Texas to work, father worked on the railroad, or el traque as they called, he had an accident and lost two toes from his left foot—he was in the hospital—when he got out the company gave him a little money and with that they returned to Crystal City and bought a few lots—I think they were thirty-five dollars each.

In 1913 there was the smallpox epidemic and many people died—they would burn the bodies. With the kind of work they did, tuberculosis was pretty common. With spinach, you worked right in the water, people would get wet clear up to their waist—women, men and children—everybody all wet and the hot sun beating down on the head—they began to get sick from tuberculosis—the doctor would say what they were sick from and they would build little shacks for them outside of town—and whole families died there from that sickness.

This letter, from Irene Castañeda to her daughter Antonia Castañeda, is from *Literatura Chicana Text and Context* edited by Antonia Castañeda Shular, Tomas Ybarra, and Joseph Sommers, published by Prentice Hall, Inc. (1972). Reprinted with permission of Antonia Castañeda.

There was no cemetery for Mexicans. They would bury them in ground that was all rocky. My father and other men collected money—they collected and gave the first payment on a piece of ground to form a cemetery. You paid twenty-five cents to dig a grave—that's how they collected to keep making the payments on the place. He took the responsibility of paying for it and he saved the papers for twenty-five years so that no one except us Mexicans would have right to it.

Mother, from seeing the poor people die for lack of medical attention, wanted to do something to help them and she learned, as best she could, to deliver babies. Sometimes on the floor with just a small blanket. Lighting was a candle or petroleum lamp—there were no electric bulbs. Sometimes she would bring pillows or blankets from home—many of the women had not eaten—she would bring them rice from home and feed them by spoonfuls. The shots were a cup of hot pepper tea—to give strength for the baby to be born—because there was no doctor. The only one had to travel to several towns and when he arrived it was too late.

There was no school for Mexicans. That's why no one knew how to read. Mother washed other people's clothes for a dollar for a big load. She had to starch and iron it. She would earn five dollars for a week's work. When she was washing clothes she would sit us down beside her and she taught us to read Spanish.

In time people began to go out to Washington to work in asparagus, corn, warehouses, in the so-called hop. Then when that work is over, they go to the coast to pick (straw)berries, then they return to the hops—the final stage—with the whole family, and from Washington they go to Idaho in September. They stay there a month, from there they go to Texas—spending four months of the year there. So the children go to school four months in Texas and one or two in Washington. They take them out of school there then they take them out of school here and the youngsters get very confused. Many learn something—others don't—and time passes and they know hardly anything.—They grow up and keep on in the same way—journeying from here to there—from there to here—and that's the reason why the Mexican hasn't learned anything and can't have a decent job.

Your father worked for fifteen years in a plant where they made ice—then they closed it and he went to work as a carpenter in a concentration camp in Crystal City—then he contracted himself with this company to go to Vancouver, Washington in 1944 and 1945 in a construction company that made boats. We stayed in Eagle Pass—that's where the three older children started school. The war ended in 1945, many people were left unemployed.

We heard the tale of Washington—that there was lots of money, that they paid real well, and we thought about coming to Washington. We didn't have a car to travel in and this man, Eduardo Salinas used to contract people and we came with him. We didn't have much money, we paid him twenty-five dollars for us and fifteen for each of the children. This was the first time we had traveled. This man said that he had housing and everything for the people, but it wasn't true. We left the thirteenth of March of 1946 and arrived in Toppenish the eighteenth. On the road the truck broke down—who knows how many times. In Utah we had to stay overnight because the road was snowed in and we couldn't travel—we all slept sitting up with the little ones in our arms because we had no money to rent a motel. We were about twenty-five people in the truck, plus the suitcases and blankets and a mattress spread out inside, and some tires—we looked like sardines. Then a heavy wind came and the tarp on the truck tore in half. They tied it as best they could—and the snow falling. We finally got out of the snow and then the driver lost his way—we almost turned over. But God is powerful and he watched over us—finally we got to Toppenish. He didn't have housing—nothing—all lies that he told us. He finally found some old shacks, all full of knotholes, in Brownstown—about twenty miles outside of Toppenish—and in tents he placed all the people. It was bitterly cold—with wood stoves and wet wood.

When the hop was over, we'd lived seven months there, the boys had gotten sick, I'd gotten pneumonia and had to go to the doctor. Well—with the fright we'd had on the road, we didn't feel like returning and we decided to stay in Washington. The work ended in Brownstown and we came to Toppenish. Then we went to live at the Golding Farm—this was made up of rows of shacks—without doors and all falling apart—there was only a wall between the next unit where another person lived. The houses weren't insulated—they didn't have floors, and we worked in the hop. They paid us women seventy-five cents per hour and eighty-five cents for the men. But since José was a carpenter he didn't work in the field. He made crates to ship hop to other places—he did other things too. That's where he had his first accident—and you know the rest—how from the time you were ten and twelve years old you worked selling pop, then in the little corner market in Granger, then in the drugstore to have money to go to school. And you know about your brothers—that they went into the service, how they went, where they went, what they did, and what they are.

SEÑORA FLORES
DE ANDRADE

Manuel Gamio

I was born in Chihuahua, and spent my infancy and youth on an estate in Coahuila which belonged to my grandparents, who adored me. My grandparents liked me so much that they hardly allowed me to go to Chihuahua so as to get an ordinary education. At seven years of age I was master of the house. My grandparents did everything that I wanted and gave me everything for which I asked. As I was healthy and happy I would run over the estate and take part in all kinds of boyish games. I rode on a horse bareback and wasn't afraid of anything. I was thirteen years of age when my grandparents died, leaving me a good inheritance, part of which was a fifth of their belongings, with which I could do whatever I wished.

The first thing that I did, in spite of the fact that my sister and my aunt advised me against it, was to give absolute liberty on my lands to all the peons. I declared free of debts all of those who worked on the lands which my grandparents had willed me and what there was on that fifth part, such as grain, agricultural implements and animals, I divided in equal parts among the peons. I also told them that they could go on

living on those lands in absolute liberty without paying me anything for them and that they wouldn't lose their rights to it until they should leave for some reason. Even yet there are on that land some of the old peons, but almost all of them have gone, for they had to leave on account of the revolution. Those lands are now my only patrimony and that of my children.

Because I divided my property in the way in which I have described (and as a proof of which, I say, there are still people in Ciudad Juarez and El Paso who wish to kiss my hand), my aunt and even my sister began to annoy me. My sister turned her properties over to an overseer who has made them increase.

They annoyed me so much that I decided to marry, marrying a man of German origin. I lived very happily with my husband until he died, leaving me a widow with six children. Twelve years had gone by in the mean time. I then decided to go to Chihuahua, that is to say, to the capital of the state, and there, a widow and with six children, I began to fight for liberal ideals, organizing a women's club which was called the "Daughters of Cuauhtemoc," a semi-secret organization which worked with the Liberal Party of the Flores Magón brothers in fighting the dictatorship of Don Porfirio Díaz. We were able to establish branches of the woman's club in all parts of the state by carrying on an intense propaganda.

From *The Mexican Immigrant: His Life Story* by Manuel Gamio (1931). Reprinted by Arno Press Inc., 1969. *The Mexican Immigrant* is a collection of interviews conducted by Gamio.

My political activities caused greater anger among the members of my family especially on the part of my aunt, whom I called mother. Under these conditions I grew poorer and poorer until I reached extreme poverty. I passed four bitter years in Chihuahua suffering economic want on the one hand and fighting in defense of the ideals on the other. My relatives would tell me not to give myself in fighting for the people, because I wouldn't get anything from it, for they wouldn't appreciate their defenders. I didn't care anything about that. I wouldn't have cared if the people had crucified me, I would have gone on fighting for the cause which I considered to be just.

My economic situation in Chihuahua became serious, so that I had to accept donations of money which were given to me as charity by wealthy people of the capital of the state who knew me and my relatives. My aunt-mother helped me a little, but I preferred for her not to give me anything, for she would come to scold me and made me suffer. There were rich men who courted me, and who in a shameless way proposed to me that I should become their mistress. They offered me money and all kinds of advantages but I would have preferred everything before sacrificing myself and prostituting myself.

Finally after four-years stay in Chihuahua, I decided to come to El Paso, Texas. I came in the first place to see if I could better my economic condition and secondly to continue fighting in that region in favor of the Liberal ideals, that is to say, to plot against the dictatorship of Don Porfirio. I came to El Paso in 1906, together with my children and comrade Pedro Mendoza, who was coming to take part in the Liberal propaganda work. I put my children in the school of the Sacred Heart of Jesus, a Catholic institution; they treated me well there and took care of my children for me.

With comrade Mendoza we soon began the campaign of Liberal propaganda. We lived in the same house and almost in the same room and as we went about together all day working in the Liberal campaign, the American authorities forced us to marry. I am now trying to divorce myself from my husband for he hasn't treated me right. He goes around with other women and I don't want anything more to do with him.

In 1909 a group of comrades founded in El Paso a Liberal women's club. They made me president of that group, and soon afterwards I began to carry on the propaganda work in El Paso and in Ciudad Juarez. My house from about that time was turned into a conspiratory center against the dictatorship. Messengers came there from the Flores Magón band and from Madero bringing me instructions. I took charge of collecting money, clothes, medicines and even ammunition and arms to begin to prepare for the revolutionary movement, for the uprisings were already starting in some places.

The American police and the Department of Justice began to suspect our activities and soon began to watch out for me, but they were never able to find either in my house or in the offices of the club documents or arms or anything which would compromise me or those who were plotting. I was able to get houses of men or women comrades to hide our war equipment and also some farms.

In 1910, when all those who were relatives of those who had taken up arms were arrested by order of the Mexican federal authorities, I had to come to Ciudad Juarez to make gestures so that Sr. Bartolo Orozco, who was brother of Pascual Orozco, should be given his liberty. I was then put into prison, but soon was let out and I went back to El Paso to continue the fight, making it fiercer and fiercer.

In 1911, a little before the revolutionary Sr. Madero became general, he came to El Paso, pursued by the Mexican and American authorities. He came to my house with some others. I couldn't hide them in my house, but got a little house for them which was somewhat secluded and had a number of rooms, and put them there. I put a rug on the floor and then got some quilts and bed clothes so that they could sleep in comfort. So that no one would suspect who was there, I put three of the women of the club there, who washed for them, and took them their food which was also prepared by some of the women.

Don Francisco and his companions were hidden in that house for three months. One day Don Francisco Madero entrusted my husband to go to a Mexican farm on the shore of the Bravo River so as to bring two men who were coming to reach an agreement concerning the movement. My husband got drunk and didn't go. Then I offered my services to Sr. Madero and I went for the two men who were on this side of the border, that is to say in Texas territory, at a wedding. Two Texan rangers who had followed me asked me where I was going, and I told them to a festival and they asked me to invite them. I took them to the festival and there managed to get them drunk; then I took away the two men and brought them to Don Francisco. Then I went back to the farm and brought the Rangers to El Paso where I took them drunk to the City Hall and left them there.

Later when everything was ready for the revolutionary movement against the dictatorship, Don Francisco and all those who accompanied him decided to pass over to Mexican territory. I prepared an afternoon party so as to disguise the movement. They all dressed in masked costumes as if for a festival and then we went towards the border. The river was very high and it was necessary to cross over without hesitating, for the American authorities were already following us, and on the Mexican side there was a group of armed men who were ready to take care of Don Francisco. Finally, mounting a horse barebacked, I took charge of taking those who were accompanying Don Francisco over two by two. They crossed over to a farm and there they remounted for the mountains.

A woman companion and I came back to the American side, for I received instructions to go on with the campaign. This happened the 18 of May, 1911. We slept there in the house of the owner of the ranch and on the next day when we were getting ready to leave, the Colonel came with a picket of soldiers. I told the owner of the ranch to tell him that he didn't know me and that another woman and I had come to sleep there. When the authorities came up that was what he did; the owner of the ranch said that he didn't know me and I said that I didn't know him. They then asked me for my name and I gave it to them. They asked me what I was doing there and I said that I had been hunting and showed them two rabbits that I had shot. They then took away my 30–30 rifle and my pistol and told me that they had orders to shoot me because I had been conspiring against Don Porfirio. I told them that was true and that they should shoot me right away because otherwise I was going to lose courage. The Colonel, however, sent for instructions from his general, who

was exploring the mountains. He sent orders that I should be shot at once.

This occurred almost on the shores of the Rio Grande and my family already had received a notice of what was happening to me and went to make pleas to the American authorities, especially my husband. They were already making up the squad to shoot me when the American Consul arrived and asked me if I could show that I was an American citizen so that they couldn't shoot, but I didn't want to do that. I told them that I was a Mexican and wouldn't change my citizenship for anything in the world.

The Colonel told me to make my will for they were going to execute me. I told him that I didn't have anything more than my six children whom I will to the Mexican people so that if they wished they could eat them.

The Colonel was trying to stave off my execution so that he could save me, he said. An officer then came and said that the General was approaching. The Colonel said that it would be well to wait until the chief came so that he could decide concerning my life, but a corporal told him that they should shoot me at once for if the general came and they had not executed me then they would be blamed. They then told me that they were going to blindfold me but I asked them if their mothers weren't Mexicans, for a Mexican isn't afraid of dying. I didn't want them to blindfold me. The corporal who was interested in having me shot was going to fire when I took the Colonel's rifle away from him and menaced him; he then ordered the soldiers to throw their rifles at the feet of the Mexican woman and throw themselves into the river, for the troops of the General were already coming. I gathered up the rifles and crossed the river in my little buggy. There the American authorities arrested me and took me to Fort Bliss. They did the same thing with the soldiers, gathering up the arms, etc. On the next day the authorities at Fort Bliss received a telegram from President Taft in which he ordered me to be put at liberty, and they sent me home, a negro military band accompanying me through the streets.

At the triumph of the cause of Sr. Madero we had some great festivities in Ciudad Juarez. The street car company put all of the cars which were needed for free transportation from one side of the border to the other.

Afterwards Sr. Madero sent for me and asked me what I wanted. I told him that I wanted the education of my six children and that all the promises which had been made to the Mexican people should be carried out. The same man told me to turn the standards of the club over to Villa who told me that they weren't good for anything. I afterwards learned that Don Francisco was trying to cajole Pancho by giving him those things which we wanted to give to Pascual Orozco.

During the Huerta revolution I kept out of the struggle, for I considered that was treason, and little by little I have been separating myself from political affairs, and I am convinced that the revolution promised a great deal to the Mexican people but hasn't accomplished anything.

In regards to my religious beliefs, I ought to say that I respect all the churches. In reality I don't believe in any of them but I do believe in a Supreme God maker of everything that exists and that we depend on Him. As for the rest, the ministers and priests, all men are alike to me. Imagine! A bishop wanted to marry me in Chihuahua.

I believe in the reality of material things which is where we spring from and I don't believe in miracles but in science and in everything that is real and can be demonstrated by seeing it and touching it. But I believe, I insist on saying it, that there is a Supreme Being who is over all things.

APPENDIX

PROFILE OF THE CHICANA A STATISTICAL FACT SHEET

Elizabeth Waldman

1. There were approximately 3.3 million Chicanas in the United States in March 1975. The majority (83 percent) resided in the five southwestern states of Arizona, California, Colorado, New Mexico, and Texas. Thus, Chicanas accounted for only 3 out of every 100 women in this country, but 1 out of every 7 women in the five southwestern states.

2. Chicanas are, on average, considerably younger than women in the overall United States population. In 1975, their median age was 20.2 years, compared with 29.7 for all women. More than one of three Chicanas were under age fourteen, compared with more than one of five of all women.

3. The younger average age of the Chicanas is reflected in their marital status. Compared with all women, proportionately more Chicanas were single (never married) and fewer were widowed. The proportion married and living with their husbands (56 percent) was the same for Chicanas

as for other women, a proportion that has been drifting down for some time.

4. Chicanas still lag substantially behind all women in formal education; that is, in education obtained in a regular school system that advances a person toward an elementary school certificate or high school diploma, or a college, university, or professional school degree. Median years of school completed by all adult women age 25 and over was 12.3 years, compared with only 8.4 years by Chicanas the same ages. The gap was much narrower in ages 20 to 24, 12.7 versus 12.1 years, and was nearly closed among teenagers 14 to 17. Thus, if the trend among younger women continues, adult Chicanas in the future may be far better equipped to compete in the job market than the adult Chicanas of today.

5. Patterns of Chicana employment and unemployment have remained much the same for several years. In 1975, the labor force participation rate for Chicanas (42 percent) was a few percentage points below the rate (46 percent) for all women, and their unemployment rate (11.9 percent) was a few percentage points higher than the 9.5 percent rate for all women. Employed Chicanas were more than twice as likely as all employed women to be in blue-collar work, mostly as operatives in textile and other manufacturing. Chicanas were

Prepared by Senior Economist Elizabeth Waldman, U.S. Department of Labor, Bureau of Labor Statistics, Washington, D.C., for the Second Task Force Meeting of the Chicana Rights Project, Mexican American Legal Defense and Educational Fund, San Antonio, Texas, September 17, 1976. Reprinted with permission from the Chicana Rights Publication Series of the Mexican American Legal Defense and Educational Fund, Inc., San Francisco, California.

also more likely than all women to be in the lower paying service occupations.

6. By virtually every measure available, the economic situation of Chicanas, on the average, is worse than for all women. In 1974, median earnings for Chicanas was $2,690, about three-fourths of the median for all women. The major reason that the earnings of Chicanas are so low is that they are concentrated in the lower skilled and lower paying occupations. In March 1975, only 42 percent of the employed Chicanas were in white-collar jobs, compared to 64 percent of all employed U.S. women. The contrast was particularly sharp in the professional-technical and managerial positions where median annual earnings for all women were over $7,000. Roughly, 21 percent of all employed U.S. women worked in these fields, but only 8 percent of the Chicanas held these higher paying jobs. In contrast, 28 percent of all employed Chicanas were operatives (e.g., assemblers, inspectors, semi-skilled factory workers), where their earnings averaged about $3,200 a year. Only 11 percent of all employed women were operatives who averaged $4,260 a year. As indicated earlier, Chicanas were also over-represented in the low paying service occupations, where their median annual earnings were approximately $2,100, not much higher than that for all women employed in these jobs.

7. Median family income in the United States was about $12,840 in 1974. The average for Mexican American families was $9,500, about three-fourths of that for all U.S. families. For families headed by Chicanas, average income was about $4,930, compared to $6,415 for all female-headed families. For husband-wife families with the wife working, Mexican American family income rose to $11,780. This was still nearly three-fourths of the average income in all U.S. husband-wife families with the wife working, but the Mexican American families were larger, thus requiring their lower income to stretch further. More than one of five Mexican American families were below the poverty level in 1974, compared with nearly one of ten U.S. families. Nearly half of the families headed by Chicanas were below the poverty level.

TABLE 1
**All Women and Women of Mexican Origin,
by Age, March 1975**

(Noninstitutional population)

Area and age	Total women	Mexican American Total	Mexican American As percent of total women
Total women (thousands)...	107,915	3,344	3.1
Percent	100.0	100.0	—
Under 5	7.3	13.1	5.6
5 to 13	15.3	23.1	4.7
14 and 15...............	3.8	4.5	3.7
16 to 19	7.6	8.8	3.6
20 to 24	8.7	10.0	3.6
25 to 34	14.2	14.0	3.1
35 to 44	10.8	10.8	3.1
45 to 54	11.3	8.0	2.2
55 to 64	9.5	4.2	1.4
65 years and over	11.5	3.5	.9
Median age..............	29.7	20.2	—
Total women in 5 Southwestern States.....	19,985	3,247	13.9

SOURCE: U.S. Bureau of the Census, Series P–20, No. 290, "Persons of Spanish Origin in the United States: March 1975," table 3.

TABLE 2
**Marital Status of All Women
and Women of Mexican Origin,
14 Years and Over, March 1975**

Marital status	Total (thousands)	Mexican American (thousands)	Total (percent)	Mexican American (percent)
Total women, 14 years and over	83,599	2,133	100.0	100.0
Never married	19,023	597	22.8	28.0
Married, husband present .	47,547	1,195	56.9	56.0
Married, husband absent..	2,941	109	3.5	5.1
Divorced	3,984	98	4.8	4.6
Widowed.................	10,104	134	12.1	6.3

SOURCE: U.S. Bureau of the Census, Series P–20, No. 290, "Persons of Spanish Origin in the United States: March 1975," table 6; Series P–20, No. 287, "Marital Status and Living Arrangements: March 1975."

TABLE 3
Years of School Completed by All Women and Mexican American Women, 14 Years and Over, March 1975

Age	Median school years completed		Percent of women completing school					
			Less than 5 years		4 years of high school		4 years of college or more	
	All women	Mexican American women	All women	Mexican American women	All women	Mexican American women	All women	Mexican American women
Total, 14 years and over.	12.2	9.4	2.9	17.0	37.3	22.5	9.0	1.7
14 and 15	8.5	8.4	.5	1.5	.2	.5	—	—
16 and 17	10.5	10.1	.1	.6	3.2	1.4	—	—
18 and 19	12.3	11.7	.4	2.0	53.3	40.4	.1	—
20 and 21	12.7	12.1	.5	2.7	46.1	37.6	1.7	—
22 to 24	12.8	12.1	.4	4.8	44.4	33.7	16.7	3.6
25 years and over.......	12.3	8.4	3.8	25.4	39.7	21.6	10.6	2.2
25 to 29	12.7	11.3	.9	8.3	45.7	32.5	18.8	4.8
30 to 34	12.6	10.4	.9	10.4	46.2	28.8	16.1	2.6
35 to 44	12.4	8.6	1.9	22.7	47.2	22.4	11.3	1.8
45 to 54	12.3	7.6	2.5	31.5	45.6	17.7	8.4	1.6
55 to 64	12.1	6.8	4.6	38.0	36.7	11.8	7.3	.6
65 to 74	10.1	4.2	7.1	58.8	24.2	4.6	7.1	—
75 years and over.......	8.8	1/	13.8	1/	18.0	1/	5.1	1/
21 years and over.......	12.4	9.0	3.4	21.9	40.3	23.8	10.9	2.3
25 years and over								
South................	12.2	8.7*						
West	12.5	9.8*						

SOURCE: U.S. Bureau of the Census, Series P-20, No. 295, "Educational Attainment in the United States: March 1975," tables 1 and 3.
1/ Base less than 75,000.
* Includes all women of Spanish origin.

TABLE 3a
Years of School Completed by All Women and
Mexican Origin Women, by Age, March 1975

Years of School completed	20 to 24 years	Age group				
		25 years and over				
		Total	25 to 29 years	30 to 34 years	35 to 44 years	45 years and over
Total, all women						
(thousands)	9,406	61,861	8,345	6,971	11,615	34,930
Percent	100.0	100.0	100.0	100.0	100.0	100.0
Less than 4 years of						
high school	16.2	38.0	18.2	22.8	28.9	48.8
High school, 4 years. . . .	45.2	39.7	45.7	46.2	47.2	34.5
College, 1 to 3 years. . . .	28.1	11.7	17.3	14.9	12.6	9.4
College, 4 or more years .	10.5	10.6	18.8	16.1	11.3	7.3
Total, Mexican American						
women (thousands) . .	337	1,350	257	206	360	526
Percent	100.0	100.0	100.0	100.0	100.0	100.0
Less than 4 years of						
high school	46.1	70.1	53.7	58.6	69.5	82.8
High school, 4 years. . . .	35.6	21.6	32.7	28.8	22.5	13.1
College, 1 to 3 years. . . .	15.9	6.1	8.9	10.2	6.1	3.0
College, 4 or more years .	2.4	2.2	4.7	2.4	1.9	1.1

SOURCE: U.S. Bureau of the Census, Series P–20, No. 295, "Educational Attainment in the United States: March 1975," tables 1 and 3.

TABLE 4
Employment Status and Major Occupation Group
of Total and Mexican Origin Civilian Population
16 years and Over, by Sex, March 1975

Employment status and occupation	Women		Men	
	Total	Mexican American	Total	Mexican American
Total, 16 years and over (thousands) ...	79,453	1,982	72,061	1,939
Total, Civilian labor force (thousands)	36,495	835	54,900	1,547
Labor force participation rate (percent)......................	45.9	42.1	76.2	79.8
Unemployment rate (percent)	9.5	11.9	8.9	12.2
Employed (thousands)	33,025	736	50,010	1,358
Percent.......................	100.0	100.0	100.0	100.0
Professional-technical...........	16.2	6.2	15.1	7.6
Managers-administrators, except farm...................	5.1	2.2	14.1	6.2
Sales	6.9	5.4	6.1	2.6
Clerical........................	35.3	28.2	6.8	5.0
Craft..........................	1.5	1.5	20.1	18.3
Operatives, including transport ..	11.3	25.3	17.5	28.1
Nonfarm laborers	1.0	1.9	7.0	14.2
Farm laborers and supervisors...	.7	1.1	1.6	7.7
Farmers-farm managers	.2	—	2.9	—
Service workers.................	21.9	28.3	8.8	10.4

SOURCE: U.S. Bureau of the Census, Series P–20, No. 290, "Persons of Spanish Origin in the United States: March 1975," table 10.

TABLE 5
Median Earnings in 1974 of All Civilians and
Mexican Origin Civilians, 14 Years and Over,
by Selected Occupation Groups of Longest
Job in 1974, March 1975

Selected occupation groups and class of worker	Women			Men		
	Total	Mexican American	Mexican American as percent of total women	Total	Mexican American	Mexican American as percent of total men
Total, 14 years and over, with earnings	$3,631	$2,692	74.1	$ 9,064	$6,421	70.8
Clerical	4,699	3,820	81.3	9,209	7,041	76.5
Operatives, including transport	3,880	3,198	82.4	8,218	7,011	85.3
Manufacturing·	4,261	3,550	83.3	8,794	7,068	80.4
Service workers, except private household	1,978	2,096	106.0	4,540	4,137	91.1
Private wage or salary workers..............	3,414	2,618	76.7	8,955	6,349	70.9
Government wage or salary workers	5,501	3,415	62.1	10,562	7,762	73.5

SOURCE: U.S. Bureau of the Census, Series P-60, No. 101, "Money Income in 1974 of Families and Persons in the United States," table 64; Series P-20, No. 290, "Persons of Spanish Origin in the United States: March 1975," table 11.

TABLE 6
Family Status of All Women
and Women of Mexican Origin,
March 1975

Family status	Total (thousands)	Mexican American (thousands)	Total (percent)	Mexican American (percent)
Total, 14 years and over	83,599	2,133	100.0	100.0
Head of household	16,772	301	20.1	14.1
Head of primary family..............	7,127	213	8.5	10.0
Primary individual	9,645	88	11.5	4.1
Living alone......................	9,021	81	10.8	3.8
With nonrelative.................	624	8	.7	.4
Not head of houshold.................	66,827	1,832	79.9	85.9
In families........................	65,491	1,806	78.3	84.7
Secondary individual	1,336	26	1.6	1.2

SOURCE: U.S. Bureau of the Census, Series P–20, No. 290, "Persons of Spanish Origin in the United States: March 1975," table 19.

TABLE 7
All Families and Families with Head of Mexican Origin,
by Type of Family, March 1975, and
Median Family Income, 1974

Type of family	Total families			Mexican American			
						Median income	
	Number (thou-sands)	Percent	Median income	Number (thou-sands)	Percent	Total	Mexican American as percent of total family income
Total families, head 14 years and over	55,712	100.0	$12,836	1,429	100.0	$ 9,498	74.0
Husband-wife......	46,971	84.3	13,847	1,155	80.8	10,434	75.4
Wife in labor force.	20,273	36.4	16,461	437	30.6	11,780	71.6
Wife not in labor force............	26,698	47.9	12,082	718	50.2	9,287	76.9
Other male head ...	1,499	2.7	11,737	55	3.8	1/	—
Female head.......	7,242	13.0	6,413	219	15.3	4,929	76.9

SOURCE: U.S. Bureau of the Census, Series P–20, No. 290, "Persons of Spanish Origin in the United States: March 1975," tables 17 and 22; Series P–20, No. 291, "Household and Family Characteristics: March 1975," table 1; Series P–60, No. 101, "Money Income in 1974 of Families and Persons in the United States," table 25.

1/ Base less than 75,000.

TABLE 8
Characteristics of All Families and Mexican Origin Families,
by Type and Size, March 1975

Item	All families			Mexican American families		
	Total *1/*	Female head	Husband-wife	Total *1/*	Female head	Husband-wife
Total persons in families (thousands)...	190,471	23,245	162,856	6,122	893	5,072
All families (thousands)..	55,712	7,242	46,971	1,429	219	1,155
Percent	100.0	100.0	100.0	100.0	100.0	100.0
2 persons	37.4	44.5	35.7	20.8	30.6	17.3
3 persons	21.8	25.5	21.1	21.3	20.1	21.6
4 persons	19.7	13.9	20.9	18.8	17.8	19.1
5 persons	11.3	7.7	12.1	14.8	11.9	15.6
6 or more	9.8	8.4	10.2	24.3	20.1	26.3
Mean number of persons..............	3.42	3.21	3.47	4.28	4.08	4.39
Mean number of own children under 18 years	1.13	1.27	1.12	1.85	1.95	1.90
Own children under 6 years	0.33	0.32	0.33	0.64	0.58	0.68
Own children under 3 years	0.15	0.12	0.16	0.32	0.23	0.35

SOURCE: U.S. Bureau of the Census, Series P–20, No. 290, "Persons of Spanish Origin in the United States: March 1975," table 18.

1/ Includes families with other male head, not shown separately.

TABLE 9
Selected Characteristics of All Persons and
Persons of Mexican Origin, March 1975,
by Low Income Status, March 1974

(Numbers in thousands)

Item	All persons			Mexican American		
		Below poverty level			Below poverty level	
	Total	Number	Percent	Total	Number	Percent
Total families	55,712	5,109	9.2	1,429	309	21.6
Families with female head	7,242	2,351	32.5	219	105	48.0
Families with male head	48,470	2,757	5.7	1,155	191	16.5
Unrelated individuals ...	18,872	4,820	25.5	331	118	35.8
Female	10,981	3,212	29.3	114	53	46.8
Male.................	7,890	1,607	20.4	217	65	30.0

SOURCE: U.S. Bureau of the Census, Series P-20, No. 290, "Persons of Spanish Origin in the United States: March 1975," tables 28 and 29; Series P-60, No. 102, "Characteristics of the Population Below the Poverty Level," tables 7 and A-3.

Note: The poverty threshold in 1974 was $5,008 for a family of 4 and $6,651 for a family of 6.
The poverty threshold for an unrelated individual was $2,487.

Source of Data. The estimates for the Mexican origin population are based on data obtained in March 1975 in the Current Population Survey conducted by the Bureau of the Census. In order to obtain more reliable data for the entire Spanish origin population, the March CPS samples of 47,000 households in the United States was enlarged to include all households from the November 1974 sample which contained at least one person of Spanish origin. This resulted in almost doubling the number of persons of Spanish origin in the sample.

Population. All estimates in the tables are for the civilian noninstitutional population of the United States, including armed forces members living off post or with their families on post, but excluding all other Armed Forces members.

Persons of Mexican Origin. Origin was determined on the basis of a CPS question that asked for self-identification of the person's origin or descent. Respondents were asked to select their origin (or the origin of other household members) from a flash card listing ethnic origins. Persons of Spanish origin were those who indicated to the CPS enumerator that their origin was Mexican, Puerto Rican, Cuban, Central or South American, or some other Spanish origin.

For further information about the above and other definitions, as well as the sampling variability of the estimates obtained from the CPS, see U.S. Bureau of the Census, *Current Population Reports,* P-20, No. 290, "Persons of Spanish Origin in the United States: March 1975."

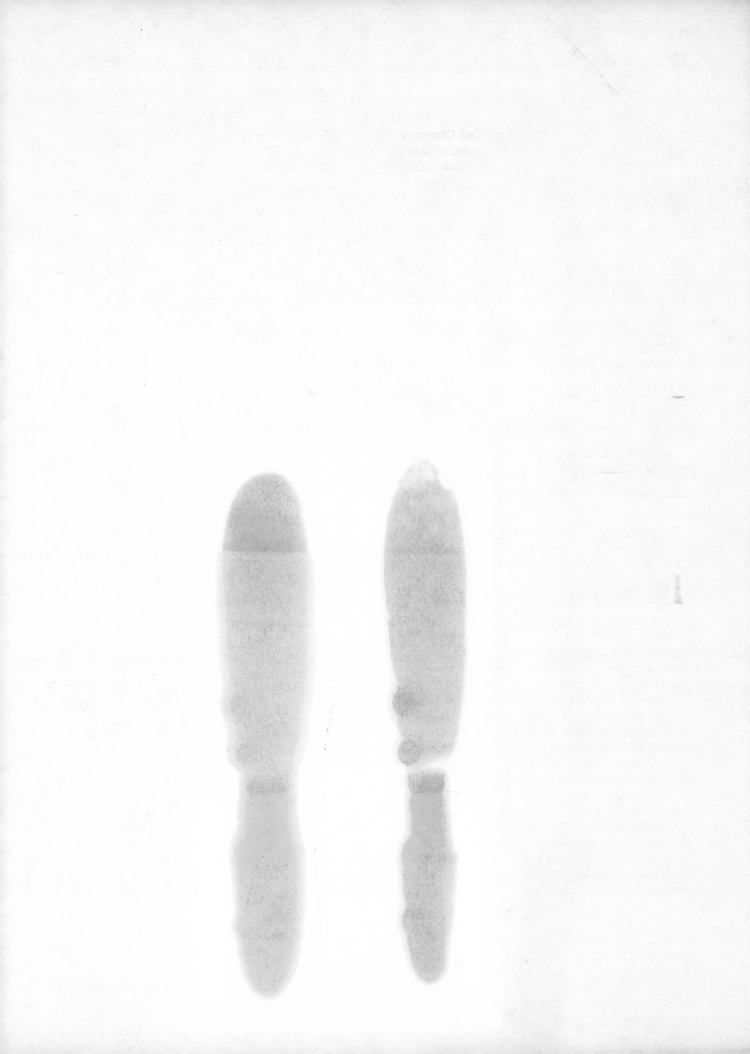